A History of Telugu Dalit Literature

A HISTORY OF TELUGU DALIT LITERATURE

Thummapudi Bharathi

Publications

KALPAZ PUBLICATIONS
DELHI-110 052

A History of Telugu Dalit Literature

Rs. 690

ISBN : 81-7835-688-0

Published in 2008 in India by
Kalpaz Publications,
C-30, Satyawati Nagar,
Delhi-110 052
Phone: 9212729499
E-mail : kalpaz@hotmail.com

Laser Type setting by: Isas System, Delhi
Printed at: Singhal Print Media, Delhi

For
All Those Who Have
Made Me

Contents

Foreword

Dalit history is yet to gain recognition as a critical paradigm in mainstream historical research, albeit Dalit literature has evolved as a distinct genre in itself, it remains to be recovered, given its rich tradition in the vernaculars. Dalit literature unlike T.S. Eliot's theory of objective correlative or experimental use of myth and allusions is multilayered narrative of experiences in the most realistic way by deploying imagery rooted in experiences. Generally, the language of mainstream literature in vernacular is predominantly oriented by romanticism, while Dalit literature has evolved in modes of representation characterised by realistic metaphysical, philosophical, symbolic and imaginative language. Dalit literature inspired by experiences of everyday life, its images and values take precedence over speculation or mere imagination. Thus, to Dalit writers, narratives are far from being illusionary or unreal as authenticity and liveliness are hall marks of Dalit literature. Because Dalit literature represents a powerful, emerging trend in the Indian literary domain. Given its overarching preoccupation with the location of Dalits in the caste based Hindu society, and their struggles for identity dignity, justice and equality, this literature is by nature oppositional.

Given these circumstances, I am delighted that a history of Telugu Dalit literature is made available to English readers by Dr. Thummapudi Bharathi. Among the valuable insights, while writing history of Telugu Dalit literature,

Dr. Bharathi finely draws a coherent literary content by locating the Telugu Dalit writings in a broad context, delineating the general currents in the literary tradition.

Dr. Bharathi's work is unusual in a sense being an exhaustive compilation of all the literary figures in the Telugu Language on the subject. So also the analysis of Dalit literature in the literary frameworks of classical, modern and the post modernist trends. Another strength of the book is its annexures and the list of Dalit writers and activists. The range of themes is fascinating as also the surprising number of verses and narratives. Dr. Bharathi's work is valuable contribution to the burgeoning field of Dalit studies, with multiple voices engaging with issues of identity, cultural dilemmas, sexuality and modernity. What is significant is that the book is evocative and a tribute to the writers' quest for reclamations of self, of human personality and an egalitarian society.

9.2.2008

(Dr. Yagati Chinna Rao)
Member Secretary
Indian Council for Historical Research
(ICHR)
New Delhi

Preface

The story of Dalits is an untold and unheard history, yet a reality. This work is a sincere attempt to make this unknown history to be known in the wide world. It is ironical to note that untouchability or caste discrimination has a religious sanction where as colour discrimination has no such sanction either in religion or in law.

The word 'Dalit' is borrowed from Sanskrit into various Indian languages. In **The Untouchables** (1948) Ambedkar used 'broken men' as an English translation of 'Dalit' to refer to the original ancestors of Untouchables. Dalit literature is deliberately used as a weapon to fight for the human rights of Dalits. Though untouchability is constitutionally abolished and equality is a fundamental right to all citizens of India, unfortunately this is not in practice. This gave birth to various movements, which include Dalit movement. The practices of untouchability, economic and social exploitation of Dalits are the black spots in the face of civilization. It is equally unfortunate to find the necessity for Dalit movements even in the electronic age. The movements started radically when the constitutional remedies failed. The literature is used as one of the weapons in the struggle.

The present work is based on written sources available, both primary and secondary. Some information is also collected by way of questionnaires, personal interviews and discussions with Dalit writers and activists. To be more convenient to the readers the meaning of the Telugu/ Indian words are either given in brackets or in glossary at the end.

There are five chapters in this thesis. The first chapter deals with the Nature and Scope of Dalit Literature. This is divided into two subheads) Stratification of Indian Society; B) Who are Dalits? The second chapter traces the references of literature from Classics to 1920. The third chapter portrayed the historic entry of Dr. B.R. Ambedkar into Dalit activities. This chapter deals with A) The Socio-Political Scenario B) Freedom Movement—Reform Movements—Dalit Organizations. The fourth and fifth chapters are titled, From the Modern to Post-Modern Literature (1921-1970)-I and From the Modern to Post-Modern Literature (1971-2007)-II. In these chapters both Dalit and non-Dalit writers are studied. The concluding chapter discussed various recent issues related to the definition of Dalit Literature, categorization of Dalits into ABCD and the effect of this division on literature etc. In the Annexures the Declarations of Bhopal and Vancouver are given for the future use of researchers. A list of writers and activists along with addresses is also given in Annexure IV for any ready reference.

I would like to thank the UGC for sanctioning this project which is very relevant today. I am especially grateful to the Dalit writers and Activists for their cooperation to complete this work.

Tirupati,
21-11-2007

Thummapudi Bharathi, Ph.D
Dept. of English
S.P. Mahila University
Email id: amma92@rediffmail.com

1

Nature and Scope of Dalit Literature

Stratification of Indian Society

Caste is an indisputable reality in India. It is a peculiar feature in Indian society that a person's status and respect is based on the caste. The Dalit experience with its chronicle of untouchability and extreme exploitation and discrimination in Indian society is at once unique and compelling. Treatment of some of their own fellow beings as untouchables is a rare and cruel feature of India alone. The exploitation of a section of people in the name of caste is a part of a continuum in the history of India for many centuries. It is a history that can neither be denied nor justified. According to Ambedkar "... the Indian society was formed with an ascending scale of reverence and descending scale of contempt and gave no scope for the growth of sentiment of equality and fraternity" (Ambedkar 47). It is very ironical and sad that a certain sections of people in Hindu society are treated as untouchables. Not only are they treated as untouchables but also as inhuman by the dominating castes. The ruling caste hegemony is the root cause for the poverty, oppression and ill treatment of Dalits. The social movements led by Phule, Ambedkar and Periyar brought a considerable change in the thinking and attitude of the suppressed. Now they prefer to identify themselves as Dalits and not as untouchables.

It is to be noted that systems of social segregation and racial inferiority are the most fixed and unchangeable in the world's culture. Of course, the basic concept for classification and division are certainly different. Whether it is Dalits in India or African – Americans in the United States or Eta (outcaste) in Japan or the Ragyappa in Tibet or Packchong in Korea or Pagoda slaves or *Para goon* of Burma, the universal factor is social exploitation based on the false ideology of moral inequality of human beings. In the age of science and technology any sensible human being has to agree that caste-segregation is based on "Pseudo-historical religious mythology" and racism on "Pseudo-scientific biological mythology". The religious, occupational and racial theories about the origin and sustainability of segregation of a certain section of people, so proved to be the biased interpretation of history.

Pollution is one of the important factors connected with untouchability or outcasts. Hence social visits, marriages, inter-dinning are strictly disdained. In India their presence is also considered pollution. It is surprising to note that all these untouchables are kept away from temples except in Burma, where the Pagoda slaves are the custodians of the temples. Of course, occupations of the untouchables differ from country to counting. But in general they are connected with butchering, leather work, removing carcass, or dirt etc. In the process of time though some groups have given up the defiling occupations, yet they are segregated and ill treated. All most all these segregated communities live in separate colonies away from the main habitation or outskirts of the village.

Not only the caste system but also the origin of caste system is a very complex issue in India. Researchers so far could not establish the facts related to the origin of the caste system inspite of a number of debates and discussions. Majumdar rightly pointed out the inability of the scholars that "It is evident from the fact that after a century of painstaking and meticulous research in the history of and function of the social system, we do not possess yet a valid explanation of the circumstances that might have contributed to the formation and development of this unique system" (Majumdar 284). Despite the existing controversies over the facts on the origin of castes, some scholars put forward their own theories to establish the origin of the caste system. Vedas, especially **Purushasukta** of the **Rig Veda** provides the main source for the traditional theory and it is well known and much criticized and rejected theory. It appears very unscientific and unnatural to accept Brahma to give birth through mouth, shoulders, thighs and feet. The scholars who supported this theory also argued that the political strategy of Brahmins to maintain their superiority over the other castes was the essential factor in the establishment of caste system.

A well established scholar Nesfield established another theory – The Occupational theory of caste and from the title it is clear that the scholar tried to establish a relationship between caste and occupation. The scholars like Sir Herbert Risley, G.S.Ghurye et al brought forward the Racial theory for the origin of caste system. They emphasized on the original diversity of races as the cause for the division of castes. They also attributed that the settlement of Aryans in India was the cause for the practice of caste system in Indian society.

The systems of castes or jatis were very concrete in the Pre-British Indian society. Before the caste system came into existence India was divided into Varna or class. According to the historians the Varna system was introduced in India only after the settlement of Aryans in the Indo-Gangetic Plains. **Rig-Veda** was the first sacred book of the Aryans, and the period of composition of the text was perhaps 1500-1400 BC. In the **Rig-Veda** the major division was between Aryans and Dasas. Kosambi in his **An Introduction to the Study of Indian History** stated that the Dasas were treated like slaves and they were not allowed to possess weapons. In a word they are the property of the Aryans. One has to make a note here that the Aryans did not enslave all the local tribes. In fact, according to Vivekananda Jha, the Aryans considered the Sutas, a friendly tribe very respectable. Dev Raj Chanana in his work **Slavery in India** reported that the male and the female Dasas, like cattle, were presented as gifts to the superior community. The historians tried to trace the roots of Shudras from the Dasas. According to Dipankar Gupta "The evidence that Kosambi and other historians have cited to show the absorption of Dasas into the Aryans fold leads one to believe that Shudras arose out of this servile population" (204).

There is no reference to the Chaturvarna system in **Rig-Veda** and perhaps it is seen in the later Vedic period, especially in **Purusasukta**. In the time of **Yajur-Veda**, the Aryan communities had the systematic existence of the four Varnas. Sharma even states that there was an overlapping of duties between Brahmans and Kshatriyas and they even fought for supremacy. According to Gupta:

> Throughout the later Vedic age and up to thee Upanishadic period, we find several instances of a Kshatriyas thirst for knowledge and increasing inquisitiveness to know the essence of nature and the world. Thus though the priest-king/ warrior groups combined to form a composite ruling class, the distinctions between them were nebulous (205).

If Kosambi attributes the theory of Varna Vyavastha to the Aryan invasion J.D. Bernal in his **Science in History** correlates the Varna Vyavastha with the technological development. Jhunjhunwala, quotes Bernal, in this context, thus:

Development of Technology	**Development of Varna Vyavastha**
Grain and Root collection	Varna -less Society
Shifting Hoe culture	Two-Varna Society
Plough and permanent Fields	Three-Varna Society
Irrigation, Bronze and Wheel	Four-Varna Society (55)

Jhunjhunwala in his work **Varna Vyavastha: Governance through Caste System** claims that **The**

Vayupurana and **The Jaina Mahapurana** have references of establishing the Varna Vyavastha. While **The Vayupurana** says that Indra established this system. **The Jaina Mahapurana** credited king Bharata for it. Jhunjhunwala refers:

> Sashampayana asked, 'Sutaji! Please tell how yajna was established? When Satya Yuga had declined and Treta Yuga had begun, at that time how was the Varnasrama vyavastha again established?'
>
> Sutaji said, 'When at the beginning of Treta vegetation began to grow subsequent to the advent of rains, people became busy in discourse of house, ashram and city, at that time Devraja Indra established Varnasrama Dharma and established the practice of yajna; at that time Aswamedha yajna was started...' (Vayupurana 57. 86-103)

It is to be noted that in **The Jaina Mahapurana** the words jatis and Varna are used interchangeably without any distinction. King Bharata explains four fold systems of Jatis thus:

> ... *Tapas* and knowledge of the scriptures is Brahmin only by birth. This jati has become the best due to its practice of charity, worship and study. *The four fold jati have been created on the basis of their livelihood.* The practice of vrata is the cause of being a Brahmin, the wielding of weapons that of Kshatriya, the earning of wealth by legitimate means that of Vaisya and those taking to lower vasana are that of Sudra.

The Varna Vyavastha was strictly practiced both in the time of the **Ramayana** and the **Mahabharata.** According to the Valmiki **Ramayana,** Rama while explaining the state craft to Bharata at Chitrakoot states: "Brahmin, Kshatriya and Vaisya live in large numbers in Ayodhya doing their own duties; you do protect such Ayodhya, do you not?" (**Ramayana** 2.100.42).

From this it is clear that during the time of Rama the Varna Vyavastha might have well established. He expresses that a king is supposed to listen to the Brahmin and help the Vaisya. There is an inter relationship among the three Varnas.

"Do you respect the elders, Vaisyas and Brahmin as your teacher and father?" (Ramayana 2.100.13).

"You are fond of the Vaisya who earns their livelihood by agriculture and animal husbandry, are you not? For, this world is happy and progresses only when engaged in agriculture and trade etc." (Ramayana 2.100.47).

During this period it is also known that a Sudra is expected to serve all other Varnas.

According to the scriptures of Sanatana Dharma every Varna has a *vasana* or desire that represents a particular Varna. The first three Varnas have 'desires' that work towards the development of society and Sudras have *bhogavasana* that works towards the destruction of the society. To be clear, it is to be noted that Brahmins have knowledge, Kshatriyas have power and the Vaisyas, wealth; and all these will be contributed for the welfare and progress of the nation. There is the incident of Sambuka as an evidence of this belief. Sambuka, being a Sudra was doing *tapas* to attain Moksha instead of serving the dvija. It is a belief that one can acquire physical powers by doing tapas. In order to prevent Sambuka from the acquisition of power Rama kills him at once. The explanation given in this context is that all the other Varnas use their power for public interest where as a Sudra uses it for his personal benefit i.e. *bhoga vasana* and this would be bad for the society. But this undoubtedly proved to be wrong in the later period as there were many saints and gurus from Sudras like Kabir, Tukaram, Tiruvallurvar, Narayana Guru, and Ravidas etc. in India.

The researchers tried to show an evolution of Varna Vyavastha in its history. They traced that there is only single Varna Vyavastha in the Satya Yuga and in the process they became four Varnas by Treta Yuga.

It is a fact that in ancient India Brahmins alone are the educated and the authority over scriptures and religion. The Kshatriyas are also educated but their education is limited. Brahmins never wanted any other Varna to know the secrets of knowledge or religion. There are some instances that indicate the kings like Viswamitra tried to become powerful by doing tapas; when the rishis complained to Indra, he invariable destroyed Viswamitra's tapas many a time. From all these one can clearly understand that Brahmins wanted to enjoy a superior place in the society. They do not allow any other person from the other three Varnas to enter their Varna. Hence they made restrictions in the name of religion that each Varna should restrict its social life within its own boundaries.

If we look at human psychology, from the time immemorial that human beings always prove that they are the superior beings and they are the masters of the universe. If we take **The Bible** for example, in the book of **Genesis** God says:

> So God created man in his *own* image, in the image of God created he him; male and female created he them. And God blessed them, and God said unto them, Be fruitful, and multiply, and replenish the earth, and subdue it: and have dominion over the fish of the sea, and over the fowl of the air, and over every living thing that moveth upon the earth.
>
> And God said, Behold, I have given you every herb bearing seed, which *is* upon the face of all the earth, and every tree, in the which *is* the fruit of a tree yielding seed; to you it shall be for meat.
>
> And to every beast of the earth, and to every fowl of the air, and to every thing that creepeth upon the earth, wherein *there is* life, *I have given* every green herb for meat: and it was so. (1:27-30)

This dominant characteristic of man is always dominant in every age. When human race as a whole try to dominate the other living beings with their "thinking capacity", on the other hand a group of people try to dominate over the other group; what ever may be the form — caste, class, race, sex, language, colour etc. Within the same group one individual tries to surpass the other. For example: leader

– follower concept, or in the family, elder – younger as per age, between man and woman, during matriarchal society woman enjoyed all power and now under patriarchy man is all powerful. Hence we understand that the superiority of one group over the other is nothing but man made. Based on the requirements of social life various professions are necessary. But in this professional division one group try to act as the best because they created an image for themselves that they are the mediators between God and man. Man from the beginning is God fearing. Hence all the remaining groups followed the dictates of the one dominant group. But in the history of human evolution, thanks to industrialization and especially the invention of printing press has brought the so far restricted religious knowledge within the reach of common people. The questioning of the superiority of one group over the other began. Charles Darwin's theory of evolution also contributed to gain knowledge of various stages of exploitation in human society.

The Indian Hindu life is directed by **Samhitas, Puranas, Upanishads, Aranyakas, Vedas** and **Srutis.** Veda in a broad sense means knowledge and Sruti literally means hearing. Very ironically all this knowledge is privatised by Brahmins alone. Whether every Brahman possesses the knowledge of these texts or not but reserves this knowledge among themselves and never impart with others. In the Chaturvarna system there are only Brahmins – considered to be the community of priests and scholars by birth, Kshatriyas – the rulers, princes and warriors, followed by Vaishyas – the community of merchants and land lords. And the last in the social hierarchy is Sudras – who are designated as servants to the above three classes. And in the process, next to Sudras in the social hierarchy a few more *jatis* are added. And all these new additions are identified as lower *jatis* or castes (Backward Castes, untouchable category etc) and assigned with mere manual work in the society. It is clear that the first three Varnas or jatis enclosed their boundaries and there by not allowing any new entries into their circles and at the same time they do not cross their boundaries to enter the other group. When some more castes/ jatis are added further to the Sudra Varna why not this happened in the other three Varnas? It reveals a clear conspiracy of the so-called privileged or dominant castes that they expand the number of groups to serve them in various forms. According to Ambedkar "A caste is an Enclosed Class" (Ambedkar 2003:19).

Who Are Dalits?

To answer this question, one has to understand different divisions in Hindu society. There are two types of the major divisions and they are Varna and Caste Systems. Both these systems are very old and they are interlinked. After the independence of India the Dalit movements have become more active than before. This led the researchers to study the subject with more seriousness. There are a good number of studies on Dalit and the related topics during 1980s and 1990s. Certainly the interest is further increasing. Many sociological studies try to dig out the historical roots of Dalits. For this study the evidences are taken from the **Vedas** and the archeological surveys. There are many more sources to rebuild the history of Dalits. One should start the study with the presumption that there is a conspiracy at a point in the history to condemn a group of people as degraded human beings. In order to reveal this conspiracy one has to unearth the possible evidence.

According to the historians **Rig-Veda** is the earliest written text used as the source of the ancient history of India. **Rig-Veda** contains ten mandalas (chapters), 1017 suktas (sub-chapters) and 10552 riks. There is a mention of two groups and one is worshippers of God, called Arya and other "deva-less" or Dasyu or Dasa. These two rival groups lived in the land of "Seven Rivers" now called the Punjab. Though the hymns of the text are addressed to various gods but a majority of them are addressed to Lord Indra.

A few examples from **Rig-Veda** may be quoted for evidence.

(1) Indra Panch Kachhatinama (1.7.9) – Indra is the ruler of five races

(2) Akarma dasyurabhi no amanturanya – varto amanus (10.22.8) which means, all around us are Dasyu without rituals; they are inhuman and following alien laws.

(3) Sa jatubharma Chhadadadhana ojo
puro vimi dannacharada vi dasi
Vidana vajirna dasyuve heti masnarya
Saho vadhrya Sumnamindar ...
Dasyu hatyaya (1.103.3,4.)
"Armed with his thunderbolt, Indra went about destroying the forts of Dasas. O Indra, throw your thunderbolt at the Dasyus, Increase the power and glory of Aryas" (Massey 25-26).

From **Rig-Veda** it is clearly established that there are two hostile groups and they are the Aryas and the Dasyas. In hymn 3.34.9 the Aryans are addressed as Varna. MacDonnell and the other scholars in their book **Vedic Index of Names and Subjects** stated, "Arya is the normal designation in Vedic literature from the **Rig-Veda** onwards of an Aryan, a member of the three upper classes: Brahman, Kshatriya, or Vaisya ... the Arya stands in opposition to the Dasa, but also to the Sudra" (64). From a detailed analysis of the **Rig-Veda** one can understand that all the negative characteristics are attributed to the Dasyus. This estimates the possibility of the Dasyus being indigenous people. When there is a reference to Indra as the ruler of five races, then the question is who are these five races? What about the popular Chaturvarna system? There are two important ideas that came forward as answers. One view is that there are five main tribes in the Aryans and they are Yadu, Turvasa, Druhyu, Anu and Puru. The other view is that an indigenous group namely Nisadas is added the Chatur Varnas and hence there are five races. One point is very clear from the text that the caste distinction was certainly not existing by then.

The historical and archeological studies agreed that the Indus Valley Civilization or the Harappa, Mohanjodaro culture, existed before the Aryans entered India. The scholars agreed that the Indus civilization is one of the four ancient civilizations in the world. The four great civilizations are the Sumerian, the Egyptian, the Indus Valley and the Chinese civilization. Well-known scholars like Wheeler Sir John Marshall, George F. Dales, Walter A. Fairservis, and Grogory L. Pussehl announced that Indus civilization is not only the oldest in South Asia but also the largest and the best civilizations of the world. It had an unchallenged and well-flourished civilization when compared with the other three civilizations. The pre-Aryan India experienced excellent unique culture and there was an evolution of culture towards the progress and development of villages. Walter Fairservis in his article **The Origin, Character and Decline of an Early Civilization** states that The Indus Valley Civilization is the beginning of the Indian Civilization. Gail Omvedt quotes him by saying:

> The Indus civilization – one of the oldest in the world with impressive achievements in two major cities and numerous towns scattered over a huge geographical region – was the starting point for what we know as 'Indian civilization'. The main Language was almost certainly Dravidian. It was clearly a stratified society, with large and small houses indicating a major division into rich and poor. (Omvedt, 38-39)

Perhaps the Dravidians are the indigenous people of the Indus valley civilization. Gail Omvedt argues that the invasion of the Aryans is not the cause for the fall of Indus civilization. She remarks:

> The Indus civilization did not fall as a result of Aryan raids, but rather, apparently, through environmental degradation associated with deforestation and changing river courses; the Aryans may have given the finishing

> touch. They appear on the Indian scene as fairly flexible groups ready to adapt to local customs. A horse-driving, cattle-herding people, they adopted not only wheat and rice cultivation from indigenous Dravidian and Mundari peoples, they also intermarried frequently. (Omvedt 40)

There are scholars who argue that Dravidians are immigrants of India. Whatever it may be, the fact is that Dravidians are living in India before the advent of the Aryans about 1500 BC. The Aryans had to face the Dravidians for their establishment in the country. In territorial context the word is used as Dravida desa, in ethnological context as Dravida bhasha. Darvida has enjoyed both the restriction and extension of meaning. In the restricted sense it is used for Tamil and in extension to mean all the Dravidian languages. Hence in later period Dravida is referred to all the south Indian states. But there are evidences that the people speaking the Dravidian languages are found all over the country. According to Hiremath:

> The majority of the aboriginal tribes in Northern India speak one or the other of the Dravidian languages. As investigation goes deeper and deeper into the interiors of the thick forests, more and more Dravidian languages are likely to be traced. Apart from India, Dravidian speakers are found even beyond ... An aboriginal tribe named Dangar in Nepal is found to speak a Dravidian language. Dangars are found in the south also, in Maharastra and Karnataka. They are mainly the shepherds. (Hiremath, 27)

He further states that people speaking Dravidian languages are found even in the southern borders of Russia, Yugoslavia, Sri Lanka, Malaysia, and Singapore etc. It is clear that Dravida does not indicate a race.

Dr.Ambedkar gives a critical and meaningful analysis of the issue on Dravidian in his **Writings and Speeches** Vol VII.

When the students of ancient Indian history delve into the ancient past they do often come across four names, the Aryans, Dravidians, Dasas and Nagas. What do these names indicate? This question has never been considered. Are these names Aryans, Dravidians, Dasas and Nagas the names of different races or are they merely different names for a people of the same race? The general assumption is that they are different races. It is an assumption on which theories like that of M Rice, which seek to explain the social structure of the Hindu society, particularly its class basis, are built. Before such a theory is accepted it is necessary to examine its foundations. Starting with the Aryans it is beyond dispute that they were not a single homogeneous people. That they were divided into two sections is beyond dispute. It is also beyond dispute that the two had different cultures. One of them may be called Rig Vedic Aryans and the other the Atharva Vedic Aryans. Their cultural cleavage appears to be complete. The Rig Vedic Aryans believed in Yajna. The Atharva Vedic Aryans believed in Magis. Their mythologies were different. The Rig Vedic Aryans believed in the Deluge and the creation of their race from Manu. The Atharva Vedic Aryans did not believe in Deluge but believed in the creation of their race from Brahma or Prajapthi. Their literary developments also lay along different paths. The Rig Vedic Aryans produced Bahmanas, Sutras and Aranyakas. The Atharva Vedic Aryans produced Upanishads. Their cultural conflict was so great that the Rig Vedic Arynas would not for a long time admit the sanctity of the of the Atharva Veda nor of the Upanishads and when they did recognize it they called it Vedanta which contrary to the current meaning of the word- namely, essence of the Vedas- originally meant something outside the boundary of the Vedas and , therefore , not so sacred as the Vedas and regarded its study as Anuloma. Whether these two sections of Aryans were two races we do not know. We do not know whether the word Aryan is a term indicative of race. Historians have therefore made a mistake in proceeding on the assumption that the Aryans were a separate race.

> A greater mistake lies in differentiating the Dasas from the Nagas. The Dasas are the same as Nagas. Dasas is merely another name for Nagas. It is not difficult to understand how the Nagas came to be called Dasas in the Vedic literature. Dasa is a sanskritised form of the Indo-Iranian word Dahaka. Dahaka was the name of the king of the Nagas. Consequently, the Aryans called the Nagas after the name of their king Dahaka, which in its Sanskrit form became Dasa a generic name applied to all the Nagas.(1990: 291-292)

Ambedkar further explains who are the Dravidians.

> Who are the Dravidians? Are they different from the Nagas? Or are they two different names for a people of the same race? The popular view is that the Dravidians and Nagas are names of two different races. This statement is bound to shock many people. Nonetheless, it is a fact that the term Dravidians and Nagas are merely two different names for the same people.
>
> It is not to be denied that very few will be prepared to admit the proposition that the Dravidians and Nagas are merely two different names for the same people and fewer that the Dravidians as Nagas occupied not merely south India but that they occupied the whole of India-South as well as North. Nonetheless, these are historical truths. (Vol.VII : 296)

If Indra is the God of Aryans, Siva is the God of Dravidians. Siva can be easily accepted as the God of non-Aryans with a snake in the neck, Ganga on the head, Trisulam in the hand and cover the body with tiger-skin. Siva is referred as Pasupati from the Indus Civilization onwards. The Dravidians and Nagas are the worshippers of Linga. Siva was a popular God before the advent of Aryans and perhaps this could be the reason for including him in the three crores of Aryan Gods. The Dvajasthamba in front of every temple is the indicator of the Linga (Phallus)-worship. It is also noticed that the Indus people worshipped bull and later it became Siva's vehicle.

The scholars through their research found that the Nagas and Dravidians are one. Dr. Ambedkar in his work **Who are the Untouchables** gave a reasonable argument for this division - Nagas and Dravidians. There is a difference in the influence of Aryans on North and South India. The Nagas of North India imitated the Aryan culture and took Sanskrit as their language whereas the South Indian Nagas retained their own culture and language. Hence the historians suggest that Nagas and Dravidians are two names for a single group. Perhaps Dravid is a linguistic reference where as Naga is the name of the race. Until 12th century the Naga Kings ruled a major part of India. Scholars like Ambedkar stated that Dravida and Naga are two names used for single race.

> The original word 'Tamil' when imported into Sanskrit became Damita and later on Damilla became Dravida. The word Dravida is the name of the language of the people and does not denote the race of the people. The third thing to remember is that Tamil or Dravida was not merely the language of South India but before the Aryans came it was the language of the whole of India and was spoken from Kashmer to Camorin. In fact, it was the language of the Nagas throughout India. The next thing to note is the contact between the Aryan and the Nagas and the effect it produced on the Nagas and their language. Strange as it may appear the effect of this contact on the Nagas of North India was quite different from the effect it produced on the Nagas of South India. The Nagas in North India gave up Tamil which was their mother tongue and adopted Sanskrit in its place. The Nagas in South India detained Tamil as their mother tongue and did not adopt Sanskrit the language of the Aryans. If this difference is borne in mind it will help to explain why the name Dravida came to be applied only for the people of South India. The necessity for the application of the name Dravida to the Nagas of Northern India had ceased because they had ceased to speak the Dravida language. But so far as the Nagas of South India are concerned not only the propriety of calling them Dravida had remained in view of their

adherence to the Dravida language after the Nagas of the North India had ceased to use it . This is the real reason why the people of South India have come to be called Dravidians.

The special application of the use of the word Dravida for the people of South India must not, obscure the fact that the Nagas and Dravidas are the one and the same people. They are only two different names for the same people. Nagas was a racial or cultural name and Dravida was their linguistic name.

Thus the Dasas are the same as the Nagas and the Nagas are the same as the Dravidians.. In other words what we can say about the races of India is that there have been at the most only races in the field, the Aryans and the Nagas (Vol.VII:300)

There are many evidences to prove that Andhra Desa was under the rule of Nagas in the first century A.D. The Skandanaga who ruled the Bellary regions was a feudatory Prince of Pulomavi, the last emperor in the Satavahana dynasty. The Nagas influenced the culture of Andhras. The signs of snakes are traced in the crowns of the sculptures of the kings and the queens that are found at Amaravathi and Nagarjuna Konda (hill). The history of Nagas was proved to be the best as people lived with happiness, peace and prosperity and they practiced Buddhism. There are many historical evidences for this fact. The names like Naaguleru, Naagalapuram, Nagamma, Nagamuni, Nagendra, Naagaptnam etc., are still present in Andhra Pradesh.

In the pre and post Independent India there were Non-Brahmin and Dalit movements. They developed their own theories of caste system in India. These theorists put forward their ideology for annihilation of caste and the involvement of the suppressed and the opposed in the abolition of caste. Dr. Ambedkar wrote on **Annihilation of Caste**: "In taking this as their goal they made certain assumptions, i.e., that caste had an origin in history and just as it had an origin it could have an end; that action of the oppressed and exploited could be effective in aiding this process" (Omvedt 22). 'Phule-Ambedkar thought' perhaps is the earliest theory that initiated the idea that the Sudras and Adisudras were the descendents of non-Aryan original inhabitants of these lands.

According to Moleworth's **Marathi - English Dictionary**, 1831 (reprinted in 1975) the word Dalit means "1. Ground and 2. Broken or reduced to pieces generally". James Massey referred **A Sanskrit – English Dictionary** by Sir Monier Williams and also **The Practical Sanskrit – English Dictionary** by Vaman Shivram Apte and stated that:

> The term *dalit* in Sanskrit is both a noun and an adjective. As a noun, *dalit* may be used for all three genders, masculine, feminine and neuter. It has been derived from the root *dal* which means to crack, open, and split, and so on. When used as a noun or adjective, it means burst, split, broken or torn asunder, downtrodden, scattered, crushed, destroyed. (Massey, 15)

One group of scholars regarded that **Jotirao Phule**, the social revolutionary and reformer of Maharastra used this word to describe the untouchables as the victims of the Indian caste-ridden society. Another group claims that it is Dr. Ambedkar who coined this word to refer the oppressed and the exploited in the society. But during 1970s, the Dalit Panther Movement popularised the word Dalit, not only with the meaning of the oppressed or broken but also with pride and militancy. Zelliot records that "The Marathi word *Dalit*, like the word Black, was chosen by the group itself and is used proudly; and even in the English Press, the unfamiliar Marathi word had to be used" (Zelliot 267). Perhaps, in the beginning Dalit is used for all those who are marked as Backward Castes, Scheduled Castes and Scheduled Tribes but today the term Dalit is used only for the Scheduled Castes.

Besides its common use, the term Dalit today is specially used for those people who, on the basis of caste distinction, have been considered "outcaste". They were "outcaste", because they were not according to the architects of the system fit to be included in the fourfold graded caste structure of Indian society ... This term for them is not a mere name or title; in fact it has become an expression of hope for them in recovering their past identity. (Massey 16)

Of late Bahujan is the new term used for the Scheduled Castes, Scheduled Tribes and Backward Castes.

Works Cited

Ambedkar. B.R "Annihilation of Caste", **Dr. B.R. Ambedkar Writings and Speeches Vol: 1.** Govt. of Maharastra: Education Department, 1989.

Ambedkar. B.R. **Writings and Speeches.**Vol : VII. Govt. of Maharashtra,1990.

Ambedkar. B.R **Castes in India:Their Mechanism, Genesis and Development.** New Delhi: Dalit Book Trust.2003.

Fairservis, Walter. **"The Origin, Character and Decline of an Early Civilization". Gregory Possehl (ed.) Ancient Cities of the Indus,** New Delhi: Vikas, 1974.

Gupta, Dipankar. **Interrogating Caste: Understanding Hierarchy & Difference in Indian society,** New Delhi: Penguin Books India (P) Ltd. 2000.

Hiremath. R.C. **The Genesis and Growth of Dravidian.** Trivandrum: The Dravidian Linguistics Association, 1984.

Jhunjhunwala. Bharat. **Varna Vyavastha: Governance Through Caste System,** Jaipur and New Delhi: Rawat Publications, 2001.

Massey. James **Dalits in India.** New Delhi: Manohar Publishers, 1995.

Macdonell, Arthur Anthony and Arthur Berriedall Keith. **Vedic Index of Names and Subjects** Vol.1. London, 1912.

Majumdar D.N. **Races and Cultures of India.** 4th ed., Bombay, 1961.

Omvedt, Gail. **Dalits and the Democratic Revolution**. New Delhi: Sage Publications, 1994.

Zelliot, Eleanor. **From Untouchable to Dalit**. New Delhi: Manohar Publishers, 1996.

2
From Classics to 1920s

In the Telugu Literature the epic **Mahabharata** has an important place. Nannaiah is the first poet who translated the **Mahabharata** and as he could not complete it the other two poets (Tikkana and Errapragada) continued from where Nannaiah left and completed the entire work. Both Vedavyasa and Nannaiah took it as their duty to strengthen the Chaturvarnna *Vyavastha* through their writings. Nannaiah very systematically tried to establish this system in the epic, that Brahmans are the supreme in the Varna system whereas the Nishadas are outside the system. The Nishadas are shown as the worst, the mixed race and the untouchables. We understand that Nannaiah the first poet in Telugu Literature portrayed the untouchables and also justified their being untouchables through his writing. In the epic he delineated the stories of Garuthmantha, Dharmavyadhudu etc. Nannaiah through his writing tried to destroy the Nishadas. This is clearly understood in the incident of Garuthmantha. Garuthmantha is the son of Vinatha, who was enslaved by Kudruva, who had one hundred snakes as her children. As Vinatha lost a bet, she became a slave to Kudruva. Along with his mother Garuthmantha too becomes a slave. He entered a pact with Kudruva that he will bring *Amrutham* (nectar) for her in exchange for their freedom. As he had to fight with Gods to bring *Amrutham,* he thought that he require strength, so he asked his mother to advise him to get more and more energy. Then Vinatha suggested him to eat Nishadas to get energy. She tells him that the Nishadas harmed all the four races hence he can eat them and become energetic. Infact this advice was not found in the original text by Vyasa. What made Nannaiah to deviate from the original text? Of course he is not translating the text but at the same time he cannot add his ideology to the original text because he is writing the same theme/text in Telugu language. So from this incident of killing Nishadas by Aryans is the creation of Nannaiah and it also indicates that the Nishadas are the original inhabitants of this land and Aryans after their invasion tried to destroy the natives. This incident clearly states the conspiracy of Aryans against natives. Perhaps the writer is indirectly giving advice to the Aryans that they have to kill the natives to ensure a firm establishment in this land. The story of Garuthmantha is in **Adi Parva** and this particular poem i.e., the killing and eating of Nishadas occurs in II: 58. Nannaiah includes a twist in this story as he gives exemption to those Nishadas who obey and serve Brahmans. Vinatha tells Garuthmantha not eat a Brahman, even by mistake while eating Nishadas. But Garuthmantha by mistake eats a Brahmin and on realization he asks the Brahmin to come out of his throat. Then the Brahmin appeals to Garuthmantha to save his wife, a Nishada woman and Garuthmantha saves her. This indicates that Nannaiah is cunning and cleaver as he hints that the survival of Nishadas depends on the will of Brahmans. So if Nishadas obey Brahmans, they are protected else destroyed.

In the story of Ekalavya, Nannaiah writes in support of Kshatriyas, who are necessary for the peaceful survival of Brahmans. Arjuna complained about Ekalavya's expertise skill in Archery to Drona. Then Drona asked Ekalavya's right thumb as *Gurudakshina* (offering or reward to a teacher on completion of a Pupil's education.) for him. In fact Drona never taught Ekalavya. Upon treating Drona as his guru in absentia, Ekalavya has to pay a high price in the name of *Gurudakshina*. This sub plot of Ekalavya clearly states that Drona, a Brahman in conspiracy with Kshatriyas, i.e. Pandavas tried to destroy the Tribals, the sons of the soil. Perhaps, Ekalavya was the first Dalit portrayed in literature who was oppressed so ruthlessly. Ekalavya's skill was annihilated and exploited by the dominant castes in the Varna Vyavastha. This reference is found in **Adiparva** V: 242 & 243 of Nannaiah's work.

The sub plot of Dharmavyadha is yet another incident in which Errapragada, in **Aranya Parva** tried to establish that Brahmans alone possess knowledge and wisdom; if at all a fellow from Panchama Varna has wisdom, the fact behind is that he was a Brahman in his previous birth. From these three references one fact is clearly established and that is the exploitation of the natives i.e., Nishadas by the Aryans and it has the sanction of literature. The writers are in support of the then aliens through their writings.

The twelfth century AD was perhaps an important period in Telugu literature as Veera Saivism became popular. The Saiva poets propagated Saivism through their writings. The Saivite poets opposed and suppressed the influence of Vedic religion and propagated Veera Saivism. A few poets among those who worked for the spread of Veera Saivism are Palakuriki Somana, Panditharadhyudu, Sreepathi Pandithudu, Mallikarjuna Pandithudu, Manchena, and Nannechodudu etc. The Veera Saivites strongly opposed the Varna Vyavastha that was severely supported by the Vedic religion. By then the Varna Vyavastha was deeply rooted in the society and the untouchability was in practice in a strict sense. The Saivism rejected untouchability. The Saivism also accepted the temple entry for Dalits and the Dalits that practiced Saivism was provided with a space in the Saiva Literature. Arudra in his **The Complete Andhra Literature**, Volume No.1 (page 286) states that the Saivism rejected the economic and racial inequalities, a majority of the lower races got converted in to Saivism instead of the higher races. There is also a reference of an inter-caste marriage between a

Brahman girl and an untouchable (a Cobbler) boy on 12th February, 1196 AD. Palakuriki Somana in his **Basava Puranam** wrote the stories of Dalits in the last part (Saptamaasvasam) of the epic. The stories of Siva Nagamaiah and Bhogaiah are good examples of this. In the process of time slowly when there was a decline in the Saivism the society once again leaned towards Vedic principles.

SREE NADHA (15th Century)

Sree Nadha in his **Palnati Veera Charitram (The Velor of the Palnati-History)** dealt with the story of the kings of Palnadu. Like the war of Maha Bharatha, there was a great fight between the brothers for kingship in Palnadu region (Macharla and Gurajala). The two principal characters on both sides are Brahma Naidu and Nagamma. Brahma Naidu was a Vaishnavite where as Nagamma was a Saivite. The differences between Vaishnavism and Saivism also contributed to the war of Palnadu. Brahma Naidu proved to be progressive by arranging communal eating and also considered Kannamaneedu, a Dalit, as his adopted son and made him the chief of the Army. The two important Dalit heroes in this text are Kannamaneedu and Theppali. By the time of this war of Palnadu, the Varna Vyavastha was in decline as the Kings of Palnadu were Sudras.

SRI KRISHNA DEVARAYA (16th Century)

Sri Krishna Devaraya, the (16th century) Vijaya Nagara emperor was not only a lover of fine arts but also a poet. Through his magnum opus **Amuktamalyada**, he introduced a Dalit character, Maladasari, a devotee of Vishnu. Samson in the **History of Dalit Literature**, records that this work has supported the Varna Vyavastha and though Maladasari is a Dalit yet the poet portrayed him as a Dalit and proved that by caste he was an untouchable, but his devotion to Vishnu was commendable. But Katti Padma Rao in his interview said that perhaps **Amuktamalyada** was the first creative writing in which a Dalit character is introduced. He tried to justify his statement that Krishna Devaraya with his constraints and limited freedom could introduce a Dalit character, which was significant by making him a special priest to the God.

VEMANA (17th Century)

In the next century Vemana (Vema Reddy, a progeny of Reddy Kings of Konda Veedu) the people's poet, wrote reformative poetry. He criticised all the evils and superstitions in the society. He also questioned the dominant castes for practicing and ill-treating the lower castes as untouchables. He recited poems spontaneously and hence all his Poetry was not available for recording. His Poems under the title **Vemana Satakam** (Hundred) later was translated into English by C.P.Brown. A good example for Vemana's analysis on social evils like caste is given here.

"Why take thy caste and pride thyself on it? Yea and what is the (twice born) Brahmin?"(208).

"He calls men sudras and says begone thou Sudra; this is a pariar worse than a pariar. If he says I am a twice born does he thereby become one?"(210).

"A pariar eats flesh, all other people eat fat – are not they one caste? They do not see that all castes are in fact one" (215).

"Why dost again and again abuse a pariar? Are not his blood and flesh and thine one? Of what caste is he who is immingled with him? The deity animates his entire works" (215)

"By slaughtering the animals that eat grass men become pariars in the earth. But what sort of caste is that, that eats pigs and fowls (as the respectable classes do) that devour the dung of all?"(216).

POTHULURI VEERABRAMAM (17th century)

Pothuluri Veerabrahmam is yet another poet who argued against the caste differences in the society. He is the poet and the prophet, who for the first time foretold and assured the Dalits' for a bright and hopeful future. He said that in future the Brahmins and the Dalits (Madiga) fight and in the fight the Dalits win and they rule the country. He prophesized that in future Dalits will dominate over Brahmans. Many Dalits were inspired by Veerabrahmam's prophecy and got connected with the religion of Brahman.

GURAJADA APPARAO (1862-1915)

Known as Gurajada, Apparao was born in the Rangavaram village of Yelamanchili taluk, Visakhapatnam district. In his writings he condemned Varna Vyavastha, and social evils and favoured social reforms. He also condemned untouchability and hoped for the casteless society. In his work **Mutyala Saramulu** (1910) he suggested that the first step towards reformation was the arrangement of communal lunches. He also proposed in this poem that intercaste marriages are the solution for a casteless society. And in **Lavana Raju Kala (The Dream of Lavana Raju)** published in 1911 he portrayed the marriage between a tribal woman, Maletha and the King Lavana. Through this story the poet conveyed that in the process of reformation only, there should be progress.

Works Cited

Brown, C.P. **Verses of Vemana**. New Delhi: Asian Educational Services, 1989.

Samson. P **Dalita Sahitya Charitra**. Guntur: Union Printers, 2000.

3
The Advent of Dr. B.R. Ambedkar

Socio-Political Scenario

When Ambedkar was born (1891) in Hindustan, nearly twenty percent of Hindus that is sixty million out of three hundred million were considered Untouchables, Unapproachables and Unseeables. These people were referred under different names in various parts of the country. "They were called outcastes, untouchables, Pariahs, Panchamas, Atishudras, Antyajas and Namashudras" (Keer 1). The then Hindustanis never allowed them to take water from the public wells and their children were never allowed admission in the schools. Barbers and washermen refused their services and Brahman priests prohibited their entry into the temple – not only into the temples but even to the outer compound wall. In short "these untouchable Hindus were treated by the caste Hindus as Subhumans, less than men, worse than beasts" (Keer 2). These are the miserable social conditions in which Ambedkar took birth and made him to take an oath that he should not die as a hindu and fought against this evil custom till his last breath. With his uncompromised struggle along with many of his ardent followers in 1950 the Constitution of India abolished untouchability. But it is abolished only on paper because even today it is strictly practiced in many parts of India.

Ambedkar was the fourteenth child of Ramji and Bhimabai. Both the families of his parents belong to the bhakti group of Kabir. He is a Mahar by caste and "Of all the untouchable communities in the fold of Hindu society the Mahars are the most robust, adaptable, intelligent, fighting, brave, virile and leading community" (Keer 8). One school of social historians is of the opinion that Mahars were the original inhabitants of Maharastra – a rastra of Mahars. It could also mean Maha –Ari, the great enemy.

With the introduction of the Indian Press Act of 1910 not only the press but the people of India also lost the rights related to personal freedom, freedom of discussion, right of public meeting etc. In short the rights of Indian Citizens and press were completely curtailed. This had a greater effect on Ambedkar and so he reflected on this repression in his work **The Evolution of Provincial Finance in British India.** Dhanjay Keer remarks: "Stating the power seldom commits suicide of its own accord, the patriot in Ambedkar describes in it how the British Government resorted to repressive measures during this period and indicts the British administration in India ..." (23).

In 1913 Ambedkar reached Columbia University for higher education with the financial support of the Maharaja of Baroda. The two important issues that impressed upon Ambedkar during his stay in USA are:

(1)The constitution of the United States and particularly, the fourteenth Amendment of the constitution (declaration of freedom for Negroes); (2) The life of Booker T. Washington, as a popular and a committed social reformer and educator of the Blacks in US. Booker T.Washington died in 1915 and Ambedkar was in the US at that time. After completing his higher studies in US he reached England in 1916 and joined in London School of Economics and Political Science to study Economics and also got admitted in Grays Inn for Law. As the period of his scholarship was over, his financial crisis forced him to come back to India in 1917, August.

In 1917, the British government declared its policy of establishing self-governing institutions to form a responsible government in India and of course that will be an integral part of the British Empire. After the declaration in the House of Commons of Britain, Montague came to India to study the effects of the declaration. A good number of organizations met him with their demands and for the first time in the history of India, the representatives of Untouchables are also among those organizations. Dhananjay Keer gives a brief but informative news about the untouchable organization. He states:

> Among those institutions which represented the Untouchables was the Punchama Kalvi Abhivarthi – Abhimana Sanga, a Madras Presidency Untouchables Association. It deprecated any political change and appealed to Government to save them from the yoke of the Brahmins whose struggle for greater share in the administration of Government they likened to the struggle of a cobra that seeks guardianship of young frogs. The Madras Adi-dravida Jana Sangha, representing 6,000,000 aborigines, made a vigorous protest against the caste Hindus who hated them as lepers and denied them any chance of betterment in their life. There was also a strong representation from the organisation of the Untouchables from Bengal. Sir N.G. Chandavarkar interviewed Montague on behalf of the depressed Classes Mission. (p 33)

In 1918 Ambedkar joined Sydenham College as a Professor of Economics. With his profound knowledge he could be able to impress the students and he became popular even among the students of other colleges, as they attended his classes with a special permission. Though he was a successful teacher he had to face bitter experience from his colleagues, just because he was an Untouchable.They did not allow him to drink water from the pot, kept for the faculty. This made him feel the ugly fangs of untouchability in the society in general and among the educated in particular. He then slowly began to contact and gather the people for this cause.

Sri Sahu Maharaj, the Maharaja of Kolhapur perhaps was the first philanthropist to be recorded for his commitment to promote the education among the lower classes and to work for the eradication of caste inequalities. Dhananjay Keer in the biography of Ambedkar noted that the Sahu Maharaj appointed an untouchable as a driver of his state elephant. Sahu Maharaj in the conference of untouchables, held at Margaon, Kolhapur state on March 21, 1920, confidently declared: "You have found your saviour in Ambedkar. I am confident that he will break your shackles. Not only that, a time will come when, so whispers my conscience Ambedkar will shine as a front-rank leader of all-India fame and appeal." (Shivtarkar)

Ambedkar was the president of the conference. The first All-India conference for untouchables was held in the last week of May 1920 at Nagpur, Maharastra. The delegates are fortunate enough to have Sahu Maharaj as the President of the conference. Ambedkar played a pivotal role in that conference. "It should be noted that with great persuasion Ambedkar could get all the sub-castes of the Mahar community and not all the Untouchable communities to dine together. It was not possible yet to make all the communities belonging to the Untouchables participate in an intercaste dinner!" . (Keer 43)

According to Zelliot Mahars were conducting conferences from 1903 onwards under the name Mahar whereas the conferences conducted by Ambedkar were in general in the name of all the depressed classes. "The Depressed classes Institute was formed after the Barshi conferences of 1924. The Scheduled Castes Federation took shape at the Nagapur conference of 1942. The Conferences that were seen as the beginning of the Mahar awakening, however, were those held at Mahad, a small town in Kolaba district in, 1927" (Zelliot 68).

In Pre-Independent India there were two types of movements – one lead by Brahmans as anti-British and the others by non–Brahmans against the Brahmanism. Mahatma Jyoti Rao Phule (1828 – 1890) founded the Satya Shodhak Samaj (Society of the Seekers of Truth) on 24th Sept 1873 to fight for social justice of Sudras. There seems to be a lasting connection between English reformism and Indian social reformers and revolutionaries. Phule's reading of Thomas Paine's **Rights of Man**, perhaps inspired him to be a committed social reformer. He not only established a school for girls as popularly known, but also worked for the welfare of the Sudras and Atisudras by actively working prohibition in the context of working people and also guiding them through his writings as well. Unlike the other reformers of his time he practiced what he preached. The first girls' school, which he established, was for Sudras and ati-Sudras. **Gulamgiri (Slavery)**, the magnum opus of Phule was published in 1873 and the last book **Sarvjanik Satya Dharma Pustak (The Book of the True Faith)** in 1889.

Phule reflected on the two ideas dharma and caste. He thought and blamed Brahmanism as the root cause of the caste system. The Vedas and the Smritis, the basis for Hinduism were created by Brahmins. He also strongly believed that Brahmins in order to retain their domination or superiority brought forward the Varna system and attributed a divine origin to it.

> Phule's thinking on religion cannot be separated from his thinking on caste ... He constructs a *dvaivarnik* (two-varna) structure, with the Brahmans and the shudratishudras forming its two poles, in place of the traditional chaturvarnya (four-verna) structure. As the brahmanical system derived its authority from Vedas, and especially from the *Purusha Sukta* in the **Rig Veda** which asserted varna superiority, it was necessary to develop a counter-discourse to it in varna terms. (Deshpande 9)

He sacrificed his life for the well-being of Sudratisudras. He accused the Brahmans in his work **Gulamgiri** that they were the founders of slavery. The Brahmans sensed that Phule with his Satyashodhak Samaj 'was a danger for them, so they supported the Indian National Congress to resist him. Against this background Ambedkar began his movement. Undoubtedly, Ambedkar's movement was a continuity of Mahatma Phule's fight for social justice.

From 1924 onwards Ambedkar was actively working for the emancipation of the untouchable castes and to establish a casteless society based on "liberty, equality and fraternity". He relentlessly strove for this till 1956 through his writings and activities.He also pressurised that Dalits should emancipate themselves from mental slavery and he also urged them not to eat the carcass. The Mahad fight occupied an important place in the political activity of Ambedkar. In order to put the ordinance of Mahad Municipality, the untouchables under the leadership of Ambedkar drank water from the village tank. Not only the tank water was purified by cow dung and cow urine but the Hindu goondas also attacked the untouchables. After this incident Ambedkar started **Bahishkrit Bharat,** a Maratha fortnightly to bring the movement into people. In this journal he wrote many thought provoking articles. In one of his writings he questioned the relationship of man and religion and also asked a controversial point whether untouchables are part of Hinduism or not. In 1927 September, Ambedkar established Samaj Samatha Sangh to achieve "social equality". In connection with this association, a journal named **Samatha** was started. Due to financial constraints these journals along with **Mook Nayak** and **Saraswathi Vilas** were temporarily stopped. Ambedkar wrote a number of articles that enlightened the readers. They also created awareness among Dalits. He bitterly criticized the injustice in Hindu society.

After giving a representation and presenting the cruel life of untouchables to Simon Commission, Ambedkar had the Poona Pact with Gandhi. **The Communal Award** in 1932 was a political victory for Ambedkar and he got this with his intelligence and wise arguments. In August, 1936 Dr.Ambedkar established the Labour Party. Through this political party, Dr. Ambedkar wanted to help not only the untouchables but all those who were economically, socially and politically exploited. In 1937, while speaking in the Annual Meeting of the Labour Party he criticised and rejected the name *Harijan* given to untouchables by Gandhi.

The year 1942 was recognised an important year in Dr.Ambedkar's agitation. He invited all the scheduled caste leaders from all over India and established **All India Scheduled Castes Federation**. During the meeting of the federation on March 30th and 31st in the year 1942, the members elaborately discussed the Proposals of Cripps Mission. The **All India Scheduled Castes Federation** organised a meeting in Nagpur on 18-19, July 1942 and in this meeting Ambedkar gave the popular slogan **Educate, Agitate, Organise** that had become a daily prayer, later for Dalits. In 1945 he established the People's Education Society and on realizing that there were only a few educated Dalits he even established schools and colleges. Siddhartha College in Bombay was established in June 1946 by Ambedkar and it became a famous college in the nation. He also established Milind Mahavidyalaya in June 1950. He also started many hostels for students. He realized the need for education because without education the Scheduled Castes can never realize their condition and Ambedkar strongly believed that knowledge is power. If Dalits are educated they work for their emancipation. On 30th September, 1956 the **All India Scheduled Castes Federation** held its executive meeting under the Presidentship of Dr. Ambedkar. In this meeting Ambedkar proposed that the Scheduled Castes in India need a powerful political party to save the nation from the Congress Party; and to have a strong opposition; and to establish democracy in the nation. Hence, in the Nagapur press meet on 30th October, 1956 he announced a new political party and called it the **Republican Party of India**.

Dr. Ambedkar's Visit to Andhra

As a Labour Member in the Viceroy's Council Dr.Ambedkar toured in South India. In that tour plan he first visited Hyderabad on the twentieth September 1944 and it is also his first visit to Hyderabad.The President of **The Hyderabad Scheduled Caste Federation** J.H.Subbaiah, his wife Rajamani Devi and Madrelu along with thousands of activists welcomed Ambedkar in the Secunderabad railway station. On the same day in the evening a public meeting was conducted and Ambedkar spoke in Hindi and the audience were very much impressed by his speech. **The Hyderabad Scheduled Caste Federation** and the women's wing of **The Hyderabad Scheduled Caste Federation** presented him the felicitation soon after the meeting.

Then he proceeded to Madras and stayed there for four days and participated in various meetings. From Madras he toured in Costal Andhra towns such as Visakhapatnam, Anakapalli, Kakinada, Ramachandrapuram, Rajhamundry, Eluru, Vijayawada, Palakollu, Gudiwada and Nellore. In all these places, Ambedkar addressed the meetings organized by the Scheduled Castes activists. The Scheduled Castes activists were happy to see Ambedkar in person and certainly his visit and speeches gave new life to the activists. Nandanaru Hari, who was instrumental for Dr.Ambedkar's visit to Andhra was with him throughout the tour.

There was social awareness among Scheduled Castes in Andhra even before the arrival of Dr. Ambedkar in 1944.The leading committed activists in Andhra were Nandanaru Hari, Eliwadapalli, Kusuma Dharmanna Kavi, Rokham Subba Rayudu, Pamu Ramamurthy, Golli Chandraiah, Jonnala Mohan Rao, Rayudu Rangaiah, Gottumukkala Venkanna, Didla Pullaiah, Geddada, Brahmaiah, et.al.

Freedom Struggle—Reform Movement – Dalit Organisations

The English education system and the western rule exposed the rigid rituals and superstitious beliefs in Hindu religion and Indian life. Many Indian intellectuals realized the existing social evils such as untouchability, child marriage and worked for social reformation. This awareness gave birth to the reform movements such as **Brahmo Samaj** (Raja Ram Mohan Ray) **Arya Samaj** (Dayananda Saraswathi) **Theosophical Society** (Annie Besant) **Sri Ramakrishna Mission** (Swami Vivekananda) and **Sarvodaya** (Gandhi).

Brahmo Samaj

Though the objectives of these reform movements are to work for the eradication of social evils, they have their own priorities. Hence eradication of untouchability was not their main objective. However, the Brahmo Samaj helped Dalits in a limited way by focusing on education for women, removal of caste inequalities among the converts into **Brahmo Samaj**. Though it was powerful in Bengal it also contributed for Dalits' education in Andhra Pradesh, then part of Madras Presidency. Raja Ram Mohan Roy (1828, August 20th) the founder of **Brahmo Samaj** advocated caste as undemocratic. The Samaj aimed at reformation of Hindu society and the religious beliefs. The Samaj was largely an elite movement as its members like Debendranath Tagore, Keshub Chandra Sen etc. were educated and westernized. The Samaj not only focused on sati, child Marriage etc., the issues related to dominant castes but also chalked out programmes for Depressed castes. These programmes mainly focused on opening schools for them and supporting their amelioration. Hence it has become the welcoming shelter for Dalits who tried to escape the cruel practice of discrimination in the name of caste. Dalits strongly believed and supported its sincere objective in building a Casteless Society. A few Dalits in Andhra Pradesh joined in these schools.

In the first half of the twentieth century itself the **Brahmo Samaj** and a few social reformers established training centres (*sevashram*) for Dalits. Sir Guduru Ramachandra Rao started one such centre at Gudivada in Krishna district in 1912. Bhagya Reddy Varma and Kusuma Dharmanna are among the active workers during 1920s. In the 45th Andhra Brahmo Samaj Poets Meet in Rajahmundry, Pathamgada Seshamma, was awarded the title **Brahma Samaj Poetess** and from 1959 onwards she worked as the President of **Brahma Samaj** Branch in Eluru.

Nama Sudra Movement (1872)

The Nama Sudra movement was started in Bengal against the domination of the upper castes. Nama Sudras are the untouchable agriculture families. To escape untouchability the Nama Sudras showed interest to convert into Islam and the conversion was at a high rate between1890 and 1910. There are many sub castes among Nama Sudras and they never had any social relationships among themselves. This movement was active between 1881 and1930. In February 1902 **The Nama Sudra Hithoshini Samithi** was started in Dhaka. They conducted meetings in every district.By 1912 the Nama Sudra Association was expanded with twenty two branches. Their first demand was that they should be addressed as Nama Sudras instead of chandalas. As a result chandala is replaced by Nama Sudra in 1891, 1901, 1911 census. From then onwards they claimed that they are desendents of Brahmin clan and started imitating the Brahmin culture.In 1911 they declared that they had no connections with the Hindu castes.They demanded the British Government a separate electorate for them like the Muslims. For this the upper caste leaders like Ambica Majumdar, Surendranath Benerjee, Aswinee Kumar Dutta stongly opposed.

Harchand Tagore born (1812) in the Chandala caste was one of the leading figures in the **Nama Sudra Movement**. Harchand decided that he should help relieve the chandalas from the clutches of Brahmins. For that he wanted first to own the land and send the Brahmins away from the land on which they are living. Hence he declared that " this is our land, we are the sons of the soil, and this is chandala's native land". He also declared that the Brahmins and other land lords had to vacate the land of the chandalas. He also called upon the chandalas to fight for the self-respect. He gave revolutionary slogans such as "study well", "work hard", "increase wealth" and "try to get government jobs". Harchand stongly believed that education alone can improve their economic condition.He asked the chandals that they should come out of the slavery from Brahmins and get the political power.

The Nama Sudras never supported the Swaraj movement and moreover they worked against **Home Rule Movement**. They have even sent a delegation in support of Britishers in 1917. Guruchand Tagore believed that the non cooperation movement against the Britishers is not only against the Britishers but also against the equality and liberty for the Nama Sudras. Later the Communists wisely encashed the anger of Nama Sudras against the Congress.

Sri Narayana Guru Dharma Paripalana Yogam

With the slogan **One Caste, One religion and One God** Sri Narayana Guru (1854-1928) established the ***Sri Narayana Guru Dharma Paripalana Yogam*** in Trivandrum, Kerala on 7th January 1903.Sri Narayana Guru was declared as the life time President and the famous poet Kumaran Asan was elected as the chief secretary. The Prime objective of the organization is a casteless society and it is open to all. Sri Narayana Guru travelled through-out Kerala and taught people to develop self-confidence and social awareness. He pointed out that people have to reform themselves towards Prosperity. He attempted various religious and social reforms through-out his missionary work. Perhaps, one could agree that Narayana Guru's creative revolution began in 1888 by his consecration of a Shiva temple at Aruvipuram. Narayana Guru emphasized on two methods i.e. modern education and sanskritization for the progress of the backward people. He strongly opposed the practice of untouchability. He strictly warned his disciples that they should never ask for the caste identification of person and asked them to practice caste equality. He found fault with the government procedure for seeking caste identification in the official documents. He was highly critical about Gandhi's belief in Chaturvarna system.

Satya Shodak Samaj

Jotirao Phule was the founder of **Satya Shodak Samaj,** (1873) a socio-revolutionary and non-Brahmin movement in Maharastra. As per the available written records he was the first who questioned the caste system and revolted against the Brahmanical dominance. He established schools and hostels for the children of low castes. He encouraged women's education. He opened schools for girls in Maharashtra and his wife Savitribai taught in the girls' school. The first school for the *Shudratishudra* girls was established by him in 1848. He was the first who demanded the special representation for the non-Brahmins in the services of local bodies; His demand was first taken up by the Maharaja of Kolhapur. After the death of Phule in 1890, **Sathya Shodhak Samaj** was further carried by Sahu Maharaj. Sri Sahu Maharaj started schools and hostels exclusively for non-Brahmin students. Sahu Maharaj's efforts on communal representation resulted in **Montague-Chelmsford Reforms** (1919).

Jotirao Phule was a committed writer and **Slavery** (**Gulamgiri**) first published in 1873 was his magnum opus. This is published before launching the movement (**Satya Shodhak Samaj**). "It seeks to identify the main contradiction in Maharastrian society which is centred around the slavery of the *Shudratishudras*. It poses the problem of slavery in historicist terms" (Deshpande 24).

South Indian Liberal Federation

The formation of the **South Indian Liberal Federation** (SILF) was decided in the Conference held on 20th

November 1916. On 20th December 1916 it is stated in **The Hindu**.

> At a conference held on 20th November, it was resolved to start a co-operative for publishing a newspaper advocating the cause of the non-Brahmin Community and also that a Political Association be formed to advance, safeguard and protect the interests of the same community. (The Hindu- 20-12-1916).

Later the S I L F was reshaped into the Justice Party. Justice Party was created as an anti-Brahmin movement. One can understand that Justice Party came into existence to fight against Brahmin dominance. In 1920 general elections the Justice Party extended their co-operation to the British to form the government in Madras Presidency, under the Government of India Act, 1919. By 1935 the Justice party had to reach its political end as they neglected the Minorities and Untouchables while concentrating on the dominant castes of non-Brahmins. As Irshick rightly remarked : "... very soon after taking office the Justice party severed its connections with the Untouchable groups. Once in power, it became almost entirely a caste Hindu party with little interest in social reform and the untouchables were gradually pushed out of the Justice party". (188-189).

Deihl in his book **Periyar E.V. Ramaswami** also stated that " . . . For all its limitations the Justice party had greatly consolidated the position of non-Brahmin caste Hindus and given them the confidence they needed"(15). Thus it is clear that the Justice party failed in its objective of representing the interests of Untouchables and other backward castes. At this Juncture, EVR left Congress (1925) and started the **Self-Respect Movement**. Though EVR started his political career with the Congress, he was very unhappy with the treatment of non-Brahmins by the Congress. In brief **The Self-Respect Movement** is anti-Brahmin, anti-Sanskrit, anti-Aryan, anti-Hindi and anti-God.

When the Aryan Culture dominated the Dravidian culture, the Brahmanism slowly crept into the Dravidian culture. At that point EVR revolted against Brahmin domination in Dravidian culture. EVR identified three evils that became cancerous to Dravidians and they are (a) God (b) Caste and (c) Brahmanism. He wanted to break these chains that have become obstacles in the growth and development of the nation. EVR lead the Self-Respect Movement, supported by Scheduled Castes and backward classes. EVR popularized Rationalism. He strongly believed and propagated that scientific outlook and rationalistic thinking are very essential for the development of the society. In December 1938, EVR was elected as the President of the Justice party with the slogan "Tamil Nad for Tamilians".

Dalit Movement in Andhra Pradesh

A separate Dalit movement emerged in1920s in the eleven districts of Andhra Pradesh (seven districts of Coastal Andhra and four districts of Rayalaseema) then part of Madras Presidency during the colonial rule. The economically developed coastal Andhra proved to be a befitting place for the emergence and development of Dalit Movement. The English education and the missionary conversions of untouchables gave inspiration to a few Hindu social reformers.

> Coastal Andhra was the site of one of the most radical elite-based reform movements outside of Bengal. Veerasalingam Pantulu was the nineteenth century pioneer, beginning with a bold widow remarriage movement and taking up issues such as dowry, prostitution, corruption of officials, and removal of untouchability. He established the Brahma Samaj in Andhra, and it was through this that the most important caste Hindu sponsorship of Dalit social advance took place (Omvedt 115).

According to Uma Ramaswamy the Government of Madras bill on education 1895, which is known as 'Magna

Carta of Panchama education' not only discussed the issues on education but also about acquisition of the land i.e. giving wastelands for institutional sites.

Though the Dalit Movement is highly activised in 1980s the roots for this movement can be traced from 1920s onwards. The origin of The Dalit Movement in Andhra is from **Jagan Mitra Mandali** founded in 1906. One is not certain about the founder but Bagya Reddy Varma(1888-1939) was an active participant since the inception of the Mandali. **The Jagan Mitra Mandali** worked for social consciousness among untouchables. It attempted to enlighten the illiterate and ignorant untouchables through one of the popular art forms of Andhra Pradesh. i.e. Harikatha. The original name of Bhagya Reddy Varma was Madari Bhagaiah, worked as a steward in a Christian family (Roman Catholic) who helped for his education. After joining **Brahma Samaj** he changed his name to Bhagya Reddy Varma i.e. the last two names Reddy and Varma (indicate Brahmanic caste) that denote the non-Dalit and dominant castes.

Bagya Reddy established **Manya Sangham** in 1911 with an objective to work for the untouchables. **The Manya Sangham** tried to create awareness among untouchables through literature, lectures, and harikathas. Some of the enthusiastic caste Hindus also supported the work of the Bhajan Madals that tried to unite the untouchables. The Bhajan Mandals under the guidance of **Manya Sangham** also provided Reading rooms and subscribed various magazines like **Andhra Patrika, Deenabandhu**, etc.

Under the Presidentship of Bhagya Reddy Varma, the **Provincial Panchama Mahajan Sabha** (1917) is renamed as the first **Adi-Andhra Mahajan Sabha**. In his Presidential address he remarked that the word panchama was not found in Hindu scriptures. There are only four varnas. As Panchamas are the natives of this land, the usage Adi-Andhra is suitable for them. From 1917 onwards the Adi-Andhra Conferences were conducted periodically till 1930s.

The details of these conferences are given here under.

Series	*Year*	*Venue*	*Chairman*
I	1917	Vijayawada	Bhagya Reddy Varma
II	1921	Gudivad	Bhagya Reddy Varma
III	1922	Eluru	Bhagya Reddy Varma
IV	1924	Guntur	Kusuma Venkatramaiah
V	1925	Anantapur	Bhagya Reddy Varma
VI	1926	Venkatgiri	Devendrudu
VII	1928	Narasapur (W.Godawari)	Bhagya Reddy
VIII	1929	Vijaywada	Audi Narayana
IX	1930	Anantpur	Devendrudu
X	1935	Rajahmundry	Kusuma Venkatramaiah
XI	1936	Vijaynagaram	Kurmayya
XII	1938	Tallanevu, East Godawari	Bhagya Reddy Varma

(*Source:* **Dalit Movement in South India (1857-1950)** by Swapna Samel, New Delhi: Serials Publications, 2004)

The projection was basically on political, economic and social issues during all the conferences of **Adi Andhra Mahajan Sabha**.

The migration to Burma is one of the important factors that contributed for education of Scheduled Castes in Godavari districts. From the last decades of nineteenth century till 1940s a majority of Dalits migrated to Burma from Godavari and other coastal districts. They came back with wealth and among them some proved to be philanthropists. Vundru Tatayya (1850-1930) comes under this category. He not only funded for schools from his revenue but also established a school at Ponnamananda, his native place in Rajolu taluka of East Godavari district in 1920s. He was a great inspirer for many Dalit leaders like Golla Chandraiah, Kusuma Tataiah, Kona Venkanna etc. The other important Dalits who contributed for the Scheduled Castes by establishing schools, hostels and training schools are Jala Rangaswamy, Eali Vadapalli, Golla Chandraih and Pandu Laxmanaswamy.

Arigay Ramaswamy, the founder of **Suneetha Balasamajam** in 1912, and a contempory of Bhagya Reddy

Varma was a committed Dalit activist in Hyderabad politics. With the inspiration of Mandippela Hanumantha Rao, Ramaswamy adopted vegetarianism and also became a teetotaler. He is well known for influencing people and working for social reforms. During The Nizam's (7th Nizam) rule panchayat system was prevalent at the grass root level. Bhagya Reddy Varma wanted to introduce certain reforms in panchayat system, which was dominated by dominant castes . Some caste Hindus approached Ramaswamy to mediate with Bhagya Reddy Varma on this issue. They both had confrontation on many issues such as Adi-Hindu organization, Social Reforms in Panchayat system etc. The **Suneetha Bala Samajam** later renamed as **Bhoomananda Swami Gurumandali**. This Mandali focused on two social evils i.e. prohibition of drinking in Social Functions and Devadasi system. The Mandali also celebrated and conducted the marriages of poor families with the organization's funds. One of the worth mentioning points of the Mandali was that they encouraged inter-caste marriages. Certainly Ramaswamy's efforts in this direction will be rememberd for a long time in the history of Dalits in Andhra.

To fight against the atrocities of Chowdaries, Ramaswamy felt the need to establish an organization. While establishing the organisation under the title **Adi-Hindu-Jatiyonnati Sabha** he invited the co-operation of stalwarts like Bhagya Reddy Varma, B.S.Venkata Rao, Baji Krishna Rao with an intention of uniting all Dalits. The organization was formed with the prime objective to extend social service to the needy in the community. Later the objectives were extended to socio-economic, educational and political issues. In the year1927, Ramaswamy renamed **The Adi-Hindu Jatiyonnati Sabha** as **Adi-Hindu Mahasabha**. One of the important social activities taken up by **Adi-Hindu Mahasabha** was setting up of Night Schools for boys and adults. A group of young committed youth with the title **Adi-Hindu Mahasabha Volunteer Corps** was encouraged to teach in this school and the organization also opened Adi-Hindu Gymnasium to help the youth to become physically fit and healthy.

By 1930s the differences between Bhagya Reddy Varma and Arigay Ramaswamy glared up very openly. The confrontation is based on caste. **Adi-Hindu Social Service League** under the leadership of Bhagya Reddy Varma was recognized as Mala organisation and **Adi-Hindu Mahasabha** by Ramaswamy was for both the Mala and Madiga Castes. The efforts of Girkala Mallesh Rao with the co-operation of Ramaswamy for the unification of Mala and Madiga communities failed. The failure resulted in the establishment of a separate organisation for Madigas. **The Arundatiya Mahasabha** especially for Madigas was formed on the first of June 1931. Ramaswamy and B.S.Venkatarao never became the members in the working of **Arundatiya Mahasabha** despite being the strong guiding force behind all the activities of the organization.

Under the influence of Dr.Ambedkar the Dalit activities increased in Maharashtra during 1930s. During this period the two important addresses of Dr.Ambedkar, the **Jat-Pat-Jodak Mandal** and **Annihilation of Caste** were made available to the public. The depressed classes' youth of Poona conducted a conference in January 1936. The conference was titled as **Maharastra Asprishya Youth Conference** and Dalits of Andhra Pradesh were invited to the conference. The prominent Dalit leaders of Andhra Pradesh like Arigay Ramaswamy, B.S.Venkata Rao and P.R.Venkataswamy participated in the conference. Certainly this conference has boosted the morale of Andhra Dalits. With the new inspiration, from the Poona conference B.S.Venkata Rao and P.R.Venkataswamy decided to start a new organisation called **The Youth League of Ambedkarites** while suspending the then existing **Adi-Hindu Mahasabha**.

The Youth League of Ambedkarites was launched on the seventeenth May 1936 and B.S.Venkata Rao and P.R.Venkataswamy were made the chairman and secretary respectively. The organization's major objectives were to support Ambedkar in his mission, to enlighten the Dalits on the evils of Hinduism, to work for the unification of Dalits etc. In addition, the League focused on the socio, economic and political issues of Dalits. With the enhanced vision and scope of the League the leaders decided to rename the League as **The Hyderabad State Depressed Classes Association**. On the thirty first October 1938, M.V. Palayam was elected as the Chairman and B.S.Venkata Rao as President of the Association. In order to incorporate new ideas and to make Ambedkar's ideology more relevant the Association organized a conference in October 1939. Unfortunately the personal differences of the leaders spoiled and destroyed the wonderful objective of the conference. As the relationship between A.R. Venkataswamy and B.S.Venkata Rao was severed, Arigay Ramaswamy with the co-operation of J.H.Subbaiah established another organisation with the name **The Hyderabad State Adi Hindu Mahasabha** in 1941. The Mahasabha not only worked for the brotherhood of different castes among Dalits but also worked for the revival of Hindu culture and tradition. With the efforts of Ramaswamy, C.S.Ethirajan and Karry Ramaswamy, all the Dalit workers were gradually brought together under the Mahasabha.

The **All India Depressed Classes Political Conference** was held in Nagpur (Maharastra) from 18th to 20th July 1942. Prominent Dalit leaders like Subbaiah, C.S.Ethirajan, P.V.Manohar, P.R.Venkataswamy, B.S.Venkata Rao, and B.Shyamsunder participated in the conference. The leaders informed of the unfortunate differences and confrontations among Andhra Dalits to Dr.Ambedkar. Dr.Ambedkar, after listening to all the arguments finally advised both Venkata Rao and Subbaiah to compromise and work together for the betterment of Dalits. The advice did not result in positive attitude; moreover a new organisation was formed under the title **The Hyderabad State Scheduled Caste (Adi-Hindu) Federation** in August, 1942.

The following members were the office bearers of the federation.

J.H.Subbaiah	President
R.Laxmaiah	Vice President
C.S.Ethirajan	Vice President
P.R.Venkataswamy	General Secretary
P.V.Manohar	Secretary
Arigay Ramaswamy	Member
Karry Ramaswamy	Member
B.G. Madre	Member
Dharma Narayan	Member
Bhasha Ganganna	Member (Samel 104)

The federation mainly focused on scholarships and freeships for Dalit students, housing colonies and distribution of cultivable land for Dalits etc. J.H. Subbaiah the President of the federation always maintained contact with Dr.Ambedkar and later he even became the President of **All India States Scheduled Caste Federations.**

As Member in the Governer General's Executive Council (1942-1946) Dr.Ambedkar toured in South India. In that tour plan he first visited Hyderabad on the twentieth of September 1944 and it was also his first visit to Hyderabad. This visit is mainly due to the tireless efforts of J H Subbaiah.

With the prime objective of working for the unity of the depressed classes the **Independent Scheduled Castes Federation** came into force on twenty third June 1945. The Federation was the creation of Shyamsunder and Ramaswamy. This Federation tried to unite all depressed classes under one organisation on one platform. According to Swapna Samel:

> A remarkable activity conducted under the above banner is submission of memorandum to Sir Mirza Ismail, President of the executive council in October 1946. Memorandum spoke about Fundamental Rights of the scheduled castes, their separate entity, about

unfair attitude of Government, Hindu-Muslim parity, infustices in the local-self Government Bodies, inadequate representation in Legislature, H.E.H.(106)

By the early 1940s the differences between Mala and Madiga further increased. Arigay Ramaswamy with the support and instigation of some Hindu social reformers established **Arundatiya Matanga Mahasabha** in 1946. Strong ill feelings were developed between **Scheduled Castes Federation** and **Scheduled Caste Association**. Mudigonda Lakshmaiah was nominated as the President of **Arundatiya Matanga Mahasabha**.

After 1930s the Dalit activities almost lost the vigour in the Hyderabad state as it witnessed Hindu-Muslim tension and Razakar's movement. By then so many Dalit Associations sprouted up. But one remarkable feature is that B.S.Venkata Rao became the Minister of Education under the Prime Ministership of Mir Laik Ali on the seventeenth of December 1947 in the regime of Azad Hyderabad.

Works Cited

Ambedkar, B.R. "Annihilation of Caste", **Dr.B.R. Ambedkar Writings And Speeches Vol 1**. Govt. of Maharastra: Education Department,1989.

Deshpande.G.P. ed. **Select Writings of Jotirao Phule**. New Delhi: Left Word, 2002

Diehl, Anita, **Periyar E.V.Ramaswami,** New Delhi, B.2. Publications, 1978.

Irshick, Eugene , F. **Politics and Social Conflict in South India,** California, University of California, 1969.

Jadhav, . R.G. "Some reflections on Dalit Literature". N.M.Aston Ed. **Dalit Literature and African-American Literature**. New Delhi: Prestige, 2001.

Keer, Dhananjay. **Dr.Ambedkar – Life and Mission**. Mumbai: Popular Prakashan, 1990

Omvedt, Gail. **Dalits and the Democratic Revolution**. New Delhi: Sage Publications, 1994.

Samel, Swapna. **Dalit Movement in South India (1857-1950)** NewDelhi: Serials Publications 2004

Shivtarkar, S.N. **The Janata.** Special Number April 1933.
Zelliot Eleanor,. **From Untouchable to Dalit**. New Delhi: Manohar Publishers, 1996

4

From the Modern to the Post-Modern Literature (1921– 1970)-I

The Modern Writers

There is a long past in the creation of Dalit consciousness in Telugu Literature. Perhaps the exploitation of life, reaction, pleading, protest, reform, progress, and revolution are the causes in the creation of Telugu Dalit Literature. Any type of awareness will not descend suddenly in the society. There are certain incidents, in general that provoke the hidden suppression. The same reason proved appropriate for the powerful flow of Telugu Dalit literature.

During 1920s and 1930s the extremist Dalits rejected their identity of *Panchama* and *Harijan* and preferred to identify themselves as *Adi Andhra.*

> The term 'Adi Andhra' arose in the post-1917 period when Dalits all over the south, influenced by the 'non-Aryan' themes of the Dravidian movement, were identifying themselves as Adi-Dravidian, Adi-Andhras and Adi-Karnatakas, original sons of the soil. For coastal Andhra, the decisive year was 1917. At this time the reformer Guduru Ramachandra Rao called a conference in Vijayawada which was labeled as 'First Provincial Panchama Mahajana Sabha', with his protégé Sundru Venkaiah as chairman of the reception Committee. (Omvedt 117-118)

Bhagya Reddy Varma the President of Maha Sabha argued for the removal of the word *Panchama* and the next day the delegates renamed it as the "First Adi Andhra Mahajana Sabha" (1917), from then onwards every year the Adi Andhra conferences were conducted till the early 1930s.

Kusuma Dharmanna Kavi an active participant of the Ambedkarite group was also the President of the Adi Andhra Sabha conferences for a few times. He was not only an activist but also a revolutionary writer and a powerful speaker; also the founder of **Jayabheri**, a weekly journal that voiced the oppressed under the leadership of Ambedkar. He became popular with his popular poem **Nalladoratanamu** (**Brown Bureaucracy**). This perhaps is the first Dalit Revolutionary poem in Telugu (Andhra) rejecting the Blacks (Indians) rule in India. He is the first Dalit writer who grew from Adi Andhra movement. He was the torchbearer in creating awareness among Dalits. Not only he but also his brothers used their pens to fight for the emancipation of Dalits. Kusuma Dharmanna Kavi was courageous enough to declare that Dalits will suffer more under the dominant caste Hindu rulers. And he voiced that "We do not want the rule of Brown Bureaucracy" in his poem **Nalladoratanam** in 1921; certainly it needs a lot of courage to voice against the Indian rulers during that period. He was the first poet to proclaim emancipation for Dalits in his **Harijana Satakam** in 1933. According to Jadhav:

> Dalit literature is the literature of politics and politics is an integral part of it, through politics could be defined in whatever terms one would like to define it. For, Dalitdom is the product of politicisation, a process that is going on continuously in every organised society. (Jadhav 37)

Perhaps Kusuma Dharmanna Kavi is the first person who propagated about Ambedkar in Andhra Pradesh.

During 1930s the Congress took initiative in organizing the Andhra branch of Harijan Seva Sangh. Harijan was the name given to the untouchables by Gandhi; hence it became very popular, even much against the approval of

Dalits themselves. A large section of Adi Andhra leadership slowly got absorbed in the Harijan Seva Sanghas of Congress. Of course a few committed and staunch writers like Kusuma Dharmanna opposed it and showed their pro-Muslim stance. Certainly Unnava Lakshmi Narayana (a non- Dalit) writing about untouchability in his Novel **Malapalli** needs a mention here. Perhaps Gurram Joshua another important Dalit writer during this period represented Gandhian thinking in his poetry. Though he was well aware of Ambedkar and his movement, and referred him in his poetry, yet his poetry appears to be a mild satire, but a strong Dalit consciousness is the underlying current in his writing whether the themes are – social, spiritual, patriotic or historical. In his popular poem **Gabbilam (A Bat)**, he selected a bat (ill omen according to Hinduism) as his messenger to Lord Siva. His writings were credited as realistic portrayals and made society to think. He opposed untouchability and questioned exploitation. The critics unanimously approved and declared that his writings provided completeness to Dalit literature. Boyi Bhimanna was a favored poet of Congress during 1930s and 1940s. His writings focused on the need for the establishment of a socialistic pattern of society. He not only showed the struggle and suffering of the Dalits in the hands of landlords in **Paaleru (A Farm Boy)** in 1940 but also argued for a casteless Hindu Society in his **Raaga Vasishtam** (1940). In this work he wanted to prove that the Harijans are Aryans by quoting the marriage of Vasista and Arundhati. Bheemanna rejected the identity of Dalit and he emphasizes that by "using Dalit we ourselves are accepting that we are separated from the main stream". He argued that Dalits have to fight from within the society for a right place

KUSUMA DHARMANNA (1821-)

Kusuma Dharmanna Kavi perhaps is considered the first Dalit poet by a majority of writers, social activists, critics and researchers. Though there are many non-Dalit writers that sincerely hoped for the betterment of Dalits, yet Kusuma Dharmanna's name is accepted as the first Dalit writer in Telugu Literature for the reasons: 1) He is a Dalit by birth; 2) He protested against the Indian leadership and 3) He wrote about Dalit life. Perhaps he was the first man of letters who strongly inspired Dalits to work for their liberation.

Kusuma Dharmanna was an Ayurvedic physician and also a learned personality in Telugu and English languages. In 1921 Garimella Satyanarayana through his popular song **We Do Not Want the White Rule** led the independence movement actively in Andhra. Taking a clue from this Kusuma Dharmanna bitterly criticized that the Indians who wanted freedom from the whites were not willing to give freedom to Dalits. His writings are: 1) **Nimna Jati Vimukti Tarangani** a presentation made on 19-3-1921, at Eluru, in the Second Andhra State Adi Andhra Mahasabha and then it was published. This booklet focused on the service rendered by Dalits to the nation and the social suffering of Dalits and suggestions for their liberation.

Nalla Dorathanamu (The Brown Lordship) published in1921 is another long poem in which Kusuma Dharmanna declared boldly that the suffering of Dalits increase if the leadership of the nation is changed from whites to the natives as the natives strongly practice caste hierarchy. He preferred whites to the native rulers. Of course, one should not come to a quick conclusion that Dharmanna is for the white rule. Actually he proposed a casteless society, but as it was not possible he preferred the white rule, which was less biased towards Dalits when compared with the Indian Government. In this poem he clearly portrayed the suffering, pain and exploitation of the bonded–labourers. He questioned the dominant castes that they divided the untouchables, by giving different names such as Mala and Madiga and they also deprived them of food, clothing and shelter. He warns Dalits to be careful against the exploitation of the caste Hindus. He openly criticised the dominant caste Hindus that they fight for national independence and not willing to give freedom to the untouchables. They take all services from them and never allow them to take water from their wells and to enter into their temples. They ask for their rights and deny the same rights for Dalits. **Nimna Jatulu – Production (The Depressed Castes – Production**) is an essay that received second prize on 25-5-1924 at Gudivada, during the second meeting of the Eradication of Untouchability, Andhra Pradesh. He also wrote **A Brief History of Harijans** that dealt with the Aryan's exploitation of the natives.

Are they Untouchables? is a collection of short stories by Kusuma Dharmanna. There are six stories in this collection and the main theme of these stories was confrontation between the untouchables and the non-untouchables. Kusuma Dharmanna, the pioneer in the Dalit struggle extended an uncompromising fight from Rajahmandry throughout his life.

BEERNIDI MOSHE (1892-1958)

Kavita Pitamaha Beernidi Moshe was born on 28th August 1892 in Vipparla, near Narasaraopet of Guntur District. His parents are Mariamma and Subbaiah. He died in Brahmanapalle on 10th August 1958. He was a *Harikath Bhagavataar* and he also wrote many *Harikathas*. None of his works was published during his lifetime. **The Harijanabhyudayam** was published by his sons in 1969 though it was written in 1949. Samson gave this date of publication based on the foreword of this work. **The Harijanabhyudayam** is divided into two parts – Chikatikeka and Veluguvaka. In the first part the poet described the suffering of Dalits in the name of Panchamas and the name of the protagonist was Panchama. In the second part he spoke about Gandhi and his involvement of temple – entry for Dalits. He also emphasized that Panchama was the son of Mother India, thereby declaring that Dalits are the natives of this land.

Moshe's other woks include **Navasandhya (The New Dusk) Yesepu Charitra (A History of Joseph),**

Puulagampa (**A Basket of Flowers**), and **Issaku Vadha** (**The Murder of Isaac**). He was also honoured with **Mrudanga Nirmata** in Music and **Kavita Pitamaha** for his literary talent.

Unfortunately not much recorded information is available on this writer or his writings.

GURRAM JOSHUA (1895 – 1971)

A contemporary of Kusuma Dharmanna, Viswa Kavi Samrat Gurram Joshua is another prominent poet during freedom struggle. He was born in Vinukonda, Guntur District in 1895 to the parents of different castes. His mother Lingamamba was a Dalit (Madiga) and father Veeraiah was a Golla. In the Indian society as per the patriarchal system, Joshua was supposed to be recognized by his father's caste. But due to petty caste–politics, he was recognized as a Dalit poet. He worked as a teacher initially and later worked in AIR, Madras. He is essentially a poet, yet he also published short stories under the title **Swapna Katha** in 1932. There are two stories in this collection. His poetry was initially published in various journals between 1924 and 34. All these poems were collected and published in 1937. Some of his popular works are **Gabbilam**, **Firadausi**, **The Life History of Christ**; all his poems are divided into seven volumes. He chose various themes for his poetry. His works dealt with various themes - social, spiritual, patriotic, historical etc. He presented the facts and the reality through his writings. He rejected the practice of untouchability and vehemently criticized religious fanaticism. He questioned the exploitation in every form. Many researchers worked on the writings of Joshua and his works are prescribed in many universities. Comparatively Joshua became a more popular Dalit poet than Kusuma Dharmanna. His **Gabbilam,** (A Bat) the best example of Dalit poetry was translated into English by Kaki Madhava Rao.

Gabbilam (1941) is divided into two parts. The first part was published in 1941 and second part in 1946. In the first part the poet tells how the protagonist was socially and economically exploited. The protagonist narrated his suffering as an untouchable and sent the message to Siva through the bat. He requests the Bat thus:

When you are hanging upside down in the temple
Quite close will you be to Siva's ear
Narrate the story of my suffering to God
Making sure that no Priest is around (9).

In the second part the protagonist awaits the arrival of the Bat. By then the untouchables were permitted to enter the temples. The practice of untouchability was reduced comparatively. The poet believed that Gandhi's teachings and the social justice of white rulers, perhaps contributed for this.

Thiruvarur temple, is thrown open to the untouchables,
Many other temples follow suit
The Gods themselves regret
That untouchables were denied access all these centuries. (42)

Joshua also wrote his biography entitled **My Story** in three parts, published in 1950, 1962, and 1966 respectively. Joshua received many Awards and titles, - **Visarada, Madhura Sreenadha, Viswa Kavi Samrat, Kala Prapoorna, Padma Bhushan** etc. The researchers considered it to be the cultural oppression as he was not awarded the Jnana Peeth.

BOYI BHEEMANNA (1911 - 2005)

Padmasree Dr. Boyi Bheemanna was born in Mamidikuru village of Rajolu Taluk, East Godavari district in the year 1911. His parents are Nagamma and Pullaiah. He started his career as a sub editor in the **Prajamitra**. He also actively participated in the Quit India Movement. He worked as a sub-editor in **Andhra Prabha** News Paper between1950 and 1955.In 1955 he was appointed as Director in the State Translation Department. The Andhra University honoured him with **Kalaprapurna** in 1971 and in 1973 he received **Padmasree**. He received Kendriya Sahitya Academy award for his poetry collection entitled **Gudeselu Kalipotunnai (The Huts are Burning)**.He was the member of Legislative Council of Andhra Pradesh between 1978 and 1984.In 1991 he was honoured with the prestigious **Raja-Lakshmi** award and in 1996 the state government honoured him. Bheemanna received **Lok Nayak** award for literature from Lok Nayak Foundation, Visakhapatnam for the year 2005. As per the announcement of Dr.Yarlagadda Lakshmi Prasad, Former Member of Parliament and the Chairman of the Foundation "a cash prize of rupees one lakh will be given to the writer in connection with the award" (**Vaartha** 25-11-2005).

Boyi Bheemanna suffered the evils of untouchability since his childhood. During those days the untouchable children were seated separately, away from the other children in schools. He started writing even from his youth (school days) and he was discouraged and insulted that an untouchable cannot write poetry. He called himself as **Mamalarishi** (taking the first two letters from both the prominent scheduled castes – Madiga and Mala). He is a versatile writer. His writings include Poetry, Prose, Essay, Drama, and research works on social, political and economic. **Paleru** (1933) a play dealing with the boned labour of Dalits brought name and fame to the writer. "It was published 18 times without the knowledge of Bheemanna" (Samson 85).

Bheemanna himself suffered as *paleru* (a bonded labourer) and hence he could portray the exploitation so realistically in the play. The central idea of the play **Paleru** is that Venkanna the protagonist of the play opposed his father's decision of making him a Paleru and goes to the town and becomes a deputy collector. Vanabala a forward caste woman and Upadesi, the school teacher inspire him and also help him to go to town for education. Through Venkanna, the Playwright narrates the cruel and slavish life of a bonded labourer. Before attempting suicide Venkanna says: "Death is the only alternative for me. I cannot live as a paleru. I cannot become an educated man. I shall put an end for this slavish life by jumping into the well. My untouchable, awkward life is a black spot on this independent, cultured race. I cannot bear this, (goes to well with folded hands) Oh, God! I am sacrificing my life by jumping into the well ..." (P.26). This play was enacted more than 100 times in the entire state. Even in 1980 **Paleru** was performed in Srikakulam. The Playwright through the character of Upadesi, the school teacher, tells Dalits about their duties and responsibilities and this gives direction to Dalits for their liberation.

> Venkanna: Master! All this is due to your blessing. You are the important person among those who worked for my development. I cannot repay your help. I pray to you to stay with us from now onwards.
>
> Teacher: That will be selfish. I have to make many people as collectors like you from these Dalit associations.
>
> Veeresam: This jati will be better if each teacher make one collector. But they should be like Venkanna.
>
> Teacher: Not just a collector! Any student that enter the school can become an engineer, a professor, a lawyer, a judge according to his desire and will. One need not violate the law. It is enough if one keeps up justice.
>
> Veeresam : It is enough if they do not forget that part (P 95)

This message by Bheemanna has an appropriate relevance. Even today this advice is applicable, as a majority of developed Dalits are not contributing their due to their fellow beings.

Coolie Raju (1946) is yet another play focused on the exploitation of labour. It deals with the just fight between the agriculture labourers and the landlords and their goondas. The agriculture labour practice, Gandhian ideology and fight for their rights and after achieving success they conduct elections for their associations.

Gudiselu Kalipothunnai (**The Huts are Burning**) published in 1973 is a prose poem. The poet perhaps hopes that if the huts are burnt, in their place, the buildings will come up. Bheemanna too accepted the annihilation of caste by Ambedkar. In the first part of the poem, very ironically and pathetically the poet reveals the fact. While introducing the burning-huts he writes:

The huts are burning
Oh! Burning!
Whose huts are they; it is a pity,
Perhaps, they are of Malas and Madigas
Who else have the huts? (P 1)

The poet takes the huts as a symbol of the ignorance of Dalits. He hopes that the ignorance of Dalits like huts have to be burnt and the non-flammable buildings i.e., the mental and physical development of Dalits should come. During those days the huts of the scheduled castes are burnt periodically. It could be either at the time of elections to gain the sympathy of the voters or out of anger. Even though the huts are burnt, they get the new huts again. But getting new huts should not be the solution. The poet expects that Dalits should think and find out the reason of this regular burning. He also portrayed that the Dalits got awareness and they even speak to the political leaders very bravely.

Boyi Bheemanna is a very powerful Dalit poet; not only had he portrayed the worst suffering of Dalits but also delineated their awareness and protest and their development through his writings. His other works are **Janmantharavairam(1988), Balayogiyam(1986), Dharmam Kosam Poratam, Paramatma, Panchama Swaram and Sankharavam.**

Boyi Bheemanna, who declared himself as *Mamala rishi* (Rishi of Mala and Madiga) refused the identity of Dalit. He said that the word Dalit with the meaning of broken or separated indicate that these people are outside the society. Hence 'Dalit' is not an appropriate word and he expressed that the caste names may be directly used. Instead of fighting from outside the Hinduism one has to be inside the ring and fight from with in. Though he does not like the word Dalit personally, his writings reflect the lives of Dalits; hence he is discussed under Dalit writing. He died on 16th December 2005.

KANTHETI CHINNA JOHA (1906 – 1980)

Kantheti Chinna John was born in Thulluru of Guntur district to Ratnamma and Ananeeya. He wrote poetry on Christian, Patriotic and Dalit themes. Out of 23 works of John only eight works are published and the remaining 15 are unpublished. The best example of Dalit writing is **Dharma Chakram (The Wheel of Dharma)**, perhaps. Though it was written before 1950s, it was only published in 1977. This poetic work dealt with the pain and suffering of Dalits.

GADDALA JOSEPH (1908 – 1970)

Gaddala Joseph's parents are Santhosham and John and he belongs to Vinukonda Taluk of Guntur district. Though he started his career as a secondary grade teacher, he later became a politician. He was a poet, and a fiction writer. The two important works **Kanniti Kaburu** (**A Tearful Message**) and **Bharathiyudu** (**The Indian**) deal with Dalit themes.

In **Kanniti Kaburu** (1943), the poet deals with the issue of education for Dalits. Dibbadu, though a Dalit wants to educate his only son. The Brahmin not only refuses education but also insists that a Dalit should not study and should remain an untouchable. Later Rayudu, son of Dibbadu, revolts against the social and economic exploitation. It resulted in his expulsion from the village along with his wife and seven children. Being an untouchable he is not allowed in any village and exposed to various sufferings. Finally, all his sons died and the daughter alone survived. Rayudu told her about the suffering and exploitation of Dalits and advised her that the Dalits themselves should work for their progress. Rayudu, the protagonist of the poem realized that even the birds and animals are cared and not an untouchable. He also questioned the creators of the untouchables.

Bharatiyudu (1956), yet another important work of Joseph, presents on the roots of the Dalits and declares that they are the original inhabitants of the nation. The poet also describes how the natives are suppressed and exploited by the Aryans. This work also proposes that if all the Dalits are united certainly they would achieve liberation. The poet also advises Dalits to fight for their rights and suggests that they shall be victorious by following the ideology of Ambedkar. **Bharatiyudu** has greater relevance today as the Dalits are neither united nor victorious in their fight for their rights so far.

ATHOTA RATNAM (1909 – 1999)

Athota Ratnam was born in Edlapalli village of Guntur district, and his parents are Nagamma and Govindaiah. The major themes of his works are Christianity and Dalit. Among his writings ten works are published and fifteen unpublished. He was a Bhagavataar and received many titles. Among his works **Harijanabhyudayam (The Progress of Harijans)** in 1970 and **Ambedkar – Adarsavadi** dealt with Dalit themes. He selected the path of Gandhi in his **Harijanabhyudayam**. He himself recited the story at many places. He traces the origin of Dalits by referring to Matanga Maharshi and their race was considered to be the best race in the early period. He also propagated through the chief character, Govind that by following the path of Gandhi and taking the help of laws one can annihilate untouchability. By 1955 he wrote and sang this at various places but Kavya Gana Kala Samithi published it in 1970. In another work **Ambedkar – Adarsavadi** he focused on the contribution of Ambedkar for the development of Dalits and focused on Ambedkar's teachings -educate, organise and agitate.

BODDU PRAKASAM (1912 – 1980)

Kalaveera, Boddu Prakasam was born in Bapatla taluk of Guntur district in 1912 to Ramanamma (Annamma) and China Veeraiah. He wrote poetry from his schooldays. He was with Gurram Joshua between 1938 and 1971. There are more than twenty unpublished poetical works. Among his works **Ambedkar Prasamsa (In Praise of Ambedkar)**, **Bharatha Varsham (The Land of Bharatha)**, **Abhyudayam (The Progress)** etc deal with Dalit themes.

In **Ambedkar – Adarsavadi**, the history and rights of Dalits are discussed. The poet also proves that Dalits are the natives of the land. In **Ambedkar Prasamsa** (1977) Prakasam said that Ambedkar like Buddha worked for the emancipation of Dalits. He is a staunch follower of Ambedkar.

NADAKURTHI VENKATA RATNAM (1915-1989)

Nadakurthi Venkata Ratnam was born to Ramamma and Venkata Swami in Govada village of Amruthalur taluk, Guntur district. He became popular with the title Govada Ratna Kavi. He wrote a poem against the untouchability and it was not published. In that poem he criticized emphatically that untouchability is not eradicated and it is a bluff. Eradication of untouchability is only in the slogans and laws but it is never in practice. He envisaged that the time will answer the problem.

ELURU APPALA SWAMY (1917 -)

Eluru Appala Swamy was born in Palamuru village of Bhimavaram taluk, West Godavari district. His parents are Chellamma and Swami and his father was doing business in Burma. Appala Swamy came to India for the first time in 1936. Among his other works, **Jaatiya Prabhodam** (1939) is the Dalit oriented work. It is first published in Rangoon and the second edition in 1991 by Dalit Open University of India, Deenapur, and Andhra Pradesh. Eluru Appalaswamy in his preface clearly mentions the objective of his writing. He states: "I wrote this small book neither to exhibit my poetic talent nor to accuse a society, but to wake up those people from deep sleep and who are not aware of the economic, social, moral exploitation by the forward castes and leading a life of slavery for ages". And there was a powerful foreword by Kalamu Narasimha Rao. In the foreword he warned "Those people for whose progress this is written, if they do not use it properly, it will not considered a book but a waste paper". (P 2)

The poet observes that though names are changed but the difference remains the same. He said that first they are named as Mala, then Panchama, then Adi Andhra, and then Harijan – It is the names that are different but they are the same untouchables. He also praises Ambedkar who appeared in Indian society like a burning sun to fight against the dominant castes and to open the eyes of Dalits and to lead them from darkness. He gave a message that sub groups in the same caste should stop the differences and work for their progress.

NAMBURI DURVASA MAHARISHI (1920-)

Born in Chintalapudi of West Godavari district, Durvasa Maharshi was a poet, a singer and a public speaker. He is imprisoned (1940) during Independence movement. Among his works **The Poorest** focuses on Dalit issues. In his preface, the poet gave the objective of his writing and he said that the society is filled with various castes and races that are unequal. The protagonist found fault with the society that though he is working hard yet in the name of caste he is kept outside the society. The dominant castes are enjoying the fruits of his hard work by exploiting him. The poet declares that the liberation of Dalits is possible only with their fight. He accuses that the law and justice is limited to papers alone.

BHUPATI NARYANA MURTHY (1921 -)

A committed communist party activist, Freedom Fighter and Dalit activist, Bhupati Narayana Murthy, was born on September 17, 1921 in Malkipuram, Rajolu mandal of East Godavari district. He is the eldest of the five children of Mallamma and Bhupati Veeraswamy. While studying in the elementary school he is slapped severely for touching a forward caste boy and that resulted in his permanent deafness. He could not continue his regular education due to this defect. During his childhood he participated in the freedom struggle along with the congressmen and he is imprisoned for protesting the tyrannical British rule in India. Later he went to Burma to join his father and worked there as a cook. During the Second World War when Japan bombed on Burma he reached Malkipuram on foot along with others. During the long walk many fell ill and died. But he is fortunate enough to reach home safely.

He is married to Kamalamma of Mori village. He is shocked to learn that Kamalamma is an illiterate. He motivated her and became his teacher. With all his inspiration she actively participated in the activities of the communist party and later she became the leader of women activists.

Bhupati Narayana Murthy is a tireless hard worker. In his early days he learned magic from the popular magician Mr. Agarwal and later studied Jyothishya. But his interest and knowledge in Marxism proved Jyothishya as false.

He took active part in the activities of the Communist Party along with Comrade Kandikatla Nagabhushanam. He is intimate with comrades Koneti Mohan Rao, Gunturu Bapanaiah and Kandiktla Nagabhushanam. He also worked with the leaders of the Communist party – Puchalapalli Sundaraiah and Tarimela Nagireddy.

In the history of Malkipuram he is the first Grama Sarpanch, elected unanimously for two terms. The credit of keeping the records and furniture of the office in the Panchayat office goes to him as they were in the houses of the dominant castes till his election. His activities as the sarpanch became exemplary as the revenue officers quoted him many a time in official meetings. By convincing the officials he got the houses constructed for the SC, ST and BCs. As he is working for the welfare of the poor uncompromisingly, the landlords and police attacked him and destroyed his house and property. His father advised him to withdraw from the activities and his son's denial forced him to commit suicide. Yet, Narayana Murthy has not changed his attitude of fighting for the right cause and for the poor. He has published books **The Revolt of Kshatriyas against Brahmanism** (2001), **The Telugu Language & Nationality**, and **Dalits: The true Nagas, The Violence against Dalits** (1993), **Reservations and the Constitution** etc., so far.

Narayana Murthy has contributed about 200 articles to various Journals and newspapers. He is a regular contributor to the Telugu Dalit Journals **Dalita Sankharavam**, Madanapalle, **Bahujana Keratalu**, Ongole, **Dalita Parivartana**, Nidadavolu, **Dalita Commando**, Nellore, **Prajadhikaram**, Hyderabad, **Nagapuram**, Ravulapalem.

Narayana Murthy also conducted many inter-caste marriages. He is an atheist. He advocates that both Marxism and Ambedkarism are necessary for the liberation of Dalits. He also produced a Telugu film, **Punya Bhoomi Kalluterichindi** in 1982 with a Dalit oriented theme. He strongly believes that one has to fight for social justice and annihilation of castes is the only solution for the true development of the society.

SURAGALI TIMOTHY GNANANANDAM (1922-)

Suragali Timothy Gnanannanda Kavi was born to Papamma and Yellaiah in Pedapenki Village of Bobbili taluk, Srikakulam district. A majority of his works deal with Christian themes. Kala Prapoorna, Gananandа Kavi has about 25 works to his credit. **Paanchajanyam** and **Akshara Puja** are the two works that deal with the themes of Dalit. His works mainly narrate the suffering, pain, and oppression of Dalits.

NUTAKKI ABRAHAM (1923 –1998)

A Telugu Pandit well versed in Sanskrit, Telugu and English literature, Abraham is born in Kolakaluru village of Tenali taluk, Guntur district. Kotamma and David are his parents. As he is one of the important disciples of Gurram Joshua, one could find the Poets' influence on him.

Muthkunam is written in 1951, and it is published in 1955 and the second edition came out in 1992. Muthkunam means a bedbug. The Poem is in first person narrative. The Poet himself is the Dalit Protagonist. He speaks to the bug and the conversation is the poem; it is perhaps modeled on Joshua's **Gabbilam** (**The Bat**). He asks the bug whether a Dalit's blood will be tasty for him? He also suggests that it should take blood from political leaders, religious fanatics and the rich. He also justifies the bugs' behaviour that it is his natural behaviour where as the selfish who are taking blood out of Dalits were doing injustice.

Paripurnudu (1989) deals with the atrocities of dominant castes on Dalits and how they treat Dalits as their enemies. He also declares that Dalits are original inhabitants of Andhra and suggests that the civilized people should think of the suffering of Dalits.

DASI BASAVAIAH (1925-)

He is born in the village Bandalai Cheruvu of Avanigadda taluk, Krishna district. He took his Vidwan degree in Telugu literature. Very few of his works deal with Dalit themes. In **Rechadu** (1965), the protagonist is a Dalit, sacrifices his life for the welfare of the nation, though he is treated as an untouchable. The poet expresses that he wants to tell the world that there are cooperative and sacrificing people among Dalits. He wrote the biography of Ambedkar in two volumes under the title **Bharata Ratna Ambedkar** (1995)

PINAPATI JERMIA (1925-)

Pinapati Jermia was a poet born in Pinapadu village of

Tenali taluk, Guntur district. Suvarthamma and Nathaniel are his parents. Being a Dalit- Christian a majority of his works deal with Christian themes. Yet the Dalit issues are under the surface. In his **Hathaasudu** (1991), the poet presents a poor Dalit who help others even if he does not have anything for himself. It is injustice on the part of the society to exploit such a Dalit. He emphasizes that the exploited Dalit shall never exploit anyone, as he prefers to starve than exploiting a fellow being. A Dalit is always honest.

PATHAGADA SESHAMMA (1926-)

Pathangada Seshamma was born in Rajahmundry of East Godavari district. Her parents are Kanipall Raamayamma and Pantangada Venkanna. She had her elementary education in Rajahmundry and from the first form to FA (first year) in Pitapuram Raja's College, Kakinada. Later she did PUC and completed her teacher training and she worked as a teacher in the training college and also as an Assistant Head Mistress.

There were regular prayers and prayer songs in the hostel when she did her high school. Naturally, she developed an interest in singing and writing poems. She is not only a creative writer but also a translator. She translated Ravindranath Tagore's **Gitanjali** (1973) and **Premanjali** (1973). She is a staunch supporter of Brahma Samaj. She deals with social reformation, spirituality and devotion in her writings. A few examples are **Brahma Vanam** (1988), **Paschaataapam (The Repentance**) in 1992 and **Ramakrishna Satakam** in 1971. She studies the works of Gorki (**Mother**), Unnava Lakshmi Narayana, Gudipati Venkata Chalam, Krishna Sastry and Boyi Bhemanna. Along with Boyi Bhimanna, Tirupati Bhupati and Kommu Damayanti Devi, she took part in the programmes for Harijans and literary meetings. She is credited as the first Dalit woman writer in Brahma Samaj. In her poem **Brahma Kanya** she writes, "There are differences and difficulties between the upper castes and lower castes, the iron-wall between the two should be broken". She says that during those days she did not find any ill treatment in the Brahma Samaj and with their inspiration alone she could produce creative works.

C. VARHALA RAO (1930—)

Known as C.V, C.Varahala Rao was born on 14th January 1930. His parents are Lashmidevamma and Chalapati Rao. He took his masters degree in Economics from Madras Christan College, Madras. He strongly advocates that he should be identified as "an Indian and only an Indian as he does not believe in caste or religion". He is a poet and a translator. C.V also recorded documents in dence of Cultural Revolution. He published a few books on Indian caste system. A few titles among the publications include—**Paris Commune** (May1975), **Kautilya's Artha Sastra** (January 1978), **Darwin's Theory of Evolution** (November 1978), **The Racism** (August 1979), **The Social Revolutionary Movements in Andhra Pradesh** (December 1981), **The Caste System in the Modern Times** (June 1982), **The Caste System in the Middle Ages** (January 1984), **Poet Kusuma Darmanna: The Poineer of the Dalit Movement** (January 2000) etc.

NAMBURI PARIPURNA (1931 -)

Namburi Paripurna was born in Bangaru gudem of Gannavaram taluk, Krishna district. Her parents are Lakhsmamma and Lakshmaiah. During her education career she stayed at Rajahmundry, Vijayawada and Madras. Her brothers are also creative writers and one of her brothers is a member in Socialist Party. Paripurna enacted as a child artist (Prahlada) in the film **Bhakta Prahlada** directed by Chitrapu Narayana Murthy in 1941. She is an active member in student unions and is imprisoned for a short while. She studied patriotic and revolutionary literature under the influence of her brothers. She read the works of Marx, Angels and Lenin and also Gorki. She began her writing career from 1965 and produced a good number of essays, novels and short stories. The central theme of her writing is the issues related to women and Dalits. Her first short novel **Maaku Ravu Suryodayalu** (**We Will Not Get the Dawn**) was published in **Andhra Prabha** weekly. In 1998 she published a collection of short stories under the title "**Untai Maaku Ushassulu**" (**We too have Dawns**). She has an unpublished novel **Polimera** that depicts the lives of Dalits.

Her story **Spurti** (**An inspiration**) deals with the problems of a working woman. Her story begins with Vimala who completely devotes her life and strength for the family and profession. Both the husband and wife are working in Zilla Parishad but in different departments. They go together and return back home together. "Immediately after coming back home he goes to the bath room washes his face and relaxes in the easy chair and reads the news paper. But Vimala goes straight to the kitchen and brings a hot cup of filter coffee to him. Then she makes some light (snacks) food for evening meal. By then children come back from schools.

After eating, again he takes half a cup of coffee and then goes out on the bike. Vimala then bathe her children and help them to do their homework; finish cooking and serve them dinner. Then she relaxes, as she is tired. She waits for Prasad with disturbed sleep".

Prasad spends his time as he wishes; either he goes to club or to a film with friends; some how reach home around 11 pm after enjoying the happiness that was "bought". Later so many changes are included and he exploits Vimala and even beats her ruthlessly and never treats her properly.

The writer shows a comparison between Vimala and her maid Mastanamma in this story. In the conclusion Vimala got inspiration from Mastanamma who boldly solves her problem and there by becomes an instrument in Vimala's decision to go to a legal aid centre, to fight against her husband's cruel behaviour.

KOLAKALURI GOPAIAH (1934 – 1996)

Popular as Gopa kavi, Kolakaluri Gopaiah was born in Narakullapadu village of Amaravathi, in Guntur district. His parents are Gangamma and Bikshalu. He worked as a schoolteacher and settled in Dharanikota. Almost all his writings dealt with Christian themes. Perhaps **Ekalavya** (1991) is the only work that deals with a Dalit issue. He took the story of Ekalavya and added the issues related to the contemporary society.

GADELAVRTHI RADHA ASEERVADAM (1935-)

Aseervadam is born in Chinagadelavarru village of Tenali taluk, Guntur district. He is a committed writer on Dalit issues. He had 15 published works and 25 unpublished works. Among his works **Agamyudu** (1979) and **Kavithalaapam** (1983) are the best examples of his Dalit literary pieces. He dealt with the early society that ill-treated Dalits as untouchables.

GOTTUMUKKALA MANGAYAMMA

Except a story **Oh! Pity!!!** Published in March 1935 in Gruhalkshmi, no other information is available about Mangayamma.. In the introduction to this story she stated that the story is written with self-experience about the untouchability as a sin. She also informed that she is a Harijan young lady. She wrote this story as she is much agonised by the insults in the form of various practices to the Harijans. The story in brief is given here.

Annapurna and Bhaskar are the young Harijan couple. One day Annapurna received a letter from her parents' home that her mother is suffering with viral fever and longing to see Annapurna her only daughter. It is a hot summer day and the young couple start their journey on foot, as they cannot afford to go by train or bus. Around the mid-day they are very thirsty. They are not given water; at the places water is kept for the public during summer, because they are untouchables. At one place a woman comes to give water but learning that they are untouchables, she curses them for approaching the water distributing shed. Through the character of Annapurna the writer criticizes the practice of distributing the water only to those rich people who take coffee or tea or Lime juice at frequent intervals and refuse water to the poor who walk in that hot summer. They enter a village to ask water, as their throats are completely dry. In one house they are ready to give water and when the servant comes and asks for their caste they said that they belong to Mala caste. Immediately they are forced to leave the Agraharam as the servant chases them with a big stick. They come out of the village and Annapurna fainted. Bhaskar was shocked and wept for their pitiable condition. With great difficulty he could bring her under a tree. The writer comments that these two lives are to be sacrificed for the evil practices of Agraharam. The story is concluded with a helping hand of a Muslim who gave them water.

Mangayamma not only projects the evil practices of the society but also questions the silence of god over such cruel issues.

NON-DALIT WRITERS

There are a few non-Dalits who contributed to Dalit literature. These writers wrote before the beginning of any Dalit movement in Andhra Pradesh. Perhaps they are committed in their concern for Dalits. Here we discuss only a limited number of writers whose writings are popular. These writers mentioned in the early literature never aspired for the welfare of Dalits. They either presented the Varna Vyavastha or justified it; but they never condemned the social evil.

UNNAVA LAKSHMINARAYANA (1877 – 1958)

Malapalli (A Colony of Malas – one of the two prominent castes among Dalits) is published in 1922 and it is banned in the same year by the government of Madras. Later again in 1928 it is permitted to publish with certain changes. It was prescribed in Andhra University in 1931 and the Government of Madras banned it again in 1935. In 1937 the Madras Government under the Ministry of C. Raja Gopalachari revoked the ban on the novel.

In this novel Ramadas, the protagonist is a Dalit and the story revolves round a Dalit colony. Ramadas is happy with a small piece of agricultural land and animals. His son Venkatadas is presented as a member in the Progressive Association. He works for the poor and kills the rich and distributes the wealth among them. Though it is judged by the critics as a Dalit novel published even before Dalit movements started, Dalit activists and writers like Bojja Tharakam refuses to see that as one of the first Dalit writing and he states that this novel did not present "Mala Palli" in a realistic way.

JANDHYALA PAPAIAH SASTRI (1912 –1992)

Karunasri is the pen name of Jandhyala Papaiah Sastri, born in Guntur and worked as a Telugu Pandit in Andhra Christian College, Guntur. He had 70 works to his credit. There are references of Dalit issues in **Udayasri** (2 volumes) and **Aruna Kiranalu**. In the first volume of **Udayasri** (1944) there is a reference to a Scavenger-girl. The poet said that her services are unrepayable and that society is cruel, which exploit the services of a scavenger girl who serves like a mother.

In **Aruna Kiranalu** (1945) he accuses the dominant caste people that they were going forward and neglecting their younger brothers (the Dalits) who were walking behind them. He also questioned and scolded for their indifference. Yet another important work on Dalits **Dalit Bharati** (1993) by Karuna Sri dealt with those characters like Ekalavya, Karna etc that are exploited by dominant castes in our epics.

MUPPALA RANGANAYAKAMMA (1939 -)

A staunch feminist, Muppalla Ranganayakamma was born in Bommidi village of Tedepalligudem taluk, West Godavari district. She used her complete name Muppalla

Ranganayakamma in her writings in 1960s. Later, i.e., 1970s onwards she is writing with the name Ranganayakamma only. A majority of her works had Marxism or Feminism as background. Her popular work with Dalit theme is **Balipitham** (1962), which is first serialized in **Andhra Prabha** weekly in 1962. She won the Andhra Pradesh **Sahitya Akademi** Award for this novel. The protagonist, Bhaskar is a Dalit and Aruna is a Brahmin. The main concept of the novel is inter-caste marriage and its consequences. He married her on her deathbed to fulfill her request to die as a *Sumangali*. After the marriage, she recovers and could not live with him; because living with him includes his relatives. She could not bear the sight of his kith and kin. Of course finally she realizes that instead of her relatives, his relatives are more humanistic and understanding. This novel is made into a film.

MANGIPUDI VENKATA SARMA

Became popular with his **Nirudha Bharatam** Mangipudi Venkata Sarma was born in Pippara village of Krishna district. **Nirudha Bharatam** published in 1915, perhaps is the first work of Dalit literature in Telugu. "**Nirudha Bharatam** means prohibited Bharathadesam" (Samson 41). The poet very clearly mentioned that reducing them as untouchables prohibited the development and progress of Dalits. He hoped for the progress of Dalits. Though a Brahmin, he fought against casteism and the domination of the other castes over untouchables. He questioned the practice of the Brahmins who are permitted to re-enter into their caste when they got polluted and why the same principle does not applicable to Dalits. Why can't Dalits enter into so-called upper caste groups? He stated that Dalits are the true sons of the soil; as Aryans exploited them it is not fair to ill-treat them as Panchamas. As early as 1915 itself Venkata Sarma showed the reasons fo conversions of Hindus into Islam and Christianity. He said that as the Hindus were ill-treating them, they preferred other religions. Had the Hindus treated them with respect they would not have left Hindu Dharma. He also advised the Hindu society that it has to cleanse itself. He also prophasised that they may try hard to suppress untouchables, but none can stop their progress; as they are being educated and employed.

Tripuraneni Ramaswami Chowdary, Garimella Satyanarayana, Puripanda Appala Swamy etc., are a few writers who touched the issues of Dalits and hoped for the progress of Dalits in the first decades of twentieth century. In the second half of the twentieth century, Unnava Lakshmi Narayana and Ranganayakamma are popular by writing novels with Dalit themes.

5
From the Modern to the Post Modern Literature (1971– 2007) - II

The Modern Writers

The atrocities on Dalits in 1970's and 1980's are the major inspiration for the post-modern Telugu Dalit Literature. Dalit literature in Telugu erupted like a powerful volcano after the incidents of Kanchikacherla (1978), Padirikuppam (1983), Karamchedu (1985), Neerukonada (1987), and Tsunduru/ Chunduru (1991). Ironically these atrocities proved to be useful for the Dalits in away, as they united all the Dalits in the state.

The Silence of Scheduled Caste Associations: Causes

Between 1930s and 1970s there are two important factors that deviated Dalits from their Associations and agitations. This resulted in the division of Dalits too. These two strong factors are Gandhi's Congress Harijan Organization and the emergence of Communists. The Andhra branch of the **Harijan Sevak Sangh** was formed in November 1932 at Vijayawada.The Hindu reformers K.Nageswara Rao and M.Bapineedu were the President and General Secretary respectively. Two Dalits namely Vemula Kurmaiah from Krishna district and Naralasetti Devendrudu from West Godavari district were elected as Joint Secretaries. These two joint secretaries played a major role in organizing the Adi—Andhra conference and also in educating many Dalits especially in rural areas. Later a large section of Dalit intellectuals turned towards Congress and are satisfied with Harijan and Hindu identity.

The working class movement under the leadership of Communists was a powerful movement during 1930s and 1940s and it was popular among Dalits till 1970s. Under this movement they organized rural poor, workers and agricultural labourers i.e. they concentrated on both the organized and unorganized sectors. Certainly these unions were successful in raising the wages of the rural poor especially Dalits. The Communists never were willing to accept Dalit identity or Ambedkar.That is to say that they were not willing to give caste identity but only class identity. Their strong belief that economic up liftment of Dalits will change their position in the society proved wrong. They could not realize that the applications of dialectical materialism will not debrahmise the Indian social system. Ironically the caste identity and caste based exploitation were even practiced in Naxalite groups. Of course from 1980s onwards a majority of Dalits withdrew from Communist Parties as well as Naxalite groups. Hence, perhaps from the year 2000 the Communist Parties accepted the Dalit identity. The first **All India Convention on Dalit Rights** was organized by CPI(M) on 22nd February 2006 at New Delhi. In his inaugural address Prakash karat said that the objective of the convention was to focus on the problems of Dalits and their rights in India. He also urged and stressed that all the party units need to study the Dalit issues and requested them to take up agitations for redressal. This convention brought out a Charter of Demands to ensure a better life for the crores of Dalits in this country. The full text of the Charter of Demands is given here.

Charter of Demands

1. Land Reforms: The central and state governments must immediately set in motion a process of land reforms whereby land will be redistributed to the landless agricultural labourers and poor peasants gratis. All loopholes in the present laws must be plugged. All schemes to reverse land reform legislation and give away land to multinational corporations and big business house should be scrapped forthwith.

2. Reservations : All the backlogs in reserved seats and posts and in promotions for SCs,STs and OBCs must be filled forthwith with special recruitment drives. The three Constitutional amendments made to correct the three OMs issued in 97 diluting reservations for SCs and STs should be implemented. The pre-1997 vacancies based roster should be restored. A comprehensive legislation covering all aspects of reservation for SCs/STs in employment and education both public and private institutions should be enacted.

3. Special Component Plan : Special Component Plan should be properly implemented in all the states with proper allotment of funds according to the population of Dalits. A National Commission should be set up to assess the real position of Dalits including reservation. The state level commissions should be set up to oversee the implementation of all schemes connected with the SCs including reservation.

4. Infrastructure Development : Infrastructure development in the scheduled caste areas like road, water, health, culture and other needs has to be given proper importance. When allotting fund for infrastructure development, a separate allotment for scheduled caste areas should be provided.

A comprehensive National Programme of Minor Irrigation for all irrigable but unirrigated lands of SCs and STs through wells, community wells, bore-wells, community bore-wells and tube-wells, bandheras, check-dams, lift, etc/., should be immediately undertaken and implemented.

5. Rooting Out Untouchabiliy : All forms of untouchability must be rooted out of the country by strengthening the relevant laws, ensuring their strict implementation and most importantly, by launching a mass movement of the people.

6. Protection from Atrocities: The central government should amend and strengthen the SC and St (Prevention of Atrocities) Act 1989, providing for special courts with judges, investigating officers and public prosecutors unburdened by any other work. Social and economic boycott and blackmail should be included as substantive crimes. Full economic rehabilitation of victims and their survivors must be ensured.

7. Employment : The privatization drive should be stopped as it leads to loot of national assets, greater unemployment, a curtailment of reservations and also a spurt in corruption. The central government should enact a bill to provided reservations in the private sector, which has been a long-standing demand of SCs and STs. Special schemes to provide self-employment to SC youth should be started. The Right to Work should be incorporated as a fundamental right in the Constitution.

8.Education : The commercialization of education should be stopped since the massive fee and donation structure of private educational managements is something that socially and economically backward students cannot afford. For this, the central government must increase its own outlay on education to 6 percent of the GDP. SC/ST students should be given special scholarships to pursue their studies. The stipends in social welfare hostels should be raised and the quality of these hostels improved. Steps should be taken to universalize primary education and expand secondary education. Special measures to curb the drop-out rate among SCs should be undertaken.

9. Agricultural Workers : The Minimum Wages Act for agricultural workers must be stringently implemented throughout the country. A comprehensive bill for agricultural workers is another long-standing demand and it must be enacted without delay. Homestead land must be provided for SCs, STs and agricultural workers.

10. Rural Employment Gurantee Scheme : The National Rural Employment Guarantee Act must be strictly implemented all over the country by involving the people., their mass organisation and the panchayati raj institutions. It should be extended to all districts and also to urban areas of the country.

11. Public Distribution System : The public distribution system must be universalized to ensure food to all. Until this is done, BPL ration cards must be issued to all poor families, many of whom are from SCs and STs. The grain under the BPL scheme should be made available at Antyodaya prices.

12. Credit : Agricultural credit to peasants and agricultural workers must be made available at 4 percent rate of interest. For SCs and STs in both rural and urban areas, credit facilities should be expanded and the credit given at concession interest rates.

13. Bonded Labour and Child Labour : The total liberation and full rehabilitation of bonded labourers must be ensured. The pernicious practice of child labour must be abolished and children properly rehabilitated and educated. Similarly, total liberation and full rehabilitation must be ensured for Safai Karmacharis who are engaged in scavenging.

14. Scavengers : Ensure total liberation and full rehabilitation for scavengers (safai karmacharis), ban engagement of contract labour in safai services and other services where SC and ST numerically predominate and instead introduce necessary improvements by involving such karamcharis; and reactivate the Central Monitoring Committee for Liberation and Rehabilitation of Safai Karamcharis and State, Municipal and District Level communities.

15. Inter-caste Marriages: Inter-caste marriages should be encouraged by giving special subsidized housing and other facilities to married couples immediately after their marriage. We should consciously try to uphold such inter-caste marriages and make them an event of big social participation and sanction.

After the Independence the Dalits are perhaps satisfied with the Positive Discrimination and hence the Dalit Associations are passive in their activities. " 'Positive Discrimination' designates the set of measures adopted by the Indian government in favour of certain disadvantaged social categories. The purpose of which is to rectify the inequities and discriminations that afflict them (Robert Deliege 192)." Three points can be high lighted under positive discrimination. (1) A certain number of posts are reserved for Dalits in the important jobs in both central and state governments. (2) The state governments give scholarships, loans, distribution of land, free medical care etc. from the state expenditure. (3) Each state has taken some special measures like freedom to bonded labourers, canvassing against the practice of untouchability etc.

Atrocities On Dalits—Formation Of Dalit Mahasabha

The rebirth of Dalit Movement during 1980s in Andhra Pradesh is a historic incident. The earlier Social movements between 1940 and 1980 argued that economic imbalance is the basis for all revolutions. Contrary to this the Andhra Pradesh Dalit Movement erupted with the proclamation of self-respect for Dalits. The cruel inhuman incidents of Kanchikacherla (1978), Padirikuppam (1983), Karamchedu (1985), Neerukonda (1987), and Tsunduru/Chunduru (1991) are the major causes for the rebirth of Dalit Movement. The seventeenth of July 1985 is the Black day in the entire Andhra history. It records the cruel slaughter of Dalits (Madigas) with axes and sickles by the landlords that belong to kamma caste in Karamchedu of Prakasam District. The reason for this violence was connected with the highheadness of the Dominant Castes. A Kamma youth washed his buffaloes in the drinking water taking of Dalits (Madiga). A Madiga woman objected for that .The youth collected other Kamma youth and attacked the Madiga Colony.Several Dalit men and women were severely beaten up and women were even molested and raped in the broad daylight.

The leaders made Dr. Ambedkar's philosophy as a guiding spirit for the Karamchedu Camp. The Camp decided to refuse the false sympathy of both the State Government (TDP) and the State Opposition Party (Congress). when Dr. N.T.Rama Rao then the Chief Minister visited the victims in the hospital and offered fruits, Veeramma said " *Ayya*! (Sir), we do not eat such fruits; you are the rulers. These fruits are yours. We live on a handful of rice we earn from our daily labour. Why do I need fruits? After you became the Chief Minister, all your relatives in the villages too became Chief Ministers. They made us their targets. We are now totally shattered. Our families are broken and drowned in blood.... Now, what do we have to be afraid?"

The camp not only reject the bureaucrats but also the hypocritic Dalit leaders. The camp became the fountain for new ideas and ideology. They banned the usage of Harijan in the camp. The leaders insisted on the word Dalit or the names of individual castes such as Mala or Madiga. They wanted to emphasize on Ambedkar's argument that if untouchables are the sons and daughters of Hari (God) then what about the upper castes? Whose sons and daughters are they? It is important to note here that even the Communists in Andhra Pradesh never opposed and they used the nomenclature labourers (*Coolollu)* and it never gave a caste identity. But this word *coolollu* too is derogatory as it refers to the low in the hierarchy. After the establishment of Karamachedu camp the nomenclature Dalit gained credibility and acceptability.

The Dalit masses, in the coastal districts donated rice, dal, vegetables and money to support the Chirala Camp. They organized *dharnas, bandhs, Rasta rokos* and large public meetings. The audience were addressed by Dalit and committed leaders of OBC.

The Dalit women showed remarkable courage and confidence. In a every struggle they were in the fore front; Perhaps the reason for their active participation could be to fight against dominant castes as their men abused humiliated and sexually exploited them in their day to day life. This gave an opportunity for Dalit unity and they found the channel to abuse and mock the dominant caste culture. Those who were at the receiving end so far began to pay in the same measurement. Certainly in every *Dalitwada*, Bojja Tarakam and Padma Rao became heroes. Padma Rao's oratory skills, his public attacks on the dominant caste culture, his way of showing the practice of exploitation in the past by dominant castes, particularly the man-woman relationships, his scathing attack on Hindu Gods, their behaviour and habits became necessary points to brood over. The dominant caste Hindus planned to kill him. Though Kathi Padma Rao was not a student of history, his construction of history was based on his knowledge of Sanskrit and Telugu literature.

On the other hand, Bojja Tarakam known for his soft speeches became popular in public meetings. His character became a source of strength to the movement. He shot a series of questions to non-Dalits. Very often he criticized that political power and leadership in Andhra State is always in the hands of either Reddy or Kamma. .Hence he questioned is it a Reddy Raj or a Kamma raj? Why should only Reddys or Kammas become the chief ministers of the state while there are about 150 castes in Andhra Pradesh? Why can't any other person become the governor of the state? He even targeted the former Prime Ministers of India. He questioned Why should only Nehru, Lal Bahadur Shastri, Indira Gandhi and Rajiv Gandhi became the Prime Ministers? Why can't a Madiga or a Mala person become the Prime Minister? Why can't a Chakali or a Mangali person become the Prime Minister? Why were all the government institutions, from village Panchayat offices to the Prime Minister's office headed by dominant castes, even though they are a minority in the population? Why did land and industries become their private property? How come the state government institutions were made their private property?

Bojja Tarakam's speeches opened a crucial debate in the *Dalitwadas* (colonies of Dalits). The people observed that unlike Kathi Padma Rao, Bojja Tarakam does not hurt the dominant castes with his language and rather he would ask for Dalits' share in everything, i.e., in the civil societal property, the state institutions and so on. The common people had an intensive debate to decide on whose strategy was correct; the youth supported Kathi Padma Rao and the ideologically oriented elderly people preferred the strategy of Tarakam. However, it is for the first time the intellectuals became their heroes and their words became a subject of discourse among all Dalits. This it self was a transformation.

This incident instigated many agitations and discussions culminating into the formation of the **Andhra Pradesh Dalit Maha Sabha** at Vijayawada on the sixth of October 1985. Here in this meeting, under the leadership of Mr. Vyas the S.P, the people gathered at the meeting place were brutally beaten by the police. Many of the leaders like Katti Padma Rao, Salagala Raja Sekhar Babu Etc., were arrested. From then onwards the **Andhra Pradesh Dalit Mahasabha** gained momentum. On July 17, 1994 Katti Padma Rao while speaking in the 9th memorial meeting of the death of the Dalits of Karamchedu said, "As the Naxalbury is for Marxist and Leninist revolutions the Karamchedu incident is for the Dalit social revolution".

The formation of a Dalit Maha Sabha certainly made a different impact in Telugu Dalit Literature. The post-Karamchedu period produced two Lyric Writers specifically from Ambedkar's point of view. They were Masterji and Pavan Prasad- one established a Dalit cultural wing, called **Dalit Kalamndali**, and the other established **Jana Chaitanya Mandali.** The **Kalamandali** and **Chitanya Mandali** consistently and consciously set a Dalit tone which mainly advocated Ambedkar's ideology all over and focused on Dalit history. For example, a particular lyric by Masterji lists Gautama Buddha, Basava, Narayanaguru, Phule, Ambedkar and Periyar Ramaswami as conscientious leaders of the oppressed..

Meanwhile, in 1989 a socio-political fortnightly called **Nalupu (The Black)** was started with Bojja Tarakam as its editor. The editorial board included people belonging to dominant castes; all these non-Dalits were politically and ideologically sympathetic to the Dalit cause. The journal was financed and circulated by the Hyderabad Book Trust, a popular organization set up for translating popular and progressive literature from English to Telugu and publishing books in Telugu. Later **Nalupu** was established a major ideological organ of Dalitology. Perhaps it is the first popular journal that included a major theoretical contributions from Dalit intellectuals. **Nalupu** published a series of articles arguing for the abolition of caste and gave inspiration to capture the political power in every organization. No doubt this journal published essays that propagated the ideals of Phule and Ambedkar. Though the publication of the journal lasted for four years (1989-93), it created a committed and powerful group of journalists, poets and lyricists. Almost every issue published a biographical sketch of a Dalit activist at grass root level or a leader. Meanwhile K.G. Satyamurthy (Siva Sagar) and U. Sambasiva Rao formed a revolutionary group called the Marxist Leninist Centre (MLC). It initiated a new debate needed for the Indian democratic revolution. This centre argued that unless the anti caste theories of Marxism and Ambedkarism are interwoven the democratic revolution cannot be achieved.

K.G. Satyamurthy, a Dalit revolutionary, and a powerful poet made an impact on the Dalit movement. Satyamurthy became a symbol of sacrifice and honesty as he had gone to the underground for 20 years. The MLC started a journal called **Edureetha** (Swimming against the Tide) that began to make attempts to blend Marxism and Ambedkarism into a new class-caste theory under the editorial ship of K.G. Satyamurthy. Meanwhile, the CPI (ML) headed by K. Rajanna (a lower rung, OBC) politically and ideologically took an initiative to treat Phule and Dr. Ambedkar as integral anti-caste social revolutionaries. Though another major revolutionary group, i.e. CPI (ML) Peoples' War Group theoretically did not spell out its assessment of Phule and Ambedkar's contributions to the social transformation, its pro-Dalit role after the Karamchedu massacre, particularly the assassination of Chenchuramaiah, the main accused, was appreciated by the Dalit of Andhra Pradesh at large.

The most significant turn in the Maoist (ML) and Dalit movements of Andhra took place with the anti-Mandal agitation (1990). The Maoists and Dalit Associations had emerged as a pro-Mandal front, and at the same time the educated OBCs began to think positively for the unification of the SCs and OBCs. The post Mandal developments, coupled with the post-karamchedu consciousness, changed the political atmosphere radically. This paved the way for Dalitism to occupy a definite place in the agenda of the political parties.

Atrocities in Andatpur

Atrocities on Dalits of Andatpur is yet another inhuman incident that is hidden from the public. Ganapathi and Manik from Madiga colony of Andatpur village, Narayana Khed Mandal, Medak district were the farm servants of the landlords Pandru Patel and Vital Rao, respectively. On 15th of January 1986 Ganapathi and Manik entered the main village to go to their colony from the cattle sheds of their masters / landlords. Manohar Patel stopped them in the middle of the village i.e. near Mahaboosab's hotel and asked for the explanation for entering the village as the entry is denied to them. When the Dalits tried to explain they were abused in filthy language and Manohar Patel took a long stick which has a hook fixed at one end (that is used to cut the branches of trees) and beaten Ganapathi on the head. Mean while Sankarappa and others who gathered there threw stones at Manik. When they found the severe injuries and bleeding on Ganapathi then the landlords withdrew themselves from the sight. This created a serious concern in Madiga colony because a majority of them have come back homes to celebrate Sankranti / Pongal from the places of migration. After a heated discussion they lodged a complaint in Manoor Police station against Manohar Patel and Sankarappa. The landlords got angry and mobilized their supporters by the evening of 16th January. They attacked the Madiga colony and burnt their houses. Not only grain, clothes, and vessels even their hard earned money was burnt. And some of the houses were looted. It was very tragic to note that in Arjun's house alone Rs.16,750/- was burnt to ashes. Even the mangalasutras and gold ornaments were snatched. The burning, looting and snatching took nearly two hours. Thus 23 houses of Scheduled Castes and Banjara Tribals were destroyed by a well organized plan of Maratha and Lingayat landlords. Very strangely the incident is reported in the press as clashes between Scheduled Castes and Backwards Castes. Just because the Backward Castes (Kurumas, Potters and Watermen) took part in looting it was misreported. As in every case of Dalits here also police supported the landlords.

Tsunduru/Chunduru : A Case Study

While the memories of Karamchedu are still fresh and have not faded away yet another cruel incident took place in Tsunduru/Chunduru of Guntur district on the sixth of August 1991. The brutal murders were reported and propagated throughout the country by **Andhra Pradesh Dalit Maha Sabha.** The proud dominant castes of Tsunduru /Chunduru massacred the Dalits with axes, sickles and swords in the broad daylight chasing them, while Dalits running for their lives. Unlike Karamchedu victims, the victims of Tsunduru/ Chundur set a historical demand to the government that a special court has to be brought to the doorsteps of the victims for the hearing of the case and the Government agreed. The Reddys (one of the dominant castes) wanted to suppress and control the Dalits (Malas) of Tsunduru/ Chunduru. The refusal resulted in massacre of Malas.

The violence aimed at Dalits in Kanchikacherla reached its heights with the brutal carnage of Dalits in Tsunduru/ Chunduru. This violent act against Dalits is the first of its kind in the Andhra Pradesh where eight Dalits were massacred and the corpses were packed in the gunny bags. Those eight victims were Jaladi Immanuel, Jaladi Mathaiah, Mallela Subba Rao, Devarapalli Jaya Raju, Jaladi Issaku, Sankuru Samson, Angalakuduru Rajamohan and Manduru Ramesh. A few days before the black day, the tension was developed in Tsunduru/ Chunduru between Dalit youth and the farmers. The incident in the cinema theatre had become the point for the eruption of the volcano. In the theatre a Dalit youth's foot touched the foot of a Reddy youth. It added fuel to the fire. Already police entered the village as there were cases in the court against each group accusing the other. The best example to show how brutal the carnage was that of, the physician Dr. Ravi Chander, after conducting the postmortem committed suicide as he could not bear the sight of the corpses. The Dalits all over the state gathered under the leadership of Katti Padma Rao, the Chief Secretary of **The Andhra Pradesh Dalit Mahasabha**. They refused to meet the then Chief Minister Dr.N.T.Rama Rao who came to console the victims. **The Andhra Pradesh Dalit Mahasabha** further strengthened the struggle by giving the slogan "Not welfare but self-respect".

Kalekuri Prasad a powerful Dalit writer wrote a poem that depicted the violent incidents against Dalits.To quote his poem here is quiet apt as he speaks for the self-respect of Dalits in the poem.

For a Fistful of Self-Respect ...

I don't know when I was born
but, for sure, I was killed
on this very soil

thousands of years ago.
Punarapi Maranam, Punarapi Jananam
I don't know this theory of karma
but I am born and reborn time and again
where I breathed my last.
Merging in the soil,
my body became Ganga-Sindhu plains.
As my eye-balls melted into tears
rivers flowed across the country.
From my veins life forces flowed
onto the land
that yielded prosperity to this country!
In Tretayuga I was Shambhuka;
Twenty-two years ago,
my name was Kanchikacherla Kotesu;
my birthplace is Keelavenmani, Karamchedu, and Neerukonda.
Now, the name tattooed on my chest
with ploughshares
by hardened cruelty of feudalism is Chunduru.
Chunduru is not a proper noun;
from now on, it is a common noun.
Now, every heart is a Chunduru, a raging tumour of a village
I am the wound of the masses,
a collection of wounds at that.
In a free country
I am the unliberated one
now, for ages.
I am the one subjected to untold suffering
humiliations, atrocities, rapes and tortures.
For a fistful of self-respect
I raised my head.
In the domain of the stinking rich,
of the caste-oppressors
I am leading a life
with my life itself as a protest.
I am the one dying time and again

in order to survive.
Don't call me a victim
I am a martyr, deathless one, and deathless one!
I am Siva who swallowed famines
to make the country prosperous.
I am the one who kicked over the head of the sun
to make the upside down morning
straighten up.
I am the one who pours forth slogans
in a blazing furnace.
I don't need your words of solace
and your tear-packs.
I am not a victim, I am a martyr.
I am the flag of defiance flying high.
Don't shed tears for me.
If you can,
you bury me in the heart of the city.
I will bloom as bamboo trees
playing life-music.
You print my corpse as the cover page
of this country.
I will pervade as a magnificent future
in pages of history.
Becoming the fury of wild fires
I will take birth again and again
in this country. (Tr. By. K. Damodar Rao)

On 10th August 1991 all those dead bodies were burned in the centre of the village and named the site ***Rakta Kshetram*** (The land of blood).When the Tsunduru/ Chundur carnage occurred on 8 August 1991, the political discourse was on the path of this new conculsion. At Tsundur/ Chunduru eight Dalits were brutally murdered by Reddy landlords, which triggered off another phase of struggle. This struggle further strengthened the Dalitization process. By that time the Bahujan Samaj Party (BSP) which became a force in north India, opened its Andhra wing in 1989, and subsequently the BSP used this newly emerging sociopolitical base for its mobilization.

After the SP- BSP combine came to power in Uttar Pradesh by stalling the Hindu communal forces (BJP) capturing Delhi, the Dalit bahujan political forces in Andhra Pradesh began to organize themselves on independent lines. In the 1994 Assembly elections, BSP contested almost all the seats. Though it could not win a single seat it created a very conscious leadership base at the village, mandal, district and state levels. In every political party and group, the question of political power to Dalit bahujans has become a mind boggling question. This undoubtedly created a definite political trend in Andhra Pradesh. It appears that the future discourse would be that of caste and class but not of one dimensional class or one dimensional caste. It would be a sort of systemization of Marxism and Ambedkarism.

The Tsunduru/ Chundur Carnage Published by **Andhra Pradesh Civil Liberties Committee**, focused on the socio-economic structure of the Tsundur/Chunduru, the sequence of events happened between the dominants castes and the Dalits in Tsundur/Chundur. And then the final assault on the Dalits by upper caste Reddys of Modukar, Dindipalem and Valiveru villages.

In this case the charge sheet was filed against 219 and before the hearing of case started 33 of them died and the remaining 179 faced the enquiry. On the 31st (Tuesday) July 2007 the court assembled at 10.30 am in Tsunduru/ Chunduru. Twenty one persons were sentenced to life imprisonment under section 302 of the IPC and thirty five others were sentenced for one year's rigorous imprisonment along with a penalty of Rs.2000/- each.

> Delivering the judgment seven days short of 17th anniversary of the gruesome attack on Dalits of Malapalli here, special judge Anis of Special Court under the SC/ST's prevention of (Atrocities) Act 1989, felt that it was not the rarest of the rare cases, which attracted a death penalty.

> In the country's first-ever special court set up for trying a case under the Act at the scene of offence, the judge acquitted 123 out of the 179 accused persons.
>
> In the case of 41 accused persons, the court did not find any evidence, while 62 of them were released on benefit of doubt. The other 20 were let off due to omission of evidence or having only single witnesses.

Found guilty

Of the 56 convicted, 21 were found guilty of charges under section 302 of the IPC.

(**The Hindu** 1-08-2007 p.1)

It took almost seventeen years for the award of the punishment after the heinous crime was committed at Tsunduru/Chunduru. Before the pronouncement of the Judgment the special prosecutor B.Chandra Sekhar argued that this is the rarest of the rare and hence the criminals had to be sentenced to death as per section 302. He also supported his argument by quoting Bachan Singh Case (1981) of the Supreme Court. But the defense lawyers Kaaiti Syda Reddy, S.Brahmananda Reddy, Garikapati Krishna Rao and K.V.Sharma stated that the Dalits and the farmers are now living peacefully and moreover the government paid compensation by giving them houses, land and employment. Hence they argued against the death sentence for the convicted. According to Ramesh Susarla and P.Samuel Jonathan:

> The prosecution is recommending to the State Government to go in for an appeal in the High Court against the judgment in the Tsundur case. Special Public Prosecutor B.Chandrasekhar and Assistant Public Prosecutor G.S.Nageswara Rao, who were appointed by State Government exclusively for this case, said the court had failed to see a conspiracy angle and common motive of killing Dalits and hence the sentence was "not satisfactory" to them.
>
> It was for the final judgment that Mandu Tulasamma, a widow at Ambedkar Colony here, has been waiting with bated breath.

> Ever since she lost her two sons in the brutal carnage against Dalits unleashed by persons belonging to upper castes on August 6, 1991 in the village, she has been waiting for justice to be meted out to her.
>
> And when Special Judge Anis pronounced the verdict, Tulasamma broke down. Quickly gaining her composure, she angrily said: "I was denied justice, as the guilty have been let off. The perpetrators of the heinous crime would still roam freely in the village". Recalling the events on the fateful day, she said: "There was no trace of my younger son the whole day. The next day, someone said that they had seen his body in a canal. My elder son Narayana broke down on hearing the news and he died of heart attack".
>
> Kula Nirmoolana Porata Samithi district secretary K.Krishna said at least 100 of the accused were let off and his organisation would appeal in the High Court seeking justice. **(The Hindu** 1-08-2007, p.12)

The Dalit Organizations in various districts of the state partially celebrated the victory and they expressed dissatisfaction at the Judgment. Gollapalli Surya Rao, the Minister for Small Scale Industries in the Government led by Chief Minister Dr.Y.S.Raja Sekhara Reddy declared that the unity of Dalits is the cause for the victory of the victims of Tsunduru/Chunduru. It is surprised to note that Katti Padma Rao, the founder member of **Dalit Mahasabha** agreed with the life imprisonment instead of capital punishment. After receiving the honourary Doctorate from Acharya Nagarjuna University he spoke on the judgement of Tsunduru/ Chunduru case in the press conference in Guntur on Saturday the fourth of August 2007. He said that the **Andhra Pradesh Dalit Mahasabha** opposes the death sentence. He said:

"We want equality in society for Dalits and upper castes, but do not believe in getting capital punishment. If any individual lawyer expresses his wish as part of his 'professional brief' it has nothing to do with the Dalit movement at large," he clarified.

"Judgment was on expected lines and now that land has been given to the victims' kin and some revenue earning means shown to them, they have come on an equal plane with Reddys and Telagas so they co-exist with dignity and conditions of those days do not exist there any more," he told reporters.

(The Hindu 5-8-2007 p. 4)

The Andhra Pradesh Dalit Mahasabha conducted a rally from Mangala Mandiram of Guntur to Ambedkar Bhavan, in New Delhi with the demands that (1). The criminals must be punished (2). The economic support and protection for the witness must be secured. On the 3rd October 1991 the rally met the Prime Minister and demanded for a special court at the place of crime and rehabilitation for the victims. It took almost a year to complete the rehabilitation work. Though the special court was appointed at the earliest possible, there were so many obstacles and hurdles for the enquiry. Finally on 1st December 2004 the enquiry started in Tsunduru/Chunduru in the special court established under Prevention of Atrocities on SCs and STs. It took almost twenty seven months to complete the enquiry.

It took two days for the massacre to come to limelight. On the second day i.e. 8th August 1991 the corpses were found in the Tungabhadra drainage, in a jasmine garden, in the New Canal near Modukuru, in Branch Canal 1 and in Aremanda Canal. Some of these corpses were packed in gunny bags and a corpse was found without eyes. A total of twelve cases were filed. Among the eight murdered people seven of them were Malas and Angala Kuduru Raja Mohan Gandhi alone was a Madiga. Out of the five injured Tanachintala Adam alone was Madiga and all the remaining four belong to Mala caste. In this case the charge sheet was filed against 219 people from four villages and the villages are Tsunduru/Chunduru, Munnagivaripalem, Modukuru and Valiveru. The people from four villages is a clear evidence that the violent action is pre-planned. Out of the 219 accused there were only two Backward Caste persons and all the remaining were Reddys and Telagas.

The first **Dalit Mahasabha** in 1985 established after the Karamchedu massacre is the turning point in Dalit literature. The literature aims at Brahminism and its injustice towards Dalits. The protest against the hegemony of upper castes, anger, self-respect, in search of roots, social exploitation etc are the themes of Dalit literature. Certainly all the writers of this category are much influenced by Ambedkarism. In the twentieth century Ambedkar perhaps, is the first Dalit to realise and voiced against Hindu Dharma Sastras. In his book on **Annihilation of Caste,** he said, "the Indian society was formed with an ascending scale of reverence and descending scale of contempt" (47). Though the lower castes are the basis for every manual work, unfortunately they are looked down. Dalits now realised their importance in the society; they want to assert their place in the society. "From the socio-cultural and aesthetic points of view, this post-80s phenomenon needs to be studied seriously and deeply" (Jadhav 39).

The above incidents proved to be the background for many Telugu Dalit writers of post 1980s.In 1995 **Chikkanavutunna Pata** (**Thickening Song**), an anthology of about sixty poets created an upheaval in the history of Telugu Dalit Literature. Later **Nisani**, **Gunde Dappu**, **Bahuvachanam** (**Several Voices**) etc followed the path. There are many powerful Dalit Bahujan Writers who are instrumental in creating an important place for Dalit literature in the main stream Telugu literature. A few among them are Gaddar, Katti Padma Rao, Bojja Tharakam, Satish Chander, Madduri Nagesh Babu, Jooluri Gowri Sankar, Masterji, Kolakaluri Enoch, Sky Baba, Challapalli Swaroopa Rani, Varre Rani etc.

A seminar on Telugu Dalit literature was inaugurated in the press club (Basheer bagh), Hyderabad on 28-7-1996. The Lokayuta publications of Ponnuru, **The Andhra Pradesh Dalit Mahasabha**, The Dalit Research Wing,

Hyderabad and **The Ambedkar Students' Association**, University of Hyderabad, jointly organized the seminar. Two important books **Racchabanda** by Madduri Nagesh Babu **Nalla Kaluva** by Katti Padma Rao were released. Important Dalit writers and researchers like Devarapalli Mastan Rao, Sikhamani, Koyi Koteswara Rao, Yendluri Sudhakar etc., spoke in that Seminar. From then onwards a majority of Telugu Dalit writers got inspiration and published a considerable number of Dalit Literary works.

A number of young Dalit writers produced powerful literature. The major themes of Dalit literature are: questioning the existing social system; bring to light the age old exploitation of the caste system; establishment of Dalits as the original inhabitants of the land; rejection of Hindu religion that sanctioned the caste system; critical and creative re-reading of the existing Telugu literature; condemning the participation of dominant castes by denying the opportunities for Dalits in politics etc

K.G. SATHYA MURTHY (1931 -)

Kambham Gnana Sathya Murthy popularly known as Siva Sagar in the literary world was born on 15th July in Adavikolanu of West Godavari district. His parents are Prasada Rao and Mary. He did his Post Graduation in Political Science from Andhra University, Visakhapatnam. He worked as a teacher in Gabriel High School at Kazipet from 1964 to 1969. Later he became a professional full-time revolutionary by associating himself with People's War. He was the Secretary of the Central Committee, **All India Peoples War** from 1980 to 1985.

Satyamurthy said that he was sent out of the People's War when he tried for the establishment of internal democracy. He didn't come out of the organization by himself. He is not only a poet but a singer too. He was actively involved with the cultural activities of the People's War. **Swetcha** Publications of Khammam brought out a collection of poems written and published by Siva Sagar from 1968-2004, in September 2004 under the title **Siva**

Sagar Kavitvam (**SivaSagar's Poetry**). In the review of this work Kasula Pratapa Reddy complimented that "Siva Sagar is one among a few Telugu Poets, who shot and can skillfully shoot poetry as a weapon". (**Vaartha,** Sunday book, 30-1-2005, P.32).

Satyamurthy is a committed writer and always concentrated on social and political exploitation in the society. He is a voracious reader and read about the revolutions of various countries for the establishment of new society. His poem, published in **Indian Literature** in 2000 is cited here.

On-going History

Sambuka with a smile on his lips
in executing Rama
Ekalavya is chopping off Drona's thumb
with an axe
Bali with his tiny feet is trampling
Vamana into the netherworld
Manu with needles poked in his eyes
his tongue cut
molten lead in his ears
is rolling in the graveyard
On the cruel sword of time stands
the roaring Chandala
inciting
four hounds onto Sankara
That's it!
The ongoing history
Is a very Chandala history. (Tr. By. Archana Chowhan)
(**Indian Literature,** Nov-Dec 2000)

In addition to Siva Sagar's poem **On Going History,** Banna Ilaiah's poem **Untainted History** proves a good example of Dalits' questioning the history.

Untained History

Are these footprints causing fear?

Is the roar of blood streams sending shivers?
These are not the footmarks of yesterday
Nor the thumb impressions
Printed in history pages by you.
From the times of the decapitated Shambhuka
To the deceptions of Gurudakshinas
Our thumbs have been used for filling history pages
From the period of rolled heads in the fields
To the borderline of the shameless present
Of forcing us eat excreta
Yours is the only route.
Ours are plain roads.
Whoever has stolen my soil-hands all these days
Whoever has taken pains to make me tainted
Whoever has imprisoned my liberty, labour and body
That very one is now focusing on humanity
Over the walls built around me.
But I am creating a tune to my song sung without it
For centuries.
I now know I am the diamond-crown over the head of
Present history.
I also know I had a history of the soil
An untained, untarnished history!

(Tr.BY. K. Damodar Rao) (taken from **Kakatiya journal of English Studies**, Vol 23, 2003).

M.A.K. Bhima Rao looked at history from a different angle and certainly with anger and protest. In the conclusion of the poem he anticipates the political power Dalits and assures that would be a meaningful democratic rule.

Ruling History

Heirs for once magnificent history,
Symbols for ruined Indus civilization
Scapegoats for Manu's magic world
Dalit brothers, to-day are our brothers
Cutting the dark blind curtains of generations
Crossing the foul pits of casteism
We are rushing thunders from the

Sacrificial stones of slavery
We had become blood drops of
Valiant revolutionary Ambedkar
who plucked the untouchable horns of caste demon
Once, you poured venom in our ears
It melted and melted opening our ear drums,
They await the revolutionary drum beats
In the place of our tongues cut by you,
We raised new tongues with vehemence
They had opened their stings with blood thirsty revenge
The clothes stitched to our long back have corroded
Now we gather arsenal to cut your mouths
Not only the nose and ears of "Surpanakha"
But also all the organs of my race were ravaged
By you upper caste Hindu enemies
Therefore,
These bats hanging in the temples
Become ravines to
Tear off your injustice
We shall bathe the lost chastity of our women with your blood
The fourth foot of Dharma which had become lame due to you
We shall resurrect it with the breath of our people
We shall keep the flame aloft with our blood as oil
The shrunken particles our body shamed by you
We will become the rulers of egalitarianism and
Rule history. (Tr. BY. Ch. Prabhakar)

Perhaps one can find justification only when one can look at these poems from New Historical perspective. History has become so crucial and central to modern humanities that one 'history' is not only insufficient but also fallible. The imperial idea of linear history has been replaced by more multi-dimensional, syncretic ones. Therefore, historians have generated 'alternate histories', 'counter histories' and 'counterfactual histories'. They prefer to replace 'history' with 'histories' since the world has to be read as a text and these readings are a 'legion' as they are many. Amos Funkenstein uses the term 'counter history' to describe the rabbinical polemics against the Gospels and applies it to the early stages of secular history as well. Thus history's roots lie in the rebellion against the convenient, self-justifying, official stories of the priests and rulers. Counter history and history are moments or stages in a continuous, conflictual process rather than substantially independent, autonomous, opposing activities with independently distinguishing characteristics of their own. Raymond Williams implies that literature itself can be read as counter history and alternate history. The counter historical mentality is visible throughout literary and cultural studies. Nothing is trans-historical and every culture is historicist either 'new' or 'old'. But the old historicism and a historicism perceived culture as synchronic but historicism in the hands of its new practitioners perceived all culture as diachronic.

In December 2004, Dr. Ambedkar People's Educational Trust, Hyderabad published Sathya Murthy's **Ambedkar Suryudu** (**Ambedkar is the Sun**). He wrote this book as a critical response to Ranganayakamma's book. He finds fault with Ranganayakamma for writing a biased work about Ambedkar without reading him and properly understanding him. At present he is taking part in Public Meetings and seminars as a speaker. He has also completed a major part of his biography. He is the founder of **Sureedu**, a political party in 2006.

THERESA DEVADANAM (1937 -)

Veena Vani is the title given to Theresa Devadanam, born in Ramireddy Thota (Madiga colony), Guntur. Her parents are teachers during pre independent days. They worked hard for the untouchables, and they opened schools for these children in Rami Reddy Thota. Theresa did her schooling in St. Joseph's high school, Guntur and St. Ann's, Phirangipuram, Guntur, Dt. She married

Devadanam in 1955 and from then onwards she is known as Theresa Devadanam. After completing her education she joined as a teacher in 1958.

From her childhood she showed interest in dance, drawing and music. After reading Vemana's poetry she imitated him in her writing. Initially she never got any encouragement for her writing from her teachers. But she was never discouraged and moreover she alone with her friends used to form a group and tune her poetry and sing very well. Later her teachers (nuns) made all the other students to sing those songs. Caste discrimination was in practice in the missionary hostels, observed Theresa Devadanam. The Dalits and non-Dalits had separate dinning places. Based on all this ill treatment she focused the miseries of the Dalits in her poems.

During the National Freedom Movement she actively participated in the activities of the National Congress. She wrote **Burrakathalu** during this period – **The Birth of Christ** (1958), **Gandhi** (1959) and **The Birth of Ambedkar** (1964). Her songs on Christianity under the title **Chraistava Geeta Maalika** are translated into English, French, Hindi and a popular musician John Billomoria tuned and rendered the songs in various Churches in India. She received many Awards from – the government of Andhra Pradesh, Andhra University, Joshua Pittam and from various youth Associations.

From 1975 to 1980 she wrote poetry mainly with Dalit Concepts. In 1980 a poetry collection, **Who are the Untouchables? Whose Mistake?** and in 1985 **The Life History of Ambedkar** another long poem are published. In the year 1985 she took active participation in the Karamchedu – agitation.

KOLAKALURI ENOCH (1939 -)

Professor Kolakaluri Enoch former Vice-chancellor of S.V. University, Tirupati was born in Vejendla village of Guntur district. His parents are Ramaiah and Veeramma. He did his B.A. (honours) in Andhra University, and Ph.D in S.V. University, Tirupati. During 1957and1959 he received prizes for best poem, story and play in Andhra University. He wrote 180 poems, 180 stories, 8 novels and 30 plays so far. A collection of his short stories **Urabavi** and **Munivahanudu** a play bagged the Sahitya Akademi Awards in 1986 and 1988 respectively. His play **Jai Hind** received the Andhra Pradesh State Government Award in 1965. The Andhra Prabha illustrated weekly awarded a prize for his novel, **Anaadha** (**An Orphan**). It is serialized in **Andhra Prabha**. He is an excellent orator. He also produced six research works and till now five M. Phil's and Nine PhDs are done on his works in the Universities of the state like Acharya Nagarjuna, Osmania, Andhra and Sri Krishnadevaraya etc. He recited poetry from various stations of All India Radio at national and regional level. The story **Talalenodu (A Person Without a Head)** is prescribed for Intermediate course during the years 1987-95. A good number of his stories are translated into English, Hindi, Kannada and Tamil. He wrote poetry in English and published under the title **"Voice of Silence"**. A poem is quoted here from this book.

You Miss Most of Me

Poetry said to poet:
"Earth is my daughter
Man is younger
than amoeba
elephant and monkey
Yours fathers learnt the language
very recently
and you understood my language
only yesterday.
You are one year old
and I am hundred years young.
You want to express hundred years
with only one year
It is natural
You miss most of me
and can't satisfy me

Our marriage has been a frustration
You are happy with one percent
What will you be?
If hundred percent is revealed"
The poet was lost in silence.

His critical work **Adhunika Sahitya Vimarsa Sutra (A Theoretical Exposition of Modern Telugu Literary Criticism)** got Sahiti Puraskaram in June 1999 from Potti Sri Ramulu Telugu University. His stories reflect the social reality. He is a writer with a "Missionary Zeal". His poetry truly reflects the life and suffering of Dalits. For example:

Worshipping Footwear

I worship the footwear
That stood beneath your feet; that made you stand;
Protecting your walk and talk;
Made your life a dusky band.
I worship the footwear
That, in violence and non-violence so far dare;
To control the lifestyles and existence of your life's mare.
In witness of the tear-drops-rainbows of "Karma Sakshi";
Of the day which bring footwear to those which stood bare;
I worship the footwear.
In witness to those
Battles that were fought; kingdoms that were upheld;
Fields loved and caressed; palanquins lifted;
Lives, wealth and health lost;
I worship the footwear.
Looking at beautiful work of 'Taj Mahal" by these bare foots;
Of people, who
Born, grown and died in foot wear
I worship the footwear.
In witness of the unfortunate race, that
Fled hither thither with no place to hide
When welkin cried the vaporous rains

I worship the footwear
In witness of those
Magnetic life spans of kith and kin;
Who flew like pristine crows?
In hunger, pain and in search of food;
I worship the footwear.
In witness of the hearts of men,
Who were refused permission to enter?
Temples that keep stones;
Power corridors slept by dogs;
Village meets sat by jackals;
I worship the footwear.
In witness of those naked penuries
Sacrificed selves to others, to the nation;
Identified themselves with their race, people and country;
To honesty and truth;
I worship the footwear.
In witness of the feminine masculinities;
Whose wonderful living capabilities;
Donated life to the nation's fifth division;
With their birth, growth and death in jails;
I worship the footwear.
In witness of those sacred fires;
Who gave birth to helpless modern "Karnas";
That stood armless, with dispassion, stillness, unmoved;
With their chariot wheels broke in the midst of their life battles;
I worship the footwear.
In witness of the lives of
Benign humane donors who wished to be sacrificed;
To the Ultramodern magicians and mandarins;
Who brought the land, sky and head in three feet?
I worship the footwear.
In witness of the luck of those
Aborigines who didn't perish;
With hermitages in tears, lives spread in thorns;

Dried waterholes and empty mouthed clouds in the village outfields;
I worship the footwear.
In witness of the country's prosperity;
That observes the raw puppetry; keeping - the helpless justice blindfold;
Tears as boons of line; poverty in bank safe lockers;
Unjust systems in parliament;
I worship the footwear. (Tr. By. Ch.Prabhakar)

BOJJA TARAKAM (1939 -)

A committed lawyer fighting for the problems of Dalits in Andhra Pradesh State High Court, Bojja Tarakam was born in Kandikuppa village of East Godavari district. His parents are Appalaswami and Mavullamma. He took B.A. degree from Pitapuram Raja's college, Kakinada and LLB degree from Osmania University, Hyderabad. He is a serious social activist. Tarakam was imprisoned during emergency (1975) for fighting for the rights of the people. He also actively participated in, and one of the leading members in Andhra Dalit Movement in 1986. He is also a writer. He published **Naalage Godavari** (**Godavari is Like Me**) in the year 2000. And **Brezil Prajala Bhuporatam** (**The Brazilian's fight for the Land**) in 2003 was published by Janapada Vignana Kendram, Hyderabad. **Naalage Godavari** consists of 21 poems. In a poem, **Ayudham Kaavaali** (**Need of a Weapon**) he says:

One-person works hard
Some one else receives the fruits
This is the order of the day
For ages!
...
There is neither an Award
Nor a reward
For the hardwork
Either today
Or yesterday
Yes,

This is not the history of today
A flow of thousands of years
...

In another poem **The Doors of the Temple**, the poet expresses his desire to touch god even by breaking open the temple doors. Bojja Tarakam also writes articles on social issues to the Telugu Newspapers.

MOTKUPALLI DAMAYANTI DEVI (1939 -)

The Ambedkar National Award winner, Motkupalli Damayanti Devi was born in Hyderabad and her education and employment too are in the capital city of Andhra Pradesh. Her parents are Galeiah and Danamma. After completing PUC and teacher training she joined as a teacher in 1965 in the government school, Sitaphal Mandi.

Damayanti Devi was inspired by Vemana Satakam and tried to write in that style. She read the life history of Ambedkar in Marathi and also read a popular Telugu Critical and Creative writer Tapi Dharma Rao. Surprised to know that there are no songs in the Telugu film **Dr. B.R. Ambedkar** produced by Dr. Padmavati, she wrote some songs on Ambedkar and released an audio cassette.

Twice in 1989 and 1992 she received **Dr. Ambedkar Puraskar** from Indian Dalit Sahitya Akademi, New Delhi. She also got **Sulochani Award** in 1998. She wrote books on Indira Gandhi, Rajiv Gandhi, Joshua, Jagjivanram and Ambedkar. She also worked as a consultant to 'Human Rights Protection cell'. She is the President of the Andhra Pradesh state wing of **Bharatiya Dalita Akademi** from 1992-96. In her poem **Kullu Vyavastha (The Rotten System)** she commented that the Hindus are slaves depending on Brahmins for every activity in life. She also warned that the Brahmanism would destroy our nation, the seat of various religions.

MAMIDI SATYAVATHI (1941 -)

Mamidi Satyavathi is born in Janagam village of Warangal district. She did her education in Hyderabad and political leaders and party workers always visit her house. Her first essay is published in 1958 in a school magazine when she was 15 years old. She often read **Jayabheri**, a journal run by Kusuma Dharmanna and **Jaibheem** by Tirupati Bhupathi. She likes Sarata's novels too. A majority of her works are published in the **Praja Bandhu** (Magazine) with her pen name "Komala". The bonded labour of Dalits, the untouchability and the feelings of women are the major themes in her writings. In her story **Tera Toligindi** (**The Curtain is Risen**) she portrayed that woman can come out of the family when there are unsolved problems

B. VIJAYA BHARATHI (1941 -)

Dr. Vijaya Bharathi was born in Rajolu of East Godavari district. Her father Boyi Bheemanna is a popular and powerful writer and mother is Nagaratnamma. Her maternal grandfather was very much impressed by Ambedkar and Gandhi and started schools on par with Christian Missionaries. During her childhood she is exposed to important Dalit social activists like Kusuma Dharmanna, who visited their house. She did her master's degree in Koti Women's college of Osmania University, Hyderabad. She is the second woman to receive doctorate in Telugu Literature from Osmania University. She worked in various capacities as Lecturer, Vice-Principal and Principal, Research Officer and Deputy Director of **Telugu Akademi.**

In 1982 she wrote a book **The Life History of Ambedkar** and in 1986 it had second and third publication. She is the first translator of Dhananjay Keer's book – **The Life History of Jyotiba Phule**. After reading Ambedkar and Phule she started critical analysis of Hindu Puranas and Vedas. As a result she wrote - **Ramayanam –The Land Struggle** and **Puranas – Caste System – Harischandra** with Dalit orientation. Her articles are published in various journals and newspapers like – **Bahujana Telugu, Golkonda**, and **Nalupu Communism, Vaartha** etc. She contributed a thought provoking paper entitled **Hindu Epics: Portrayal of Dalit women** in the book **Dalit Women: Issues and Perspectives** edited by P.G. Jogdand in 1995.

SUREPALLI MANOHAR (1942 -)

Surepalli Manohar was born on 22nd June 1942, in Pinnelli of Guntur district. His parents are Kataiah and Janamma. He did his BA in Nalgonda and he worked as a Junior Lecturer in Telugu and retired in 2000. His poems are published in various Telugu Magazines. Manohar also contributed various articles to Telugu Newspapers and Magazines. He published a long poem entitled **Nallagonda Naayamma** in 2002. He also wrote and enacted in the play **Kanniti Mantalu**. He is the scriptwriter for **Ee Charitra Cheripeddam** that won **Nandi Award** from the Government of Andhra Pradesh for the Best film under the Documentary section. He also wrote the script for **Pragati Padham lo Nallagonda** another documentary film produced by Nalgonda friends. His poem is given here.

Reformation

You're a pride into the nation
You waged a war against the fanatic religious presumptions
And the conceits of caste pride
You operated on the cancerous/ cankerous tumour of untouchability
Fought unto death for the upliftment of the Dalit
Ambedkar, you're my country's pride;
Emancipation of the oppressed was your motto.
Establishment of a new social order was your goal.
Destroying the demon of untouchability was your revolution.
Women's progress was your cherished aspiration.
And a caste free society was your dream.
Educate! Organise!! Agitate!!!
Is the slogan you gave to the nation

A clarion call for revolution
Its echo is whirling on earth, in the sky,
In water, in air, in fire, reaching
The very far ends of the four directions shaking them
When we think of the remarkable agitation
You rose those days
Against the caste system
Against the religious fanaticism
Against the inhuman heinous social practices
Against the rotten, stinking stigmatic social evils
Against the unquestionable iron laws
When we think of your courage
That fought a social war singularly
When we think of the unflinching boldness
With which you hankered the caste-ridden
society into pieces
That courage, that rage, that commitment
It boils our blood and the heart
Springs up in raptures
That agitation
That fury
That distress
That efficacious shouldering of a social cause
When we think of it, it raises
Volcanoes in the heart
Waterfalls from eyes
And flames of fury allover the body
It needs guts
It needs courage
It needs self-confidence and self-esteem
It needs efficacy
To cremate the 'Manusmruthi'
The world was stunned
The world revered you more than
Martin Luther who burnt the Sale of Indulgence*
You are lauded in the world history
As a great social revolutionist, a daring and dauntless
one

Ambedkar, you're my country's pride
You championed the cause of the downtrodden into death
You aspired for a casteless society
Your sacrifice will be remembered forever
Let me end with an aphorism of yours
"In an oblation they sacrifice
lambs but not lions".

* In the Roman Catholic Church granting of freedom from punishment still due for sin after sacramental absolution

(Tr. By. P. Naga Jasmine)

SARELLA VENKATARATNAM (1944 -)

Sarella Venkataratnam, popularly known as SAVERA (formed with the first letters of his name and it also means 'dawn') was born on 15th July 1944 in Tummalapalli of Allavaram Mandal, East Godavari district. He did his Graduation from S.K.B.R. College, Amalapuram and B.Ed, at Comprehensive College of Education, Rajahmundry with High Second Class. He has Diploma in Kannada Language from S.R.L.C, Mysore in distinction. He has written and published nearly twenty literary works in different forms like poems, Lyrics, Free verse, Mini Kavithalu (Short Poems), Deergha Kavithalu (Long Poems), Ballets, Prose, Translations, Biographies, Children's literature, Novel, Satire etc., and a few among them are: **Sumaanjali** (1974) (a collection of poems, lyrics and free verse), **Brindaavanam** (1978) a Geya Kaavyam depicting the glory and beauty of Mysore Brindavan Gardens in Mysore, **Velugu Baata** (1979) a ballet depicting the child labour, **Dalita Jaatula Dharma Yuddham** (1991) a Geya Kaavyam prescribed for M.A., Telugu (Correspondence) Andhra University. **Dalita Chaitanya Lahari** (2004) is a collection of essays that are published in various News Papers and Journals and broad casted in All India Radio. He published biographies of Kanshiram and Balayogi under the titles: **Bahujananetha Kanshiram** (1994) and

Adarsha Lok Sabhapati Sri G.M.C. Balayogi (2002). He also wrote to create Awareness among people on various issues: **Dr. Ambedkar Jeevitamlo Mukhya Ghattaalu-Rachanalu, Dalitulu - Okanati Bouddhulu** etc. He is the Founder President of **S.S.N. Rao** (his only son under missing from 1991) **Cultural Trust**. In the name of this Trust, merit students are rewarded with Dalit literature, mementoes and certificates of appreciation. This Trust also conducts competitions in elocution and essay writing. The winners are rewarded in cash and kind. The poor and needy pupils are presented dictionaries and grammar books.

SAVERA received the **Best Teacher Award** in 1985 from Andhra Pradesh state government. He is a committed social activist and an inspiring teacher. His poem on Ambedkar is quoted here.

Human Jewel -Ambedkar

Who is the one, picked venomous tongs of caste serpents; and spread equality and Humanism?

Who is the one, made the freed Mother India's Constitution?

Who is that pious man who had put the Dalits
from sheer penury to progressive route?
Who is that honourable one, become path finder
for women's freedom and nation's progress?
Who is the one applauded by every one on earth?
Who is that Manu's killer and Modern Buddha?
The one with universal fame, Dr. Ambedkar
I salute him with all humility.
The one who swam across the seas of troubles and stood on the waves of victory
The one who ingested all sciences and shone with knowledge
The one who wrote works to awaken masses and become the best writer?
The one whose learned counsel won over the best Judges

The one who become the best Minister in the Victory's cabinet
The one who is the lighted torch for work force?
Jewel of Universal men, Dr. Ambedkar
I salute him, with open heart.
He is the one who fought for human right of "Mahad Tank" water
He is the one who burnt the unjust lettered Manu Smuriti
He is the one who made the caste walls of "Kalaram Temple"
He is the one who preserved the Dalit's rights in Round Table conferences with his
Arguments
His life was an eternal battleground
His breath was egalitarian society
He is the one most respected and admired
Human Jewel, Dr. BhimaRao Ambedkar, I salute him
Caste trough swords had cut his heart
Untouchability had burnt his foot
Yet, he is the one who fought for a share in Power for Bahujans, Patriot, BhimRao.
Afraid of separate constituency for down castes
Bapuji himself started fast unto death
It's BhimRao who gave life to him, who else?
When it's difficult to achieve merit in one field it self,
In different fields he achieved greatness, won world fame
BhimRao, I salute him. (Tr. By. Ch. Prabhakar)

TALLURI LABAN BABU (1945 -)

Laban Babu was born on 11th August, 1945 in Pedaravur of Tenali Mandal, Guntur district. His parents are Daniel and Leyamma. He did his Master's degree and joined in Reserve Bank of India in 1975. Later he entered into NABARD, an offshoot of RBI as ADO and retired on 30th June 2003 as Assistant General Manager. He is not only a prolific writer but also a social activist. Many a time he submitted useful suggestions to the state government on developmental activities related to Dalits and Farmers. After his professional retirement he is busy with writing and publications. He started Publishing Books on no-profit and no-loss basis from his firm Kusumanjali Publications, Hyderabad.

Laban Babu's books are published from 1980s onwards. His first book **Jaya Bharati** (poetry) published in 1983 and **Yuga Dharmam**, a collection of three plays in 1986. His other works include **Maha Nirgamam (The Great Exodus)**, published in 2001, **Laban Geetalu (The Songs of Laban)** in 2002, and **Bhahujana Vadam (The Doctrine of Bahujanism)** in 2005. His magnum opus, **Madigavari Charitra (The Chamârs of Andhra Pradesh)** is first published in 2001 and it is reprinted in 2002, 2003 and 2005.

Undoubtedly **The Chamârs of Andhra Pradesh** is a research work. It provides a Historical and Social background to study Dalit Movement in a total perspective. In this book he traced the chronological study – beginning with 'Jambudweep' to the present Dandora Movement. He discussed the entry of Aryas, race and caste systems. He declared that "caste system is obnoxious and ignominious" (20). He presented Gurram Joshuva and Jagajjivanram under different chapters.

Laban Babu's latest book is **The Doctrine of Bahujanism**. This book is divided into two parts. In the first part there are three chapters and the first chapter is by B.S. Ramulu, second by Katti Padma Rao and the third by Laban Babu himself. The second part consisting of six chapters by Laban Babu began with the Creation of Man and discussed the man in relation to various aspects like society, institutions etc, concluded with bahujanism as a model ideology. Talluri Laban Babu also edited a book entitled **Nomenclature of Christian Women in Telugu** (2002), written by his father. One of his poems is given here.

At the Dusk

On that evening—

Chakkraponali from the temple
Chakkrakeli in his home
What to eat first?
Is a problem to a *poojari*
On that evening—
In a palatial residence
a serious dilemma on a future programme
whether to steal the chief idol in the temple
or to grab the glebe-land
Is a problem to a land lord
On that evening—
What to hide in the cellar
and what to keep in the shop
Is a problem to a trader
At the dusk—
If he enter the temple
to fulfill the vow made
for his sick child
they will kill him;
If he does not go
his child will die
How to solve...
Is a great problem to a Dalit.

Notes:
Chakkrapongali : a sweet dish made of sugar,rice and milk—offering to god
Chakkrakeli : one variety of banana
Poojari : a hindu priest (Tr.By. T. Bharathi)

Boya Jangaih (1947 -)

Dr. Boya Jangaiah popularly known as Jatara Jangaiah was born in Telangana. His first novel **Jathara** (1988) won the **Best Novel Award** from Potti Sreeramulu Telugu University in 1989 and he has been acclaimed as Jathara Jangaiah since then. He wrote his first play **Kasta Sukhalu** in 1963 and has been writing rather tirelessly since then. He is a prolific writer who has several plays, short story collections, poems, novels, Children's literature and biographies to his credit. He received several Awards and honours such as – **Sri Sri Memorial Gold Medal, Dr. Ambedkar Fellowship, Swarajya Lakshmi Award** and **Pratibha Award** from P.S. Telugu University. In the year 2003, Potti Sreeramulu Telugu University of Andhra Pradesh bestowed on him the D.Litt degree. Some of his writings are included in the syllabuses of Mysore and Sri Krishna Devaraya Universities. Jangaiah participated in many conferences and seminars and the important among them are – **Second World Telugu Conference** at Malaysia in 1981 and **Short Story Convention,** Chennai in 1991. He took a cultural literary tour to Rajasthan in 1994 with the financial assistance of the **Sahitya Akademi**, New Delhi. He remarked, "Touring the country and observation of the people is the main objective of his life". He has vividly portrayed the theme of common man's suffering in the poem **The Anguish of a Man – for the Morrow**

The Black stone I sculpted
Became a God in procession.
The person I elected with my ballot
Became a minister and forgot me.
The former gets gifts without asking
The latter gets garlands and
obeisance at every step.
But, I their creator,
stood gazing,
and waiting and pondering
over the morrow. (Tr. By. Dr.M. Neeraja)

Dr. Jangaiah gave a meaningful interpretation to the statue of Ambedkar in his poem entitled **Ambedkar.**

Ambedkar

With just your pointing finger
You wiped out the caste monster.
With just a stroke of your pen
You bettered our destinies.
The slavery of the have-nots for the haves

Will end hereafter.
Baba! Had you only lived for ten more years,
The destiny of entire India
Would have changed for the better.
(Tr.By. Dr.M. Neeraja)

GEDDADA KASTURI (1949 -)

Sahiti Siromani Geddada Kasturi was born in Gantikothapeta of East Godavari district. Her parents are Surya Prakasam and Savithri. She is a graduate student of St. Theresa's college Eluru and Arts College, Rajamundry. She writes with the pen name *Radhika*. During her childhood she developed interest in literature and in her husband's house too, she is exposed to literature and experienced the environment of Brahma Samaj. Her first story **Ammayulu Jaagratha (Girls! Be Careful**) was published in **Andhra Prabha** illustrated weekly in the year 1977.

Kasturi wrote free verse, poetry, short novels, plays and essays. She also wrote about children and social issues. She won many awards and honours such as – **Kala Sahiti Award, Madireddi Sulochana Award** and honoured by literary personalities like Malati Chandur, Ravi Sastri and Karuna Sri. In 1999 on the occasion of the golden jubilee celebrations of UNESCO, She received **UNESCO Sahiti Siromani Award**. In her story **Oh Blood! What is your Caste?** she portrayed the predicament of intercaste marriages in the name of social reformation.

GAJJARLAMUDI NIRMLA RANI (1950 -)

Gajjarlamudi Nirmala Rani's parents are Prasada Rao and Mary Rajamma. As her father was an employee in railway, they had to move in the entire state and that resulted in Nirmala Rani's education in various towns like – Vijayawada, Rajahmundry etc. She is a graduate of Sri Padmavati Women's College, Tirupati and did M.A. history in S.V. University. She received encouragement to write from her teacher and her father. Her father used to recite Tagore's **Gitanjali** at home. She preferred to teach school children though she is invited to teach in a college.

Nirmala Rani is writing from 1990s with a Dalit perspective. She received special recognition for her article on **The Successful fight of Dalit Women** in 1995. With her essay, **Are the Issues of Women Personal?** published in the **Vaartha** newspaper, she is established as a feminist writer. Her writings are published in the Telugu Journals like – **Andhra Bhoomi, Andhra Jyothi, Andhra Prabha, Aruna Tara, Bhoomika, Praja Sahiti** and **Mahila – Margam**. In her works she portrays women's issues with the back drop of the physical and political environment of Rayalaseema. She is also a social activist and worked as a vice president for the Association of Rationalists and connected with Jana Vignana Vedika, a people's Organisation.

DASARI SIRISHA (1952 -)

She is the daughter of famous Communist leaders Dasari Nagabhushanam and Namburi Paripurna (She is already referred in this book). She is the niece of the well-known Dalit poet Namburi Srinivasa Rao and Numburi Durvasa Maharshi. She is very much influenced by literature as she is brought up in a family of communist and Dalit activists and writers. Sirisha's first story **The King and the Queen** is published in 1968 in the **Yuva Jyothi** journal. Being a committed writer she always presents a social issue or the life style of poor and middle class families in her stories. She released her first collection of short stories **Samidhalu** in 1995. She received **Chakrapani Award** for the story **Samidhalu**. Her novel **DuuraTeeralu** is serialized in **Andhra Prabha**. Regarding Dalit problems she argues that the Dalits' problems are not only the problems of Dalits but also of the dominant caste. They too need to think of the Dalit related issues.

Dasari Sirisha is also a Dalit social activist and she started **Youth World** an organization for the welfare of women and Dalit children including Scheduled Tribes, in Puttur of Chittoor district.

CHILUKURI DEVAPUTRA (1952 —)

A popular Dalit writer from Rayalaseema, Devaputra was born on 24th April in Kaluvapalli village of Beluguppa mandal, Anantapur district. His parents are Sarojamma and late Aseervadam. He is at present working in the Revenue department of the state as Senior Assistant in Anantapur district.He is essentially a fiction writer. He began his literary creation with short stories in the year 1977. His first short story **Manavatvam (The Humanity)** is published in **Prajasakti**, October 1977. So far he has published about 100 stories and some of these stories are translated into English, Hindi, Marathi, Oriya and Kannada languages. His stories are included in the short story volumes published by Sahitya Akademi, New Delhi and Visalandhra. So far Devaputra's stories are published in three volumes.

Chilukuri Devaputra is more known for his novels. He has published only four novels yet he gained popularity as a committed Telugu Dalit novelist. His four novels are **Addamlo Chandamaama** (1989) **Panchamam** (1998), **Kakshasila** and **Cheekatipuulu.** Among these four novels except **Chıkeekatipuulu** the remaining three novels deal with Dalit themes. Devaputra's more popular novel **Panchamam** received third prize from ATA (American Telugu Association) in 1998. An amount of Rs 30000/- is given as cash prize which includes the publication cost of the novel. This novel also bagged **Undela Kalapita** award, (Hyderabad).

Devaputra's first published novel **Addamlo Chandamaama** focuses on the failure of the scheme of distribution of land to the landless. The rulers practice the double standard in the distribution of land to the poor and the downtrodden. Around 1985 the Andhra Pradesh government decided to distribute the wetland to the landless. The name of the scheme is *Maagani Samaaraadhana.* The futile attempt of the scheme is the central idea of the novel. The novel is situated in Kothapalli village in Anantapur district. Rachapalem Chendrasekhara Reddy in his review stated that unless there is a social change the government schemes will never be successful. In this novel the chief minister comes and distributes the land to Dalits of that village. The landlords organize the function in a grand scale and the chief minister of the state appericiates the landlords Tippeswamy and Dharmaiah for voluntarily donating their land for distribution. On an auspicious day the Dalits go to fields for tilling the land. The landlords by appointing *goondas* hindered their entry into the field. The Dalits complained the matter to the chief minister, the collector, the other revenue officials etc. With the help of the police the Dalits try to occupy their land and it resulted in a big fight between the Dalits and the *goondas*. During the fight the Dalit leaders Hanumanthu and Chinnodu are brutally murdered. The remaining Dalits ran away from the fields. Sanket in the Sunday supplementary of **Andhra Jyothi** Daily Newspaper, while appreciating this novel comments that Devaputra portrayed a wide subject on a small canvas. He says that **Addamlo Chandamaama** cannot be a novel but a novella. Hence he suggests that the novelist could have written a full length novel and then he would have justified the theme.The title of the novel is quite apt. In **The Ramayana,** when Rama cries for the moon it was shown in the mirror to pacify him. In the same way here in the novel all the welfare schemes for Dalits are limited to government orders only.

In this novel Devaputra used typical Anatapur dialect. Vallampati Venkata Subbaiah in his work **The Modern Literature in Rayalaseema;A Socio-Cultural Analysis** (2006) finds fault with the novelist for his unauthentic geographical description.

Panchamam is a more acclaimed novel of Devaputra. Undoubtedly this novel reflects the contemporary reality. This novel is centred round the rise and fall of the protagonist Sivaiah, a Dalit. He passed Intermediate in first division and later got selected in APPSC Group-I competitive exams as RDO (Revenue Divisional Officer). The landlords tried for the appointment of Sivaiah in their division so that they can safe guard their lands. Sivaiah wishes to do justice and help the poor and Dalits. But he lost his job due to the conspiracy of the landlords. Finally the novel concludes with the victory of Dalits in getting the land from the landlords. There are a few sub plots in the novel and they are complimentary to the novel as they portray some of the other problems that the Dalits face in their day today life. Unlike the ending of **Addamlo Chandamaama** the Dalits in **Panchamam** never yielded to the conspiracy of the landlords and more over they got their land back and are ready to fight back landlords, unitedly if necessary. Vallmpati Venkata Subbaiah judges that ther is a progress in the novelist from **Addamlo Chandamaama** to **Panchamam.** One can find maturity in the novelist as the former novel ends in failure the later in success. The novelist also speaks of self-respect for Dalits in his works.

Through the story **Uudalamarri (The Banyan Tree)** Devaputra tried to emphasize that reservations for Dalits are only for name's sake and in practice the fruits of reservations proved null and void. This story deals with the Veerapuram panchayat elections and it is reserved for Scheduled Caste. For about thirty-five years Bheemappa is the panchayat president. That particular year it is reserved for SCs. Hence Bheemappa selected his servent for the post. Bheemappa also explains the reason for his choice. He says that if somebody else is elected they will become independent and will not be under his control. Hence he selected Obulesu who will be a president in name and Bheemappa can enjoy the real power. In the evening the election officer by force make Obulesu sit on a chair and take pleadge as a president. In the evening Bheemappa beat him badly for sitting on a chair in front of him. In such circumstances one can imagine what would be the predicament of Obulesu as a president.

Chilukuri Devaputra's story "Son of the Soil" was pulished in **Indian Literature**(Vol. XL VII Sep-Oct 2003),a reputed Journal published by Sahitya Akademi, New Delhi is given here under.

Son of the Soil

"Come and eat sankati," Obulamma called her husband impatiently.

Lost in thought, Ramachandra sat on the pial outside the hut staring into space inattentive to her call. By then their neighbours had eaten sankati or something and sat under the streetlights gossiping. The children were playing game of run-and-touch, yelling at one another.

"Sankati gets cold. Come and eat it, "Obulamma was impatient. She came out and shook her husband by the shoulder.

Ramachandra was startled. "Have you finished cooking?" Getting up he said, "You have just begun it!" Without replying to him, Obulamma went into the hut.

Ramachandra stood up but did not move. Obulamma brought water in a big brass container and gave it to him. Ramachandra washed his hands, feet and face and drying himself with the checkered towel on his shoulder, moved into the hut.

"Ramesh! Suresh! Where are those rascals? Call them," he told her as he sat down for food.

"They have already eaten and gone out to play."

In the glimmer of the lamp, he looked at the plate. A big morsel of Sankati of millets occupied much of the plate, and a substance like chutney nestled in one corner. He touched a little of it with his forefinger and put it to his tongue. It tasted sour.

"It's tamarind chutney again," he said with a distasteful expression on his face.

"Yes, you have been earning a lot. Saving everything greedily for myself, I am preparing only tamarind chutney for you," Obulamma shouted at him.

"Why do you shout? I just said that you have been serving tamarind chutney everyday. Is it wrong to say so?" Swallowing hurriedly handfuls of ragi sankati, Ramachandra said. "It's difficult to talk to you. I don't know what irritates you."

"Yes. It is difficult to live with me," Obulamma looking angrily at him replied without lowering her voice. "You know how to silence me. Others think that I am a nagging woman. You speak softly but do everything silently, looking innocent." He mumbled with a smiling face, a morsel of sankati in his mouth.

"Yes, I have come here all the way because I am a wretched woman. It's six months since we have come and settled here in Bellary. And you never pay heed to me," Obulamma continued. "I told you many times to sell away the ten acres of land in the village so that we can buy a piece of land here and build a small hut. But it never gets into your head. You feel happy paying a hundred rupees from your wages as rent for this hut every month." Tears filled her eyes. "Since morning I have been sitting outside as I could not bear this talk. You have started it again. Whatever you say you come back to the ten acres of land," Ramachandra said. "You know about my father. Will he allow me to sell the land as long as he is alive?" He questioned.

"Don't utter those useless words. Tell him outright that you would sell the land. Why your father? Even your grand-father would accept it," Obulamma replied. "You become so meek when you face your father that you won't say anything to him. What have you grown like a tall tree for? Can't you convince him that nothing will grow in that land where only the chameleons lay their eggs? For the past five years have we ever got a yield of more than ten bags of groundnuts? We dump bags of grains into it and look at the sky for rains. Had it been fertile, why should we have come here all the way to earn our livelihood? But won't you ever think about it?" "Keep quiet. Without regard for my father's age you speak against him," Ramachadra said.

Obulamma could sense the harshness in his voice.

"Aged! Yes, its only due to that I have been silent all these days," Obulamma said "What's great about age? Even a stone in the street will be old enough." As she continued Ramachandra stopped eating, got up angrily and hit Obulamma on her back with his fist a couple of times.

With this unexpected turn, Obulamma, sorrow welling in her started crying in a screeching voice.

"Do you speak this way without any regard for your father-in-law? All the time I tolerated it somehow. But you go on without any restraint." Ramachandra kicked the plate he was eating in with his left leg, as if to make his anger effective. The plate flew in circles, hit the wall with a thud and fell on the floor. Ramachandra washed his hands and sat on the pial outside. He could faintly hear Obulamma's weeping from the hut.

"Ramachandra!" As he heard the call, he turned in the direction. A person who was around forty came to him smiling. He was lean, and was wearing a white panca and a shirt. His partially grayed bushy moustache appeared to have been fixed on his face.

"How are you? Narayanappa! Are you all right?" He dusted the place next to him. "Come and sit here." "You have to come tomorrow. We are laying the foundation for a house in Kaul Bazaar," Narayanappa said as he sat on the pial.

Obulamma's wail was not heard from the hut. "She saved me from embarrassment," Ramachandra thought. Narayanappa was the head of house-construction workers. Ten years earlier he migrated from a village, Kaluvapalli in Anantapur district to Bellary in search of livelihood. He began his life there as a coolie carrying stones. Soon he became the head of a gang of construction workers, well-known in Bellary. Nearly half-a-dozen labourers worked under him now. Seven years ago, he had a small hut in the site given by the government, which now had turned into a big building. He had two Godrej almirahs, a sofa set, a colour T.V. and other valuable things in that building. He bought a house-site of twenty cents on the Sangankallu road in Bellary. It costs around three lakhs now.

"Tomorrow I have work at home. If you want, I can come the day after tomorrow," Ramachandra said. "It's all right, Ramachandra! I will send for some other worker," What rent do you pay for this hut?"

"A Hundred rupees."

"One Hundred! For this small hut?" Narayanappa said. "You said you had some land in the village. You can sell it and buy some place here and build a small house. You don't know how good it is to have a house instead of land these days? In Guntur or Vijayawada one will be considered rich if he has ten acres of land. They are such fertile lands and they work hard to raise crops too. But in our area even if a farmer has twenty-five acres of land, he has to face problems throughout the years and it is difficult even to lead a normal life. Our lands are barren? In our village, Kaluvapalli my uncle has twenty acres of land but it is difficult for him even to feed his family. Consider my case. I don't have even an acre of land. But are they equal to me? Nowadays cultivation has become a gamble or betting in a cock-fight, "he said. "Expecting rains in time, the farmers would somehow buy the seeds and sow them. Then, if there are normal rains, the former would survive. Otherwise he would be at the mercy of moneylenders. The fate of agriculture depending on rains is always so." Narayanappa told Ramachandra and went away saying, "Take my advice. You sell away your land. Don't take me amiss Ramachandra. I'll come again."

The whole street was deserted.

The streetlights were glowing brightly.

Ramachandra lay on a mat on the pial rolling this way and that. He was unable to sleep. He felt remorseful for beating his wife. He had never beaten her. Yet he hit a woman who had so much of love for him. If she talked the way she had, it was due to circumstances. It was difficult enough to live though both of them worked and earned wages. How difficult it was to send money to his father in the village for his expenses and also pay a rent of a hundred rupees for the hut! The children, Ramesh and Suresh, were in ragged shorts, as they had no money to buy new ones for them. Of the three saris Obulamma had, all of them were in tatters.

Suddenly anger against his father engulfed Ramachandra. Only because of his father he had to face all these difficulties. He would not live with them there. It was true that the old man was very fond of the land. There was reason to be so, if it was a fertile one. He did not understand why he had so much of attachment to that arid land. He wished his father dead so that, weeping for a while, he could dump him once for all in a pit. As he thought about his father he felt like killing him. He would no more remain passive. He would certainly sell away the land, at any cost, without caring for the wails of his father.

The moment he came to that conclusion, he got up involuntarily. Thinking that his wife would be happy to know this, he went into the hut pushing the door. In the glimmer of the lamp he looked all around. The children were fast asleep. At a slight distance from them Obulamma was lying on the floor curling herself up. He silently went to her and knelt near her.

"Obulamma," he called her.

`She rolled to the other side. Then it became clear to him that she was awake.

"Ei! It's you I'm calling," he said and placed his hand on her shoulder.

She pushed it away angrily.

"Abba! How can a woman be so angry? Please listen to me," he pleaded.

"So have you come again to beat me? Come on, hit me. I am the only one who will tolerate everything," she said weeping, her eyes looking into his.

"I haven't come to beat you. When you talked badly about my father I was unable to control my anger and hit you." Ramachandra forcibly took her hand in his and said, "I promise I would not beat you again." He observed that her grief had subsided.

"I will need your advice. I will sell away the land. Let the old man wail as he wishes. Are we happy though we have that property?" Shall we go tomorrow?"

"All right," Ramachandra kissed her on her forehead and said, "Let's go tomorrow."

It was noon. The hot Sun was shining brightly.

"Oh, Ramachandra. Have you come just now? You have set out in the hot sun!" Chennappa welcomed his son, daughter-in-law and grandsons looking at them with great affection. "How big they have grown! Come to me! Ramesh... Suresh!" he said, holding them in his arms and happily showering kisses on them

Ramachandra took away the old metal box from his shoulders and placed it in front of the hut. "How are you, Father? Is your health all right?" Ramachandra asked. "You have grown thin."

"I am all right," Chennappa said. "Look at yourself. You have become skinny. Even she and her boys have become lean."

"As you see us after a long gap, you feel so...Mama," Obulamma said.

"Papa... Narasakka!" he called the girl from the adjoining hut. Despite his torn vest and soiled panca he was wearning and his unshaven grey beard, his face was glowing with joy.

"Yes, tata!" A thirteen-years-old girl with tasseled hair, and in green dirty dress, came out from the next hut. She was related to Chennappa: a grand-daughter. Moreover, due to his good nature, she helped him in his household chores.

"Your uncle, aunt and their children have come. We don't know when they had food last. They must be hungry," Chennappa said to the girl, "Cook some rice for them and give some water first for washing their feet, my dear." He instructed her.

Smiling shyly, she went into the hut to cook food.

After an hour, they had food. The day was declining.

It was always cool there even when it was hot summer, as there was a densly grown neem tree next to the pial in front of the hut. He felt it risky now to ask him to sell away the land. How should he put it? Moreover how to begin the conversation?

Chennappa was still smoking a beedi.

Lying on the end of the sari spread on the floor, Obulamma was staring at her husband. Suddenly Ramachandra looked at her."Come on. You begin it," she gestured to him. "Wait a while," he suggested to her with his look. "How much of groundnut will we get this year?" Clearing his throat, he began hesitantly, unable to know how to initiate the conversation.

"Yield. . . Had it rained at least twice by this time, it would have been different. With the attack of pests almost all the crop has withered. Even if it rains today or tomorrow, the yield would be just enough for seeding. It is not only here. This is so everywhere. A gentleman told me this today...he had been to Hindupur, Kadiri to look for a match for his son," Chennappa continued. "But how is life in Bellary, Ramudu... have you learnt any brick-laying work?"

"Yes. I am still learning," Ramachandra replied in a low voice.

"I always worry about you. But for the failure of crops you would not have left the village to live in a far off place as a labourer," Chennappa said in a choked voice.

Unable to raise the topic of selling the land when he was so concerned about their welfare Ramachandra suddenly got up and said, "I will go down the street to talk to Mallesu and Thippanna mama, father." He went away.

Obulamma who had been looking at them intently to know what would happen became furious. "Thu... What a man is he! Just when he was to speak out, he went away. He has no guts to talk to his father, but he is ready to argue with me," she mumbled to herself.

Night. It was time for food.

The rays from the street lamp next to the hut spread light over the pial like moonlight. While eating, Ramachandra thought many times as to how to talk about the selling of the land with his father. On the pial outside Chennappa was gossiping with his grandchildren, laughing loudly at times.

"Ramudu! These rascals are very clever. You have to be careful," Chennappa said to Ramachandra as he came out after finishing food. "Otherwise they will sell you both in the Bellary Market for three bottlu. How intelligent these fellows are!" he said looking affectionately at them.

Ramachandra smiled awkwardly. His mind was on the matter he wanted to raise.

"I heard the Reddys have sold away their lands,"Ramachandra said to his father as a prelude to the issue.

"Reddys?" Chennappa was still engrossed in the delightful company of his grandchildren.

"I heard that Thimma Reddy has sold his thirty acres of land to the people of Uravakonda at twenty thousand rupees an acre."

"Yes. After selling away all his land here Thimma Reddy is doing some business in Anantapur. They are all very big people. They do not care for their village or mother. They can live anywhere. Anantapur or Hyderabad... they are ready to settle anywhere and live happily," Chennappa said as he took out a bundle of beedis and a box of matches from the pocket of his vest.

"But we stay on here whether it's famine or crop-failure. Which God told us to be here, father? Why should we find fault with them? Our fate is so."

"You son of a ..., Howmany times have I told you not to raise this question," Chennappa said. Ramachandra sensed that his father was more furious from his words but he did not want to retreat. "You are mad. About the land. Because of it we have come to this ruined stage." Ramachandra continued, "You raised a loan of fifteen thousand rupees to dig a well and only a boulder appeared at the bottom. For a bore pump you spent ten thousand rupees and it ended in vain too. No water but only debts to repay. By the grace of the Rain god we reaped groundnut crop for two years and repaid the loans. Otherwise, could my children and I have repaid such a heavy loan?"

"Why do you talk so strangely now?" Chennappa questioned him angrily. "Have you come all the way from Bellary to sell this land?" He became furious. His grandsons got off his lap frightened and ran to their mother sitting at the door.

"Why do you become so angry whenever I suggest you to sell the land?" Ramachandra shouted back at his father.

"Yes, I do, because it is my life. Selling it is like selling my mother... You always talk about the amount spent on it. Think a while. Without it my father, grandfather, you and me... all of us would not have lived a respectable life in the village," Chennappa went on, "It is all due to this land. I wish you weren't born to me. You are a person without any gratitude. Had your mother been still alive, you would have sold her too when she could not do any work. You... wretched fellow," Chennappa spoke with a strange expression on his face.

"I don't care for all that. You have to sell the land and come to live with us, that's all." Chennappa sensed recklessness in his son's words.

"I won't come with you and I won't sell the land. Do whatever you want to. You are so rude because you send me some money for my expenses every month. From now on you need not send me anything," Chennappa said in an agitated voice, lit another beedi and began puffing it vigorously.

"If you speak so I will lose my temper," Ramachandra said irritated.

"Why should you be angry? Have you lost any of your father's earnings? What are you furious about?" Chennappa shot back. "I won't sell the land, whatever you say."

As their quarrel reached its culmination, the neighbours gathered.

"Ore... Ramachandra. Why do you raise the issue of selling off the land now?" An old man in the gathering said in his shivering voice.

"Since all of you support him he has become so adamant and refuses to sell it," Ramachandra said loudly.

"See... He talks without any regard for me... his father," Chennappa was shivering in fury.

"Mama, why do you get so irritated when we ask you to sell the land?" Obulamma said.

"So, you are behind all this. It's because of you he is talking so. My son had never talked so harsh with me. It's enough to have a daughter-in-law like you to break a family," Chennappa said vengefully, though he had never uttered a word against his daughter-in-law since she came to live with them.

"Your son has no courage and so you hold the land fast, ruining us in the process," Obulamma said spitefully.

"Being a woman you should not talk so against your father-in-law," an old married woman said.

"Atta... you know nothing about our family. We want to sell it only to look after his welfare. See how he behaves," Obulamma said.

"If you don't care for his wishes, why should you worry about his welfare?" another married woman questioned.

Obulamma became furious and retorted sharply, "Why do you worry about our family problems? It's no concern of yours. We have not asked you to deal out justice for us."

"All right... we have nothing to do with you. You can do as you wish," the old, married woman left the place feeling unhappy.

"I will see how you can stop me from selling the land. Or else you give me my share." Ramachandra spoke as if he was parting with his father forever.

Chennappa turned to his son as he felt it unpleasant to hear those words. Tears filled his eyes. Was it his only son who said all this? Was he the one whom he brought up so affectionately?

"Ore... Ramudu Why speak of your share and mine? All is my brother to share it with me," Chennappa continued in mournful tone. "Take all of it. I can fill my stomach by begging in the village. Do as you wish." He moved away as tears rolled down from his eyes.

Ramachandra and Obulamma did not expect this and they remained stupefied.

For some time silence filled the air.

"Amma. Tata is going away," Suresh shrieked.

Obulamma did not say anything.

Where will he go? An old man... He will come back after he cools down," a middle-aged person from the crowd commented.

"He will come back. Where can he go?" Others echoed.

The day was just dawning.

Ramachandra did not sleep the whole night. He was worried about his father. Many times he thought and repented that he should not have been so harsh with him.

Obulamma also was remorseful. She sent Ramachandra to search for her father-in-law in the houses of their friends in the village. She enquired about him in the street. She was distressed that she was rude towards her father-in-law who used to call her Papa affectionately.

Ramachandra's eyes were swollen and red, as he was sleepless. Thoughts swarmed in his mind like bees from a disturbed hive. The thought that his father might have ended his life frightened him most. That was why he had been looking for him in the gardens and wells since morning. Some of the villagers accompanied him in the search. It was morning.

"Ore... Ramachandra!" he felt as his father had called him affectionately from a distance and he looked around vaguely. No one was there. He decided that he would never say anything against his father's wishes. He felt like falling and weeping at his feet if he found him. He would never ask him to sell the land again.

"O... Ramachandra anna," Rangaiah came gasping to him and said, "Anna... your father... dead. There, in your land." He pointed to his land. A body in white clothes was lying in his land a few tracts away.

As if he had heard a thunderbolt striking, he rushed to the land, shivering all over.

Amidst the withered groundnut crop Chennappa's body lay serene and free from sorrow, like a child sleeping in the lap of the mother.

Dazed, Ramachandra fell on the dead body

(Translated from Telugu by T. Sreenivasa Reddy, **Indian Literature**, Sept-Oct 2003)

Chilukuri Devaputra received a number of awards for his fiction. A few important awards among them are: **Nutalapati Sahiti award** in 1996, **Dharmanidhi Puraskar** from P.S.Telugu University, Hyderabad in 2000, The **Visalandhra Golden Jubilee Puraskar** in 2003 etc. So far two M.Phil thesises are awarded on his writings in the P.G.Centre of S.V.University and University of Hyderabad. Research work is being done on his writings in the other universities like Kakatiya, Acharya Nagarjuna, Sri Krishnadevaraya etc. The Telugu Department of Sri Krishnadevaraya University prescribed his novel **Panchmam** and **Bandi** a short story in the M.A syllabus for the academic years 2001-2004. **Panchmam** is also prescribed in the M.A syllabus of the University of Hyderabad in 2005.

GANDHARI SRI RAMULU (1952 -)

Gangadhari Sri Ramulu is known only as Mastaarji. It is not exaggeration to say that many people know him only as Mastarji but not as Gangadhari Sri Ramulu, because he entered the literary career with his pen name Mastaarji.

Mastaarji was born on 7th September 1952 in Bolaram, Secundarabad. His parents are Rajaiah and Sattemma. Though he is brought up in Bollaram he had to face many hurdles due to caste differences. He withstood many obstacles to complete his school education. He took his

Postgraduate degree from Dr. Ambedkar Open University and B.L. from Siddanti Law College in 1995. His work **Dalita Geetalu (Dalit Songs)** is published in 1994 by Om Sai Lazer Graphics, Narayanaguda, Hyderabad.

During his childhood there was a great scarcity for drinking water in Bolaram. The situation was even a worse for untouchables. From all this experience he realised that the root cause for all this exploitation is the caste-based society. As a child he also thought that higher education and a good employment will help him to occupy a higher place in the society.

Later he understood through experience that "Art is the right weapon to get recognition in the society". Then he started his attempts in writing songs and poems.

Who do You Think He is?

Who do you think he is?
He is the first one, the ancient man
the authentic one.
He is Madiga!
He belongs to that phase
when the earth took its shape
when the animate began to breathe
when the first man appeared on the scene
That's why,
calling him Adipurusha
rishis, sages sent the wives of impotent men
to Kardama for their progeny!
He is Dharmavyadha
who preached millions of deities
you pray today!
He is the Chandala
who provided moments of revelation
to the Sankaracharya
who groveled in the darkness of ignorance!
He is Matanga
who created the veena

to make you flow in the ocean of music,
to provide succour for your life
ridden with agonies and wailings!
He is Madiga!
He is the one, who shaped the poornakumbha,
which inspires you to lead your lives
auspiciously, always!
When your days are numbered
and you breathe your last,
he is the Veerabahu
who performs funeral rites for your useless bodies
in the grave-yards!
He is Madiga!
He too is –
Adi Jambava
Valmiki, Vyasa!
He is the origin of all those beings
who have existed on this earth
from it's very beginning!
He is the first source of
human existence!
He is the cause of historical truths
progressive paths in the evolution of culture!
Devoid of him, history is emptiness!
The one who loves emptiness
is like the rocks!
He is the one who influenced
each part in your body
all fields of your life!
But for his existence, devoid of him
nothing is there in your life!
(Tr. By. K. Damodar Rao,**Indian Literature**, Nov-Dec 2000)

KATTI PADMA RAO (1953 -)

The rationalist convert to Dalit Movement, Katti Padma Rao was born in the village Eetheru of Guntur district. His parents are Subba Rao and Manikyamma. He is a writer with commitment and wrote with historical and social background. He is a poet and a critic. He took initiation in the formation of Dalit Mahasabha after the Karamchedu (1985) incident. He resigned his job as a Sanskrit lecturer in Ponnuru and turned as a full time worker in the Dalit Movement. He along with Bojja Tarakam toured the entire state in propagating and establishing the Dalit Mahasabha. Katti Padma Rao is an eloquent speaker. He is imprisoned for his active participation in the Dalit Movement against the government. His **Jailugantalu (The Prison Bells)** published in 1988 consists of nine poems and deal with the Karamchedu massacre, exploitation of Dalits and the responsibility of Dalit leaders etc. **Vimukti Gitam,** published in 1988 speaks about Dalits as the original inhabitants of this nation and the exploitation of Dalits as untouchables in the name of casteism.

Padma Rao in his introduction to **Nilikeka** (1998) declares that his poetry is a loud cry and "it is a dark song for centuries". **Nilikeka** is a collection of Sixty-eight poems that reflect a variety of themes – **Mother, Love letter, Black Day, Myself the Crown** are some of the poems in this collection. Lokayuta Publications brought out **Ambedkar-Buddudu,** a Politico-Philosophical discussion, by Katti Padma Rao in the year 2002. In his foreword to this book, B.S. Ramulu credited "Padma Rao as a powerful Philosopher after Ambedkar and Padma Rao showed the relevance of Buddha to the present day society where as Ambedkar spell out the principles that are necessary for the reconstruction of Indian Society. This book is a present day Philosophical need". **Mulla Kiritam (The Crown of Thorns)** is yet another collection of poems filled with the poet's sensitivity and his concern for the common. There are sixty-five poems and it is also published in 2002. Katti Padma Rao as a committed creative writer and social activist certainly has a right way of understanding women. This angle of his is proved with the publication of **Pitruswamya Vyavastha lo Stree (Woman in the Patriarchal System)** in 2003. The publishers informed that the work is based on a decade's research.In August 2007 Padma Rao received honorary Doctorate from Acharya Nagarjuna University.

KONDAPALLI SUDARSANA RAJU (1954-)

Kondapalli Sudarsana Raju was born on 29th April 1954 in the village Moparru of Amartalur mandal, Guntur district. His parents are Kondapalli Zakariah and Ratnamma.He is a graduate of VSR and NVR college of Tenali and his Master's degree is in Telugu Literature from Nagarjuna University (1980). He took his M.Phil from University of Hyderabad (1983) and Doctor of Philosophy from Andhra University, Visakhapatnam(1989).In 1986 he got his Diploma in Hindi; in 1988 a Senior P.G. Diploma in Sanskrit and in 1992 a P.G. Diploma in Translation.

At present he is working as an Associate Professor in the Department of Telugu, Andhra University Visakhapatnam.He is also teaching a paper on Dalit literature for postgraduate students. It is worth noting that he has successfully guided four Ph.D theses and three M.Phil dissertations on Dalit Literature. In1983 he published **Kavi Raju Natakalu: Hetuvada Drukpadam (The Plays of Kavi Raju: A Rationalistic Perspective**) and the author claims that it is the first research work on Rationalist angle in Telugu literature at the university level. **Pauranika Natakalu: Bhava Viplavam** is his second research work published in1990. He compiled and edited the first collection of Dalit poetry in 1991 and it is the publication of Andhra University. This collection includes Dalit and Non-Dalit writers' writing on Dalit themes. In 1992 Sudarsana Raju published a book on Dr.B.R.Ambedkar's pointing finger with the title **Chupudu Velu (The Pointing Finger**). **Adhunika Satakam** (1994) consists of one hundred poems on Dalit issues. He also published two collections of critical essays—**Sudarsani** in 1995 and **Sulochani** in 2001. Being a scholar critic he wrote a book on **The Rationalistic Perspective: The Famous Playwrights** in 2005. In recognition to his contribution to

Dalit literature, he received **Bharatiya Dalita Sahitya Akademi Award** (New Delhi) in 1991. He also received **The Rajani Kundurti National Award** (Hyderabad) for poetry in 1987. He is a committed Dalit writer and researcher. He presented research papers on Dalit literature in various seminars and published articals both in jounals as well as in newspapers. Often he makes presentations on Dalit literature in All India Radio, Visakhapatnam. During 1990-1994 he also worked as Research Associate in the UGC Major Project on Dalit literature. Dr. Kondapalli Sudarsan Raju is the Chief Secretary of the Dalit Sahitya Pitam that was founded in Visakhapatnam under the guidance of the founder president Dr.Velamala Simmanna in the year 1991, the birth centenary year of Dr. B.R. Ambedkar.

JHANSI K.V. KUMARI (1954 -)

Jhansi K.V. Kumari was born in Kakulapadu village, Gannavaram taluk of Krishna district. Her parents Yohan and Ratnadanamma are teachers. She studied in St.Theresa's College of Eluru for her degree and took M.A. in English Literature from Andhra University. Her first employment is in Hyderabad as a telephone operator and later joined as a Programme Officer in All India Radio in the year 1976.

Jhansi Kumari faced a mixed environment in her home – The combination of The Congress Party, the Communist Party and the Christian faith etc. The exposure to a variety of ideologies contributed her intellectual growth and broad-mindedness. As she works as the prompter in the rehearsals of the cultural activities of the Communist Party she almost got by heart of the plays – **Paaleru, Jnanasundari** and **Maharaji**.

Jhansi K.V. Kumari's first story **Niseedhi (The Darkness)** is published in 1974 and later she wrote many articles on Milton, Shelly and Keats and they are published in the Souvenir brought out by Arts College of Andhra University. Her first employment is in Hyderabad as operater. Later as a Programme Officer in All India Radio, she had to write essays on the eve of Republic day, or on Religious Harmony, National Integration, The Status of Women, Child Labour etc. She said that this sort of work also contributed for her becoming a writer. She confessed that she learnt to study the society after reading Dr.Ambedkar's Writings. She has brought out a volume of Poetry in 1998 with the title **Nissabda Sangeetam (The Silent Music)** and a collection of stories in 2001. From the collection of poetry, **The Mirage** is quoted here.

The Mirage

How many festoons of hopes
did we hang on the door?
How many rows of lamps
did we light securely
in the heart's nest ...
How much we waited
that you are coming
Indeed you are coming
How much we decorated...
How madly we searched thinking...
Probably in dusk
when we are just about to sleep
you have come
Behind the platform
in the middle of the house
at the turn of the street
on the *rachhabanda*
under the shade of the banyan tree
in the thorny bushes
in villages
Towns ...
Pch ... it's only our madness
Why would you come?
Cross with us
No ... no

Angry with us you went away!
Yes, indeed
hide and seek with you?
You respond when we call you
If we give a seat you will sit elated
If we give a space of a jasmine bud
You will emit fragrance full of our hearts
If we desire
Wholeheartedly ...
You will curl up like a bird
in the fist-sized heart!
Did you ask for a property?
Or wealth ...
Isn't it only sacrifice or selfishness?
that you begged!
It's enough to grow
from "I" to "we"
It's enough to transcend
from homogeneity to plurality
It's enough to turn
from religion to humanness
You will become ours forever ...
Know not
What our misfortune is
Peace ... we cannot rescue you
...we cannot make you our own.

(Rachhabanda – A stone bench, where the elders hold council in a village)

(Tr. By. K. Suneetha Rani)

GUDA ANJAIAH (1954 -)

Born on first November 1954, Guda Anjaiah is working in the State Government, Department of Pharmacy. He was born in Lingapuram of Dandapalli mandal, Adilabad district. His parents are Lasumaiah and Lasumamma. He started his literary career from 1970s onwards. He is also a singer and an actor. He acted in the character of a judge in the film **Erra Sainyam (The Red Army)**, as a freedom

Fighter in **Dandora** and as a factory labourer in **Chikati Suryulu**. Many organizations and Associations like – **Ranjani Telugu Sahiti Samiti**, Hyderabad in 1988 and **Visala Sahiti**, Jagityala in 1996 honoured him. On the occasion of the celebration of 2nd Anniversary of the Pratyusha Sahiti Monthly Magazine in 1991 honoured him. He is awarded with **Sahitya Ratna** in 1998 by the cultural Academy of Adilabad district and **Dr. MalayaSri Sahiti Award** by Navya Sahitya Parishad in 2004. He has published a collection of Poetry written from 1970 to 1978 with the title **Udyamam (The Revolution)** and **Swetcha** (1990, June) another collection of poems and a book of songs in 1999 entitled **Uurumandira (The Village is Ours)**. He has published a novel, a play, a collection of short stories and two collections of poems.

Guda Anjaiah is certainly a powerful writer with commitment for the betterment of the oppressed.

K. SANJEEVA RAO (1956 -)

Sikhamani is the pen name of Dr. K. Sanjeeva Rao, born on First January 1956. He did his post graduation in Telugu Literature and Ph.D in Modern literature. He is a poet, critic and a researcher. He published four critical works – **Prayogavaadi Pattabhi, Vividha** (Essays on Modern Literature), **Dalita Sahitya Tatvam (The Philosophy of Dalit Literature)**, and **Aneka (**Essays on Modern Literature**)**. His poetry collections are: 1. **Muvvala Chetlikarra (Hand stick with Ornamental Bells)**, 2. **Horugali (Howling Wind)**, 3. **Chilakkoyya**, 4. **The Black Rainbow** 5. **Kirrucheppula Bhasha (The Language of Creaking Footwear)** and 6. **Nallagetu Nandivardhanam Chettu (Collection of Poems)**. His poems are translated into English and published in various journals like **Indian Literature, The Mosaic, and Voices of Wings** etc. He has edited 8 works so far. From the year 1989 he is writingwith a Dalit Concept. His first Dalit poem is "He is the 'Filthy' human being" (1989). One of his best Dalit poems is given here.

Iron Nibs are Sprouting Up

In my high school days
when asked for water
in the *Anyam's* house
When they poured water
lifting the jug high
I got doubt then itself.
When my heart is peeled off
along with the knee cap
as the other person
called me son of a Mala bitch,
When a dispute rose amidst the games.
I got doubt then itself.
Intermediate Interviews
When *Chayanlugaru* questioned
saying foreign shirt, pilot pen
Bata Chappals for a reservation fellow
I got doubt then itself.
When I tried to interfere
in the literary discussions
as couple of my brahmin friends
satirically simpered
saying in a language incomprehensible to me
a poetic outpouring of *'Arasi kaya'*
I got doubt then itself.
As a child, on *Sankranthi* festival
At my maternal grandma's village
As I brought the eatables from the adjacent Wada
My fellow children gathered round me
mocked at me saying
Are Madiga's eatables, *'Yak'*
I got doubt then itself.
That a conspiracy has already taken place
I have been separated
not only from other castes but from my own too
I got doubt then itself.
When a gentleman appraised me

Saying Is Sikhamani SC? ...
Looking at his poetic style, I thought he is OC.
I was hurt by
the confidence in it that a particular caste
alone can write good poetry
than the compliment
I want to have the details now:
How my house moved
to the outskirts
which must be in the
open place for deification
a cemetery to burn the corpses
The country that separated
not only my house but also even my cemetry
looks like a Hindu graveyard.
I want to have the details of the desert giants
that enhanced the water distance
between me and the streams,
The saliva of the earth's mouth.
I am immersed in the work of cutting the pointers
that pointed us the bogs
for the sin of begging for a drop of water
with parched tongue.
Tying the palm leaves round our griddles
as you tie them to the donkey's tails
the crores and crores of our foot prints
you wiped off from the land
each one becoming a foot of steel
are ready.
The spit we spit
in the pots tied to our mouth
is secure still.
The day has come to pour it off.
Inevitable is your drifting away
like broom sticks in that flood.
You demanded Thumb as a *Guru Dakshina*
For the teaching you haven't taught
In the place of thumbs

Iron nibs are sprouting up.
They will certainly rewrite the story
Then the people who poured boiling led
into our ears
know, the day has come for them to use the ladders
To pluck the hair sprouted in our ears
What illegal law
that commanded our tongues to be cut
that law, now has become a slip of palm leaf
to take off the dirt on our tongues
The sword that cut the Sambuka's head
is as sharp as it has been
for centuries.
But, now it changed hands
Surely it recognizes you
Now no Manu can save you.

Anyam: The surname of a family
Sankranthi: A Hindu Festival comes every year in the second week of January (A festival of new harvest).
Wada: arrow of houses, a street
Guru Dakshina: Offering or reward to a teacher on completion of a Pupil's education.

(Tr. By. Dr.Sheela Swarupa Rani)

Sikhamani is the recipient of many Awards and a few important Awards among them are: **The Literary Award** of Telugu University in 1988, **Free Verse Front Award,** Hyderabad in 1987, **Garikapati Sahiti Puraskaram,** Kakinada in 1996, **Regency kalavani Sahiti Puraskaram** in 1997 and in 2004 the **Andhra Pradesh Government's Language Award** from Andhra Pradesh Adhikara Bhasha Sangham. His contribution to Indian Literature is recorded in **Who is Who of Indian Writers,** in1999, published by Sahitya Akademi, New Delhi.

Sikhamani is a popular poet in general and a Dalit poet in particular. He reminds the romantic poets of England who brought the common man and ordinary themes to the limelight. Siva Sagar, in his foreword to the **Kirrucheppula Bhasha** (2000) said that he was remained of Gothe when read Sikkhamani's poems on 'Mother'. He quoted from **Faust** about the Maternal Goddess:

All things corruptible
Are but a parable;
Earth's insufficiency
Here finds fulfillment;
Here the ineffable
Wings like through love
Eternal womanhood
Leads us above

About Sikhamani, the poet, Professor C. Subba Rao remarked "the person of the poet and the persona of the poet are one and the same". (Foreword: **Kirrucheppula Bhasha**), certainly one can find simplicity, commitment, sensibility and poetic beauty in Sikhamani's poetry. At present he is teaching in Potti Sreeramulu Telugu University, Hyderabad in the department of Comparative Literature.

MOKA RATNA RAJU (1957 -)

Moka Ratna Raju working as a Postman at present (Maharanipet, Visakhapatnam) published two collections of poems in the year 2000 and 2002, respectively. He was born in Manepalli of East Godavari district on 25th January 1957. His parents are Moka Veeranna and Mahalakshmi. He is also a social activist and conducted many social marriages. He received the prestigious **Dak Seva Award** from the Postal department in October 1989. He received First Prize in story writing in March 1988. In 1996 he got first prize for his **Amma Amaram (Mother is Eternal)**, at State level Writers competition conducted by Rajani Cultural Association. In April 2001 Bombay Telugu Akademic Association, on the occasion of the 110th Birth Anniversary of Bharatratna Baba Saheb Ambedkar, felicitated him and in June 2003 he received **Ugadi Puraskar** from Visakha Cultural Academy for "his mammoth contribution to Indian Art and Culture through his writings".

The first collection of Poems, **Neevu-Nee Staanam** published in 2000 (**You and Your Place**) consists of 53 poems. A famous critic in Telugu Literature, Addepalli Rama Mohan Rao wrote the foreword entitled **Diksuchi** (**The Compass**) for this collection. He commented: "Ratna Raju's poems clearly reflect the present day social problems and they are in simple expression, diction and impressive". G. Subba Rao, a contemporary poet and the Secretary of All India Postal Employees Association, stated that "His poetry is influenced by unemployment, poverty, ignorance, social evils and evil practices".

Another work **Gunde Kolimi: The Pleading of Ratna Raju** (November 2002) is a collection of 48 short poems. Dr. Addepalli Rama Rao, a popular Telugu literary critic remarked, "These pleadings are the best examples of comic-satire" (38). A good example for the poet's concern for the common man is given here under.

POEM: 12

If you drink arrack, country liquor,
brandi, whisky or gin
their inebriating effect
disappears the next morning.
When will the drunken discriminatory
stupor of caste, religion and class,
which is infused into every nerve
of man for generations together,
which has turned man into a beast,
quit man and lead him to
the path of humanity?
It is enough if one in a hundred
listens to my truthful, intrepid appeals.
Can anyone tell me?
Is Brahma who bore?
children through his multiple
reproductory organs ¾ face, shoulder,
stomach and soles of the feet ¾

a male or female?
It is enough if
one in a hundred modern Brahmas
listens to my truthful, intrepid
appeals. (Tr.By.P.Hari Padma Rani)

PRATTIPATI MALLESWARA RAO (Sambuka) (1958 – 1995)

Prattipati Malleswara Rao, popularly known as Sambuka was born on 19th December 1958 at Nidamarru of Guntur district. He could not even complete his school education due to dire poverty. He founded **Charvaka Youth Organisation** in 1975 to create awareness among the local youth. He was a supporter of Left Parties till 1975 and later he joined the Indian Atheist's Organisation in 1976, as he was vexed with Leftist ideology. At that time he met C.V (C. Varahala Rao) and read his works and became a true revolutionary. In 1977 he was selected as a constable in the 6th Battalion of APSP, Mangalagiri, Andhra Pradesh.

Based on his knowledge in the ideology of Marx, Lenin and Mao, Sambuka started studying the police system. In 1979 the police had gone on a nation-wide strike. In response to the strike, he wrote essays, songs and poems to inspire the police. Though he was a police constable yet he worked for the Peoples War. After the unfortunate incidents of Karamchedu and Tsunduru/Chunduru in 1988 Sambuka published a historical work in 1988 with the title **Andhra Pradesh lo Communist Udyamam pai Kula Prabhavam (The Influence of Caste on the Communist Movement of Andhra Pradesh)**. This work did not see the light of the day due to the jealousy and conspiracy of Boddu Rama Krishna Rao. He published a collection of Poems **Poyedemi Lenollam** in 1992 and **Charitra lo Kraistavam (Christianity in the History)** in 2004. He roared against the injustice done to Dalits from times immemorial, in the name of Vedas or Varna dharma.

The Roaring of the Dalit

Even before I fell into this world,
When I was still in my mother's womb
I grew as an untouchable.
I opened my eyes on this sacred 'Bharath'
with the stamp of a low caste fellow,
'What I am' was decided in my mother's womb (it self)
My hut, my surroundings speak of my caste
My hut which looks hurled away
Away from the mainstream, near to the graveyards,
It stands a symbol to my caste;
My hut speaks of my caste
My caste is reflected in my hut;
Comrade, Manu called me a Sudra
He said I am a Chandala
an Untouchable, a Pariah, the least of the mankind
He said it suits the *Varna Ddharma* to let
me remain an illiterate,
and to wait on the high caste.
He said it was ordained by God
through Vedas, Upanishads
through epics and ethics
through Brahmanism and Varna dharma
In the name of the deeds of the previous life,
In the name of fate and Destiny,
and on thousand and one pretexts,
they over ruled my life and commanded me
Drilled nails into my intelligence
and plotted to make me
a permanent slave to the high caste.
I've just one thing to tell you my comrade,
He debased me in the name of Varna Dharma
and you're taking over me in the name of *Varga Poratam';*
He shackled me in the name of Fate
and you are dodging me in the name of unison.
You both throw me into a state of confusion;

He, with his Sanskrit slokas
You with your stock Marxist jorgan.
Let me tell you one thing,
You know swimming and you're swimming
in the favourable currents;
But I, I'm swimming against the currents.
I am bearing the pain of piercing thorns;
While you have no experience of pricking even,
How can you understand the severity of the pain?
Only the one who is burning in
the flames of caste discrimination
alone can understand it.
Your analysis of the situation is pedantic
But mine is the agony of personal suffering;
Let me tell you one thing
In a cunning ruse to safegaurd
the privilege of leadership
You stamped me as one without merit;
Under the straps of party's discipline
You chained me into dumb slavery;
pegging me down, you are safeguarding
your own position.
While he treats me as a sinner
you treat me as a dunce;
Caste is his weapon
Marxism is your weapon as well as shield;
I'm the foot stool to his luxurious life
I'm the base for your merit;
In a way he is a bally-hoo of casteism
and you of leadership
Let me tell you one thing
I'm neither the surface layer nor
the foundations as you say;
I'm just a person from oppressed caste
set out to bring down the dominance of high castes;
I'm a person from exploited caste
Out on putting an end to your games;
I'm an ignorant low caste dunce

Out on driving away
the modern barbarism law – bearers of Marx
Let me tell you one thing
I want neither the heaven he is luring me with
Nor the liberation you are beguiling me with
I don't want any sacrifices from you
Which you are so ready to make
while enjoying the benefits of leadership.
Let me tell you one thing
Liberation from your dominance is the first thing we want
We know it pretty well that for you
To lose the privilege of leadership is
as hard as it is for the landlords
to lose their rights, authority and property;
In the long run of seven decades
We've learnt that revolt is the only way to stop exploitation
We need to revolt to counterfeit
the aggression of the high caste
We need to revolt to bring you down,
from the alters where you
instilled yourself as our lords
Comrade! I know it's irksome to you
to be called a comrade by me
Since I questioned your high caste leadership
I've become a caste fanatic
Casteist I am
Oh! High caste comrade,
Being a caste discriminated fellow
I least wish to have a caste
I don' t need it.
It's you, who need it, for you enjoy it,
The honour, the dignity, the prestige
that the caste bestows upon you
The philosophy of caste and its
existence are your needs
As a down trodden one

as one put to humiliation on the basis of caste
I am not for caste identity
It's you who nurture the caste system,
And yet you act as a communist with no caste
You deserve to be in the Ginnis Book of World Record
For your acting (Best Performance)
The documents and the commissions you have been writing for seven decades are an example of your diplomacy and double standards
Comrade of High caste,
I've just one thing to tell you
However you name it, whatever colours
you paint on it
Let me assert that caste is the
only weapon for us to fight
against the aggressions of the high caste
You are a Marxist, an illusionist for saying
that there is no caste
You deceive yourself by saying
that there are no castes in Indian sociaty
Let me warn you of one thing
You may stamp us as you fancy
But we affirm that we are of an oppressed caste,
oppressed casteists;
But we will be the architects of
a new socialist society that will drive away
the dark kingdom of the exploiting high caste;
we are the chariot drivers
of the oppressed and suppressed caste
We're the off spring of the pioneers of the Modern Revolution
We're the builders of a caste free society.

(Tr. By. P.Naga Jasmine)

YENDLURI SUDHAKAR (1959 -)

Dr. Yendluri Sudhakar was born on 21st of January 1959 in Nizamabad of Andhra Pradesh. His parents are Devaiah and Shantha Bai. He did his M.A. Telugu literature in 1988 and received his doctoral degree in 1993. Before entering Potti Sreeramulu Telugu University in 1990, he worked as a Grade I Pandit in Wesly Boys School, Secunderabad (1985 - 1990) for five years. A good number of M.Phils and Ph.Ds are awarded under his guidance. His doctoral thesis is on the literature of Gurram Joshua. He has received nearly 18 Awards and important among them are **The National Level Ranjani Kundurthi Award** in 1988, **Free Verse Front Award** for **Varthamanam** in 1993, instituted exclusively for poetry, P.S. Telugu University **Dharmanidhi Puraskar** in 1995, **Kavikokila Gurram Joshua Visista Sahiti Award** in 2000 and **Acharya N.G. Ranga Centenary Literary Award** in the year 2000, ***American Telugu Association Award,*** Texas, USA in 2002 and **Detroit Telugu Association Silver Jubilee Award** in 2002.

Dr.Yendluri Sudhakar published fifty research articles, about one hundred poems and thirty short stories. The important among his works are **Varthamanam**, a collection of poems, **Kotha Gabbilam (The New Bat)** a long poem, **Malle Moggala Godugu**, the stories of Madigas and **Nalla Draksha Pandiri – Darky**, a bilingual poetry collection published in June 2002. The Poem **Darky** speaks about the life of an untouchable girl. The poem has poetic sensibility and it is an answer to the critics who vehemently denies the poetic sensibility in Dalit Poetry. The poem is given here under.

DARKY

O my *Chandalika* !
Epic heroines of yore pale
Before your silver anklets!
O my Black Bird!
Tomes of Beauty take to heels
At lightnings of your black earth.
I wouldn't on the sly say –
You're a tender slender creeper languishing lean.
O the blossom of my race, my blue diamond!
Today I've captured the language

That has cast your beauty out.
I bet it on your marigold bun!
It hit the pot in the sling
Held high in the sky outside the village.
O my *Matangini*!
Making you a kite
I fly you on in the beauteous sky
The iron bowl heavy on your head
Mocks at even the Miss World's Crown.
As a sharp sickle or a cheeta
You go reaping at harvest time,
All nature's colours around bow down to you
As you stand half drenched under the Palmyra umbrella,
Dry clouds come down cuddling you.
One look at you,
Even old corn cobs sprout warm seeds again.
When you set your foot on the moon in the rivulet
Fish in clustered waters kiss moonbeams of your toes.
As you fix your Sari in truss and sling
The catapult from the crop dais
All the four directions startled, salute your strong calfs.
As you call up *'bho, bho, bho'*
All the fighting cocks with red crests
Fall at your feet splashing their wings
Forgetting rice grains at the taste of your sweet call.
As you spread out a leg lusciously
Grinding millet in the hand mill,
Flour powder on the fold of your black waist
Shines like a silver girdle.
Sneaking at the red streaks in your eyes-
The folk festival night you drank Palmyra toddy,
This very world reels round and round.
In the black cotton soil of your body
Moves slowly the black sheen of pepper creeper.
The moon, seeing your beauty
As you lie on the string cot out in the open,
Tells your sensuous secret to the sun in his ear.

The sun, right at dawn runs to watch you
And puts his diamond ray of ring under your pillow.
O Beauty of my Black Vine Grape!
My Black Vine canopy! My star *Arundhati*!
As my fingers feel the warm drum cheek
My throat sings sleepy songs.
I've seen the dance of stars in the sky of your blue eyes
From the tepid circles of light blue flames.
My Black Beauty!
On the throne of Black Aesthetics
I anoint you with all reverence of poetry
I announce you heroine
Of my Black Poem.

Chandalika : An out cast woman

Matangini : Of Madiga community, wedded to God. Yet, she can have intercourse with any one of her choice.

Arundhati : A star named after the wife of the sage Vasistha; At marriage ceremonies Arundhati is invoked by the bridegroom as a pattern of conjugal excellence. The hereditary occupations of Arundhatiyas is cobbling and playing music at village ceremonies.

(Tr. By. 'MO')

In another poem **Ostracized,** he narrates the pathetic and unwanted life of an untouchable in this country. He concludes the poem with a new hope that "... but a fearless voice to state our choice/ a new book of law, a new country/ a new land and a new sky". **Low Caste Script** is yet another important critical poem that speaks about the brutal treatment of Hindu fundamentalism.

Low Caste Script

Jesus once again died of burns.
Can you touch the leper with love
As gently as you touch a flower?
You become stale food offered to your stone legged diety.
Can you ever hug a hungry orphan like Mother Teresa?

You run to milk feed the mouth of an image.
Can you give life to the babe in the dust bin?
In your very orange vengeance lies a spiteful spite,
You can neither serve mankind
Nor worship God.
You are an Indian ocean of violence.

II

Who knows where from
Yet, Jesus came into our ghetto
In the place of my spittoon
He gave the honour of a Cross to my neck.
Buddha, son of the soil
Sounded on my torn tongue the
Tripitakas unflinchingly.
Install the statues of the
Father of the Constitution not in Dalits streets
But at the thresholds of casteist VIPs
Time will prove
Whether flower garlands fall
Or pairs of *cheppals*

III

Believers are offering prayers of fasts.
At midnights as birds on olive branches.
With frightening hisses of slogans like snakes
A crowd of caste enemies fell on the birds.
The dinner of the Lord turned red with blood
Sisters became Crosses of rape.
Tears of blood ooze in Virgin Mary's eyes.
A golden sentence shinning like a candle of blood
Among the fallen walls of the church –
'Love thy neighbour as thyself.'

IV

A final tomb for the last autocracy
Self respect, the foundation of my race.
Mine is the civilization of Chindu dance
I'm a Synonym for merit.
All the five elements know my skill.
Mine is the blue signature on the blue millennium

From now on, our own ward bards are the leaders of the age
An explitive in the alphabet is
Not an untouchable lass of insult.
Enriching poetry is an age old art of we the outcasts
Saraswati has now and for all time to come
Become the daughter-in-law of our ghetto.

V

Rama is not my saviour. He is my slayer.
A burning throat can't sing a
Suprabhata Sloka.
The moment he set his Aryan foot on my earth,
I became the cheated oout son of the soil
I lost my all.
Fangs of History became red with my blood.
Sanctum Sanctorum untouched by my feet
Became barren.
Notify all out cast hamlets as liberated
Before I become an untouchable nation and
From then come out universal men.

Tripitakas : Collective title of three Buddhist sacred texts.

Chindu : Dance of the untouchables.

Saraswati : Wife of Lord Brahma; Goddess of speech and learning.

Suprabhata Sloka : Invocation song to Lord Venkateswara waking him up from sleep.

The Jesus figure in the poem is Graham Steins burnt alive along with his two sons by Bhajarang Dal fundamentalists.

(Tr.By. 'MO')

Undoubtedly Yendluri Sudhakar is a powerful, promising Dalit poet.

DARLA RAMACHANDRA (1960 -)

Darla Ramachandra was born on 15th November 1960 in Gollacharla village of Dornakal Mandal, Warangal district. His parents Devaiah and Ellamma are agricultural coolies. He did his M.A. Telugu in Osmania University, Hyderabad in 1992 and B.Ed in Ekasila B.Ed College of Janagama, affiliated to Kakatiya University. At present he is working as Junior Telugu lecturer and Vice-principal, APSWR Junior College, Husnabad Karimnagar district. So far he published thirty stories in various journals. Social change is the broad spectrum of theme for his poems and stories. From 1985 onwards he is writing poetry. He received the honour at state level for his poetry in 1997 from Madhira Sahiti Samstha, Khammam district and **Dr.B.R. Ambedkar Literary Fellowship** in 2001 from Bharatiya Dalita Sahitya Akademi, New Delhi. The Visala Sahitya Akademi published his first volume of stories in September 2002 with the title **Kirru Cheppulu**. B.S. Ramulu a sincere Marxist and the founder of Visalasahiti wrote the foreword for this book. There are fourteen stories that reflect his life connected with his untouchable caste, family, his village etc. As he is born in a poor Dalit family he has to face uncountable hurdles even to complete his education. He has to fight with social injustice at every point of his life.

JUPAKA SUBHADRA (1962 -)

Jupaka Subhadra was born in Damaranchepalle of Regonda Mandal, Warangal district. Her parents are Narasimha and Kanaka Veeramma. She took M.A. and M.Phil degrees in Telugu Literature from Kakatiya University, Warangal. In 1988, she got employment in the Secretariat of Andhra Pradesh. In her childhood she wrote small poems on the subjects like – nature, friendship and beauty. In the year 1997, her poems, **Nagaramlo Naagu** and **Palle Koila,** and **Shuddicheyale**, a story brought her name and recognition. Her writings are published in magazines and newspapers like **Bhoomika, Andhra Jyothi, Ekalavya, Udyoga Kranti, Vaartha** etc.

Subhadra is the first Dalit woman who contested in the Employee's Association in the Secretariat of Andhra Pradesh. In 1992 she started a Women's Association for the first time for the women employees of the Secretariat. Her story – **Shuddi Cheyyali** written in 2001 depicts the physical hard work done by a Dalit woman.

PUTLA HEMALATHA (1962 -)

Putla Hemalatha, a Christian by faith is the wife of a popular Dalit writer Yendluri Sudhakar. Her parents are Manashhe and Manoranjitam. Her first story **Tirigirani Payanam** is published in the magazine **Kristu Rahasyam** a Christian journal in the year 1975 while she was studying ninth class. In 1990 she wrote a novel **Guudu Cherina Guvva** and it is serialized in **Spandana** a religious magazine. She recited her poems many a time in All India Radio, Visakhapatnam. Hemalatha strongly advocates that the Dalit and Women's movements should create a platform to express themselves from the lowest rung of the people in the villages. She wrote about three novels, twenty stories and thirty poems in freeverse. Her writings are published in **Eenadu, Andhra Boomi** etc. Her poems are included in **Niili Meghalu,** a famous anthology of women's writing. Though initially she wrote with Christian perspective, slowly she started writing with Dalit and feminist angles. A good example of her writing is:

Veils of Memory

In childhood
Warmth of the sari end that mother covered me with
becomes a memory
And encircles me
like a shawl around my shoulders
She is somewhere away
like a Yakshini personified
But I look at
the sweetness of affectionate calls
through binoculars of memories
When my heart flutters
like a kite in tree branches
When I slip away like a baby
from life's shoulders

mother caresses on my back
like gentle breeze
The plantain leaf-hands that fed me milk rice then
are becoming the whetstones
building the walls of pain and pleasure
Sometimes
my heart slips
and falls down with a thud like an almond in the courtyard
Loving calls
becoming ancient remnants
lie rusted under the roof-edge
When I get fed up
repeatedly patching up
the wounded hearts
an unknown feeling
winnows me from top to toe
Now
Becoming solitary in a crowd
I curl up like a baby crow
under the wings of vacuum
Only my mother
makes me a human being
and shows me the path of life
holding my mother's little finger
toddling
I measure the boundaries of lifelines.

(Tr.By K.Suneetha Rani)

JAJULA GOWRI (1962 -)

Jajula Gowri was born in Lotukunta of Secunderabad and her parents are Mallaiah and Lakshmi. She got married when she was studying VIII class and has to discontinue her studies due to her marriage. But later took BA degree from Dr. Ambedkar Open University, Hyderabad and studied journalism in Potti Sreeramulu Telugu University.

From her childhood Gowri developed interest in listening songs and writing poetry. Her first poem

Karshakulu (1980) is about her parents. From 1980 onwards she wrote about 300 poems on the themes of poverty and child labour. When they are rejected by many journals, later she started writing from Dalit perspective. Her poetry brought to light along with the Andhra Pradesh Dalit movement. Her poems on Dalit concept, **Dalit Samrajyam** and **Utiki Aarestha** are published in **Ekalvya** in the year 1994.

Jajula Gowri is the first generation Dalit woman writer from Telangana region. She writes in Telangana dialect. In her unpublished story **Kanche (The Fence)** written in 2001, she depicted the young girls who have to do physical hard work while studying in the school and the physical abuse they are exposed to.

Gowri published her stories with the title **Mannubuvva** in 2005. It is published by Visala Sahitya Akademi of Hyderabad. The stories reflect the writer's clear understanding of society. They also deal with the social exploitation of Dalits from various angles. In her poem **Utiki Aarestha (I Will Wash and Dry Them)** she declares:

...
From the madigas life
Declaring revolution
I clean dirt in the family
And false pride in the society
Now, I wash and dry...!

In another poem **I As Myself** she speaks about the social exploitation in the name of caste.

The system of chaturvarna made me the fifth one
And pushed me out from the town
The theory of fatalism made me
an untouchable and left me to loneliness
The Brahmanism betrayed and annihilated me
The political diplomacy of the rich
dragged me into the streets
Enfacing occupation on me
They weighed my labour in an unjust balance

They made me the needle of the balance
and pierced mine own eyes with the same.
Excommunicating even from the Sudras
They smeared the fifth 'Varna ' on me.
- In the name of bonded labour
They sucked out the last drop of my blood
What remains are bones
And my own comrade is after them
pounding them into flour chanting
the mantra of unison.
- I can bear it no longer
It's time I thought of my own place
Co-existing with people inhuman
I'm deceived time and again
Crushed among yesterday – today and tomorrow
I'll keep myself as myself (Tr. By. P. Naga Jasmine)

MADDELA SANTHAIAH (1963 – 2002)

Maddela Santhaiah, who worked actively in the agitations against the attempt murder on Gaddar and the capital punishment to Chalapati and Vijayavardhanam, was born on 9th August 1963. By the time of his death on 14th March 2002 he was a lecturer in the P.S. Telugu University Hyderabad. He is not only a poet but also a singer. He is certainly a very committed Dalit activist. His university lectureship was never a hurdle in his participation in the Dalit activities. Like an ordinary activist he pasted the posters and distributed pamphlets many a time. Santhaiah had some family problems and along with that his ill health worked together to put an end to his life. His simplicity and commitment for his community made him a good friend to one and all in the creative field as well social and political life. His friends under the guidance of Sikhamani are formed into Maddela Santhaiah Memorial Trust in the Hyderabad and brought out a souvenir with the title **Santhaiah Kosam** (**For Santhaiah**) in 2003. The trust also collected the poems of Santhaiah and brought out a collection entitled **O.C. Kreestu**.

KALEKURI PRASAD (1964 -)

Kalekuri Prasad was born on October, 25th in Kanchikacherla of Krishna district. His parents are teachers and they are Srinivasa Rao and Lalita Sarojini. He is a freelancer, literary critic, creative writer and Dalit activist. He came out of Peoples War Group in 1987 and out of VIRASAM (The Revolutionary Writers' Association) in 1991. He is very much touched by the Karamchedu and Tsundur/ Chunduru incidents. He wrote a song "Karma Bhoomilo Pusina O Puvva!" in 1987 and it became a successful and a popular song after including it in the Telugu film **Sri Ramulaiah.** A famous singer Jesudas (Kerala) rendered this song for the film. His poem **For a Fistful of Self-Respect** is published in **Indian Literature**, Nov-Dec, 2000 and it is prescribed for the Post Graduate students of Sri Krishnadevaraya University. His poem **Untouchable Love** is yet another example that presents how untouchability is an obstacle in love.

Untouchable Love

Although my injuries were writhing in pain
didn't I carry your footprints on my heart.
Although death was about to pounce on me
didn't I long for life with you
If I could not live for love
at least I wanted to die for love
my dear!
As the mornings curd rice
that you gave me as the evening meal is my witness
shall I tell you the truth behind my death
my dear!
Do you know how my heart, blood and language
longed to call you thus as long as I was alive
except addressing you madam –
when your people dragged me to the village court
binding me to the pandal pole
battered me like a beast
I laughed
how I pitied my people who stood

pathetically bowing their heads!?
if your people asked me what the issue was
I thought I would proclaim that I love you
but the village court accused me of theft
and you were the witness, weren't you
I know how to cremate corpses
but your people burnt me when I was alive
'father forgive them for they
do not know what they are doing'
I remembered Lord's words that Father spoke
again and again.
The sleepless nights that we spent together is my witness
If a single tear were to flash in your eyes
I would have forgiven you and your people
The furnace that you blew in my heart
The kerosene fires that your people lit on my body
I can't say now
Which is more painful
My dear!
While the flames engulfed me
I felt as if you were embracing me.

(Tr. By. Dr. K. Suneetha Rani)

K.Suneetha Rani of University of Hyderabad translated this poem **Untouchable Love**. His short stories and literary reviews are published in various magazines. He translated Swami Dharma Thirtha's **History of Hindu Samrajyavadula Charitra** for Hyderabad Book Trust in Telugu. He translated other works too. He delivered a research based oration on "Dalit Movement – Dalit Literary Movement" in 1999 at Telugu University in the conference on Dalit Literature (29th & 30th Dec). Later **Sakshi**, **Human Rights Watch**, and **Andhra Pradesh** published this speech. This is a critical analysis, certainly useful for researchers in Dalit literature. On the last page of the essay Kalekuri Prasad also gave suggestions to Dalit writers. He used **Yuvaka** as pen name for his poems.

Kalekuri Prasad also tried his hand at short fiction. In the story "Malletita" **(A Type of Weed in Tobacco field)** published in December 1996, he wrote on the child labour and how Dalits are exploited by the land owners when they go to work in their field. He not only presented the problem but also gave a befitting solution; when the elders among the Dalits after taking liquor from the landowners supported the dominant castes. Dalit youth questioned and rejected the decision of their elders. And also refused to work for a long time. Kalekuri through his writings, project the self-respect of Dalits.

MADDURI NAGESH BABU (1964 – 2005)

Madduri Nagesh Babu was born on the independence day of India in 1964, in Rudravaram of Sattenapalli taluk, Guntur district. His parents are Zakaraiah and Jonnalagadda Anasuyamma. He is a graduate of Andhra Christian College, Guntur during 1985-88. He took his M.A. degree in English literature (1988-1991) from Andhra University, Visakhapatnam and completed his M.Phil on **Comparative Literature – The Concept of Protest in Modern African Poetry and Indian Dalit Poetry** from Potti Sreeramulu Telugu University (1991-92). He registered for PhD in the same institution on **Indian Dalit Poetry** and he could not complete it due to his sudden demise on 10th January 2005. He died while working as a Mandal Revenue Officer at Nadendla of Guntur district.

The year 1985 is a turning point in the lives of Andhra Pradesh Dalits in general and Madduri Nagesh Babu in particular because from then onwards he became a committed Dalit writer. Many Marxist writers are turned into Dalit writers and Dalit writers in turn became Ambedkarites. The year in which the Dalita Mahasabha came into existence and many powerful writers started writing Dalit Literature; Madduri Nagesh Babu is one of those committed writers who started writing Dalit literature vigorously. **Naraloka Prardhana**, **Meerevutlu**, **Rachabanda**, reflect the poetic sensibility and his agony for the fellow Dalits. With the Christian background he attacked the Christian authorities and priests for giving untrue and irrelevant messages to the poor. His poetry is full of fire sparks. His **Naraloka Prardhana** is a collection of Dalit Christian Poetry published by Alice Publications, Narasaraopet. **Rachabanda** is a long poem published in 1996 and in 1998 the ASMITA brought out his poems under the title **Meerevutlu**. Nagesh babu also wrote powerful short stories with Dalit themes. In **Kottam (The Cattle-shed**) he delineated how Dalits are used and exploited by the landlords. The protagonist is also a narrator of the story. He begins with the statement "I died in a strange situation. "Strange" because I did not die normally. More over, it seems I died by committing suicide due to unbearable stomach-ache, unknown to me". He was a bonded labour and as his landlord is a drunkard and always spend his time in town, he became the victim for the land lady's sexual desire. When the landlord came to know about the relationship of his wife and Paleru (bonded labourer) in the beginning he did not react. Later the husband and wife with some understanding killed him and converted the murder into suicide. The protagonist explains how he was exploited and how his son who will become 'paleru' in his place would be illtreated. The writer shows the mental struggle and pain the servant had because he never wanted any physical relationship with the lady and moreover he undergoes severe mental trauma because the landlord knowing well never said a word nor showed anger against him.

A poem is quoted here.

Dalit Mother

In front of the corpse shop of any government hospital
Did you see a pool of tears – that is my mother
Among the graves of any yard did you ever see a lonely rock
That grew on a grave without deserving even a

tombstone ¾that is also my mother
My mother is not Yashoda
She is not even Kausalya
When I cried bitterly because of hunger my mother did not take me in her arms
And showing me the moon did not feed me thumb morsels from silver vessels
When I threw a tantrum for *noojeedi* she kicked and scolded me
But my mother did not lovingly feed me baby biscuits
Where is the trace of single lamp being ever lit in her eyes!
About such a mother of mine tell me what shall I write
If everyone is knitting poetry on their mothers
Their mothers are royal mothers milk mothers in whose stomachs the buttermilk did not
churn
What is there about my mother
She did not even have a name except for 'ase' 'ose'
She did not deserve any honorific except to be called 'prostitute' or 'bitch'
She is one mad woman who all through her life worried and lost hope just for a palmful
of gruel
For poetry on such a mother of mine
Do you think the words would agree?
Do you think the rules would obey?
When everyone else's mothers were sleeping happily
My labourer mother was molested among the mounds of harvest
When all the rich mothers received the rewards of the best mothers
My mother from our locality was paying a penalty for drinking a handful of water
When everyone else's mothers became leaders and were ruling
My cheap mother was doing a dharna in front of government offices

To anyone 'mother' brings to mind the picture of her feeding milk or singing a lullaby
But I am reminded of my mother taking out the weeds in the fields carrying mud baskets
Starting with the crow of the cock till Father's touch at night
About my coarse mother who did not even remember that she was actually a woman
What do you ask me to write
My mother never sang a lullaby for me
Her voice had been lost with hunger long ago.
My mother never even patted me to sleep
Her hands had changed into agricultural tools long ago.
When all the children were going to picnics holding their mothers' little fingers
I shrivelled into the abdominal valley of my mother and slept, Sir!
When all the children were praising their mothers as living embodiments of God
I was abusing my mother with my wrath for she did not pay my fees
When all the sons were disturbed by just the headache of their rich mothers
I grumbled why my disease-ridden mother had not yet died, Sir
What to say!
Coming drenched in rain to dry myself when I caught my mother's pallu
Crores of faded patches mocked at me
With a parched throat when I thirstily touched my mother's breast with my mouth
Her rib bones pricked me
Whatever happens, Sir!
Among the lakhs of mothers who are being abused as animal mothers
For giving birth to animals who looked down upon fellow-humans as animals

To talk about my mother who was nothing but human
This language this poetry will never be enough, Sir!
(Tr. By. Archana Chowhan,**Indian Literature**, Nov-Dec 2000)

BANDI SATYANARAYANA (1965—)

Doctor Bandi Satyanarayana was born on 15th January 1965 in the village Vilasaravigunta cheruvu near Amalapuram of East Godavari district. His parents are Veeramma and Vanamaiah. He did his post graduation in Telugu Literature from Andhra University. He received a cash prize from the Social Welfare Department of Andhra Pradesh for the first rank in M. A. He is awarded Ph.D in the year 1994 by the Andhra University, Visakhapatnam. He is an employee of All India Radio.

Bandi Satynarayana is an upcoming poet and his **Gundepagilina Sabdam** , a collection of poems is published in the year 1997 by Sahiti Samakya of Kothagudem. G.Subba Rao a Telugu poet and critic reviewed this collection. In the review Subba Rao remarks that the deep pathetic emotions and serious thought provoking ideas are inter twined in the poetry of Bandi Satyanarayana. In one of the poems the poet laments that all are human beings in spite of the difference in colour and features is the saying from ages. But in the society the reality is contrary to the saying. In the poem **Chiguraku (A Tender Leaf)** one can see the despair in the poet.

Born in the poverty of darkness
So you never had sufficient food
Only in dreams you had good sleep—
Then how will you have
Smooth cheeks and long black hair?(Tr.By.T.Bharathi)

NETALA PRATAP KUMAR (1965 -)

Netala Pratap Kumar an upcoming poet in expedient short poems under the name **Na Neelu**, was born on 13th August in Vijayeswaram of West Godavari district. His parents are Satyam and Santa kumari. He is a postgraduate in Telugu literature and did Bachelor of Law from C.R.R. College, Eluru. He is working as Telugu Pandit (Grade – II) in U.P.P. School, Ramachandrapuram, Janga Reddy Gudem, West Godavari district. He worked as a journalist in **Vaartha** and **Vijetha** Newspapers ard as a columnist in **Eepaksham**, a fortnightly. He published a few articles in the newspapers and magazines especially on Women's issues. His first book of poetry entitled **Palakanki** is published in 2003. He is also planning to bring out another collection of **Na-Neelu**; he is a first Dalit poet who used this Prakriya.

CHANDRA SRI (1967 -)

Chandra Sri was born in Chirala of Ongole district, though her roots are in Telangana. Her great grand parents migrated to Chirala from Warangal district to join in Army during colonial period. Her father Jaya Chandra is a Mandal Cooperative Divisional Officer and mother a craft teacher. She discontinued her studies in the Intermediate course to join Radical Student Union in 1984. She was arrested and imprisoned in the central jail, Hyderabad as she participated in the meeting of Royat Cooli Association. She actively took part in the cultural wing of the Association. She is a good singer. She was very much upset with Karamchedu massacre of Madigas on 17th July 1985. Against this incident she supported and participated in the programme drafted by the People's War Group. Along with her husband she went to underground and led a secret life for about eight years. She even worked in the revolutionary groups along with her husband. But later due to her ill health she came out and started working as an activist to the legal cell of Jananatya Mandali. She is one of the prominent woman activists among a limited number of woman activists in the cultural wing in the state. She sings folk songs as well as classical songs. She inspires thousands of audience when she sings with corresponding dance steps. Her writings reflect her experiences and the history of the Movements. Her writings are published in

Bhoomika, Vaartha, and **Ekalavya**. The issues related to women too appear in her writings.

PILLI RAMBABU (1968 -)

Pilli Ram Babu was born on 31, December 1968, in Ainapalli Lanka of Konaseema and settled at Ramachandrapuram as a teacher. His father is Pilli Saheb and mother Leelavati. He did his bachelor degree in Science. He is interested in studying the roots of the Dalits and writing the true history of them, as he believes that the present history gives a false witness to their existence. He published **Adi Bharatiyulu** and **Chandala** in April 2005. In **Chandala** the writer accuses that Brahmins created a false theory that Vedas are above the questioning and silenced the true history for centuries. Due to this concept people could not gain knowledge about Hinduism. The writer questions those who try to establish that Aryans as the natives of this country against the historical declaration that the Aryans as invaders and he even suggested that DNA test may settle this dispute. His unpublished works include 1). **Is Gupta's Age a Golden Period** 2). **Nagavasam** and 3). **The Ramayana, The Mahabharata, The Bhagavat Gita – A Review**. He received Sahitya Ratna award in 2005 from Jnana Dharma Prachara trust, Eluru and received Visista Puraskar from Bharatiya Dalit Sahitya Academy, New Delhi.

GUTAM SWAMY (1969-)

Dr. Gutam Swamy was born on the first of June in Ganti, Kothapet mandal of East Godavari district. His parents are Santaratnam and Tatarao. He is a post graduate in Telugu Literature and his doctoral thesis is on " A Study on War Poems". He worked for eight years in AMG Junior College, Bommuru, near Rajahmundry as Telugu Lecturer. At present he is working as a Telugu Pandit in M.P.U.P School, Edida Kothpet of Mandapeta Mandal in East Godavari District.

Gutam Swami's works include **Ekikaraniyan** (2005) a long poem, **Yasodhara** (2006) a novel and **Neelipathaaka** (A monologue of a Dalit) a long Dalit poem published in October 2007. In this poem the poet selects a bat as his messenger being a conscientious mammal. The poet requests the bat with blue flag to convey the pain, the suffering and the agony of Dalits in Andhra Pradesh to the Chief Minister. The poem is a first person narrative. The poet being the protagonist depicts the plight of Dalits in the state to the bat. Gutam Swamy advocates Ambedkar's philosophy for the betterment of Dalits and emphasizes the need for self-reliance among Dalits. He also published **Swamy Sathakam** in 2008. His other unpublished works include **Boduru Kappalu** a collection of short stories and **Hridaya Spandanalu** a collection of poems, **Chitti Kathalu**, stories for children and **Vyasa Manjari**. He also contributed essays and articles to various Journals and News Papers.

Gutam Swamy participated in more than twenty seminars so far. For the past ten years he participated in various social activities and a member in Swarnaandhra Cultural Association and GMC Balayogi Charitable Trust. He received **B.R.Ambedkar National Fellowship Award**, New Delhi in 2006, **Kalalaya Visista Puraskaram,** Palakollu in 2007 and **Padmabhushana Mahakavi Joshua Visista Sahitya Puraskaram**,Tenali in 2008.

KANDALA LILLY (1969 -)

"Jwalita" is the pen name of Kandala Lilly. She was born in Tallada village of Khammam district. Her parents are Swamidas and Kanaka Lakshmi. She took M.A. and Ph.D degrees from Osmania University, Hyderabad. At present she is working as a Telugu Pandit in Social Welfare Gurukul School, Vaira.

Lilly is writing poetry since her school days. Her parents and grandfather were singers. She is interested in ancient Telugu literature with Dalit Perspective. Her writings are published in various magazines and newspapers, like – **Vaartha, Prajasakti, Andhra Pradesh** and **Krishna Patrika**. She did her research on **The History of Dalit Literature**. In this work she accused the caste Hindus for recording the history in their favour. In her poem **Vipra Vinodam** she writes:

...
This Country!!!
The Altar of the weak
The Scaffold of the poor
Which Sastra's sinful-creation is this Untouchability?
The castes are the dark seeds sown by Vedas ...

GOGU SYAMALA (1969 -)

Gogu Syamala was born in Peddemul village of Rangareddy district. Her parents are Balaiah and Anantamma. She took her degree from Dr.Ambedkar Open University, Hyderabad. Syamala joined in the programmes of Radical Student Union since 1984. Later in 1989 she became a full time worker in the organisations working for the Royat Coolies. She worked on issues related to equal pay for equal work, Minimum wages Act, Creating Awareness among Women Workers etc. Her first essay **Poorudaarullo Strivimukti** (**Emancipation of Women Through Revolution**) is published in the journal **Nalupu (The Black)** in the year 1990. From 1990 onwards her writings are published in **Bhumika, Vaartha** and **Nighu**. She contributed to **Nighu**, a regular feature depicting her day-to-day experience under the title "Diary of a Dalit Woman". She participated in the Durban Conference against racism in the year 2001 and as a participant she wrote a poem – **Varadagudu (The Rainbow**)

I am the sufferer of this nation
I am also the revolutionary
...
My anger smashes the casteism.
I am the rainbow that grow plants in desert
By keeping my stomach empty I filled other stomachs
I enhanced the national income by my hard work

I am so hungry that I can eat mountains
My mother is Muthamma, Phulandevi is my sister
My aim is to hit the caste; Durban is my victory
...

Gogu Syamala is the editor of **Nalla Poddu** an important research work on Dalit Women's Literature, 1921-2002. This project is taken up by Anveshi, Research Centre for Women's Studies, Hyderabad. The research team needs an appreciation for doing a wonderful work.

VINODINI (1969 -)

Vinodini was born in Guntur and her parents are Devasayam and Sarojini. Her father worked as a head master. She took her M.A. and M.Phil degrees from Potti Sreeramulu Telugu University, Rajahmundry.

Vinodini chooses the themes for her writings from her observations of life around her. In her colony she observed that the boys of upper castes fall in love with Dalit Christian girls and marry them and after some days these men leave them and disappear and the unfortunate women remain single. Based on this background she wrote her first story **Mugimpu (The End)** in the year 1985. Her poem **Onti Nittadi Gudese** that dealt with the existence of Dalit Christian women is included in **Padunekkina Pata** (1995), one of the early collections of Dalit Poetry. This poem is translated into English and published in the Magazine **Chandrabaaga**. She is essentially a Dalit Christian woman writer and she feels that she gets satisfaction only after writing about Dalit Christians. Her poem **All Indians Are My Brothers and Sisters** published in 2000 focuses on the atrocities of Hindus on Christian Minorities.

JANGA GOUTHAM (1970—)

Goutham was born on 15th August 1970 in Sitaramudthota, Nedurumalli post, Ainavalli mandal of East Godavari district. His parents are Meeramma and Krishna Murthy. His started his career as a Dalit Activist on 17th July 1985, the black day on which the atrocities committed on Dalits in Karamchedu. He also actively participated in Mandal Movement against Babri incident. Goutham declares that while The Dalit Movement progressed from Self-Respect to Social Justice and then now for the political power, he too got transformed from a Dalit woker to an active participant and now turns to be a leader. Meanwhile he worked as a staff reporter and sub editor in **Vaartha** daily newspaper. He resigned from the job, as he wanted to be a full time activist and a leader in Dalit –Bahujan political movement.

In the process he joined in Bahujan Samajvadi Party (BSP) and withdrew from BSP as it had political alliance with BJP. Goutham believed that the basic problems of Dalits would be solved with the political power only. Hence he joined in the foundation of Bahujan Republican Party along with K.G.Satya Murty (Siva Sagar). He also contributed many articles and cover stories to **Ekalavya** a monthly Magazine under the editorship of K.G.Satya Murty. Goutham was also a member in the editorial board in this magazine.

Goutham felt that K.G.Satyamurty was not serious in the construction and planning of Dalit Bahujan activities. He also found fault with Satyamurty for his misusing the Party for mere advertisement but not seriously committed for the Dalits' wellbeing. Hence Goutham criticized and oppossed him for his non-commitment and came out of Bahujan Republican Party.

In the meantime Goutham tried to unite all those groups who share the similar ideology and by the time of State Assembly Elections in 1999 he took active participation in forming a political party named Mahajana Front in which associations of various castes are members. He worked as the chief secretary in Mahajan Front. Later this Mahajan Front is converted into Mahajan Party. The objective of this Party is to ensure political power to SCs, STs, BCs, Muslims, Women and the Poor Classes. With this objective he is now continuing as a fulltime activist and the founding chief secretary. He is participating in various flatforms discussing the issues related to Dalits and Bahujans and also contributed articles on this to various magazines. In connection with the party he started **Mahajana** a monthly magazine and he is the editor.

Goutham supported the Madiga Dandora Movement fighting for social justice and equal opportunities though he is a Mala by caste. He stongly opposed the Dandora activists when they focused Malas as their enemies.

So far Goutham published about 35 poems. They are published under the title **Nalu Dikkulanunchi Randi** in 2006. He is a powerful and committed poet. One of the best poems is quoted here. This poem gives an anlysis of Dalitism.

Conspiracy on pointing finger

First they migrated to riverbank Sindhu and subsist
conspired against the indigenous hosts and drive out

Feeling heavy with defeated psyche they seep into
Buddhism hijacked and buried the social egalitarianism

Poured into saivism, Jainism like secret agents
proclaimed Manu's arguments as ubiquitous

In the cloak of reincarnations sudra kings were quelled
popular kingdoms toppled and axed...

Defeated, they became ministers... if victorious,
Messengers of god... and grabbed the villages and owned
them

Scared at the British power, paved the way for English
fired the rebels and hanged the courageous

When times are ripe they talk freedom and struggle
When independent, grabbed the seat of power and that
of opposition too

Red rose on a white coat, rolled the capital on the red

carpet get left by sneaking into Marx's beard and Lenin's heart

What they think is progress, rest is casteism
Embraced Russia's weapon, China's arms, Mao's brain
Played facts to fiction like Gireesaham
Wagging tails of Simian army... down the way ....

If not like a feather on a tail...fleas on the feathers
All the story of evolution is monotonous

******

We spoke truth and lost life; its our history let us give witness
By the people...for the people...is ruler's voice
People build history and destiny of tyrants
Who are people? what's their history?

Unscary of excommunication, courageous tradition is our's let us give witness
Belligerent Parusurama's descendants heading the peace talks
Hindu imperialist facilitators naively talk of self-reliance

Land distribution is a conspiracy
Brahmanism behind the land issue is conspiracy

History a conspiracy...historical events are conspiracy
Media is conspiracy....progressive thinkers are part of conspiracy

Parliamentary democracy cherishing the four headed Hindu caste snake is a big conspiracy
Brutes enrolled us the in list of traitors let us give witness

Down the line of history conspiracy on indigenous people

Conspiracy on the pointing finger of the revolutionary son of the soil
Conspiracy on the fragrance of social democracy....
(Tr. By. P.V.Ranganayakulu)

He wrote a poem on the capital punishment of Chalapati and Vijayavardhanam in conncetion with Chilakaluripet case of burning the state government bus. Though the media presented them as worst murderers to burn the bus along with the passengers but the accused said that it was an accident.

The Gallows should be Hanged

On the dunghill of untouchability
The country proudly gave birth to two buds
Chalapathi and Vijayavardhanam,

Merciless and dire poverty
sacrificing these two
Consumed one bus in flames.

Stones shed tears for them
The walls of jail imprisoned
their pangs of hunger.
The Law of Manu awarded them
Death sentence in the name of humanity

Hey Scoundrel!

It's not Chalapathi and Vijayavardhan
who should be hanged
But, hunger and untouchability. (Tr.By.Dr.M.Neeraja)

At present, in addition to his political and editorial work he has taken up an appropriate research project i.e recording the Dalit movement in the past two decades (1985-2005). Let us hope that a useful and meaningful record will come out from the committed Dlit activist.

GYARA YADAIAH (1970-2004)

Gyara Yadaiah was born on 12th May 1970 in Marriguda

village of Nallagonda district. His parents are Ramulu and Lakshmamma. He studied Telugu Literature at undergraduate and postgraduate level. He has published his poetry collection in 1996 with the title **Gutam Debba** (Dalit Songs). He is exposed to Marxism as well Ambedkarism. Yadaiah is honoured by the then Chief Minister of Uttar Pradesh, Mayavati and the Bahujan Samaj Party Supremo, Kanshi Ram. He worked hard to earn his living during his student days. He worked as a teacher in a remote village near Devarakonda of Nalagonda district. He not only writes poetry but also essays in Dalit literature. His other works are **Rampekota** a collection of his songs and **Erkoshi**, a long poem published in 2001 and 2002 respectively. He proved to be a singer too. Yadaiah participated along with the popular singers, Gaddar, Mastarji, Gorati Venkanna, on many occasions. He worked as a strong activist in the changing society. He actively participated in Dandora Movement. He maintained good relationship with the other members in Movement and with the other writers. He is a good friend of Vemula Yellaiah, the author of **Kakka**; a representative Telugu Dalit novel from Telangana. Yadaiah died on 17th November 2004 as a bachelor.

CHALLAPALLI SWAROOPA RANI (1970 -)

Challapalli Swaroopa Rani, a powerful and effective Dalit woman writer was born on May 25, 1970 in Pyaparru of Guntur District. Her Parents are Mantraiah and Mariamma. She writes poems and short stories. Some of her writings are translated into English and Hindi. She also published research articles as she teaches in Potti Sreeramulu Telugu University. She also participated in students' agitations and social activities. She also participated actively in public meetings, seminars, workshops related to Dalit and women's issues. She took Ph.D degree from the University of Hyderabad in History. An Anthology of her poems are published under the title **Mankena Puvvu** in 2005. There are thirty poems in this collection. The title poem **Mankena Puvvu** is selected here to show Swarooparani as a powerful Dalit woman poet.

Mankena Puvvu*

I am a Kingfisher
suffering agonies
in an entangled thorny bush.
If I stir any side
it's me that the thorns prick.
These thorns are not of today
They are shackles placed around me
for generations together...
Permanently caught between
the well and the pit
I am always haunted by danger.
Let me ask, when have I lived
my life myself ...?
At home male ego has slapped
me on one cheek while
in the street, caste supremacy
has slapped me on the other.
For daily wages
when I went to the fields
when the sexually blind master there
waited in ambush to even, me along with my sweat
I wanted to sow myself burying
me in the earth.
Deprived of education for
years together,
I walked into the
lap of a hostel.
There too unable to withstand
the hungry looks of the warden.
I felt like holding my body
in my fist and flinging it away.
When they said in my childhood
that I had no 'bindi' and
on growing up when they said
I had no caste,

I felt like clamping my nose tightly
at the stinking village.
When I who was useable for sex
was not useable for living with.
I felt like hiding myself
in some gutter.
Fighting hard against all these insults
When I learnt the alphabet
and got a job,
On my way to office,
unable to hear the whispers "reservation category".
I felt like plugging my ears with lead.
When patience dies
even a blade of grass
can poke like a needle.
I have no patience to run anymore
I would wash my life in the
flames of these hardships
and bloom like a mankena puvvu
I will run past all the
Adverse jungles like a stream.

Note: Mankena Puvvu: a red colour flower found in the fields and forests. Here it is used as a symbol of revolution.

(Tr. By. Dr. P. Hari Padma Rani)

In the poem **Banned from History** Swarupa Rani delineats the predicament of a female in this country beginning at the status of foetus and how a girl child is unwanted and prohibited.

Banned from History

Even as a foetus
I was branded untouchable.
I was born with the stamp of a mean caste
On the very day of my birth.
I was identified as impure
Flung into the gutter of superstitions
and meaningless customs, I have been

deprived of life.
My childhood which should be filled with
joyful singing and love
sings melancholy tunes
even without sprouting.
My youth, which should be
drenched in the care and concern
of parents, is introduced as
a "doll in the market"
even as the Goddess in the temple
stands as an eyewitness.
In the shameless modern era
Where we are taken naked
on a procession,
where we were force-fed shit
with our youth lynched
mine is a typical tale of woe.
I have been enduring the disgust
Of generations and the indifference of ages
As my (rightful) heritage
I enjoy the distinction of
being a "slut" even before I could open
my eyes on the earth.
I do not know in which
chapter of this great country's history
my story, at which
the cyber revolutions
should bend their heads in shame
into the stone age, will find place.

(Tr.By. Dr. P. Hari Padma Rani)

Swarupa Rani shows feminist attitude in her writings and very critical out look she developed towards issues related to women. She is a keen observer of the contemporary women's problems. The poem given here under proves her commitment for the cause of Dalit women.

Flowers and Thorns

Phoolan

My obtund grass flower elegance!
As you walk uprightly
On the uneven lands
like a fathom high weapon,
slaughtering the Keechaka darkness'
encompassed round your life
The Chambal valley saluted
Your valour.

Wearing the bullet girdle round your waist
As you did marching
On the fattened Brahmayees[1]
My cracked mud lips
Crushed in the master's hay stalk
Greedily kissed your red boots.

My scooted sky reddened
As you blazed like a lethal weapon
At the Manu's endeared parts
That cannot see us as a
Fusion of mind and flesh
Except as a 'particular part'
The rachabanda[2] sahibs
that fix the price for our virtue and lives shuddered
as they read in the newspapers
that you are distributing Moses' law
in the Northern villages
tightening the law in your fist.

Phoolan Singh?
My flag of valour!
Your death
Stirs my healed wounds
Your body fallen lifelessly to the ground
Saying hello to my heart.
No need for us to remain
Casually
Like parts

In the system where we are not seen as human beings
Except as thieves...witches
Or else Mathangies.
Just as the blind rose wore the crown of thorns
For self protection
Whether the phoolans here
Or Maddikera Marthammas
Must become walking arsenals!

Note:Rachabanda: A stone bench, where the elders hold council in a village

(Tr.By. Dr.Sheela Swarupa Rani)

At present she is working on a critical evaluation of **Dalit Movement in Post Independence Period** and certainly she can bring out a meaningful work as an insider.

BHUTAM MUTYALU (1971 -)

A teacher by profession Bhutam Mutyalu was born on first of June in Tirumalagiri of Nampalli Mandal, Nalagonda district. **Gumpu**, the Literary, Association of Nallagonda published his first book of poems entitled **Dugili** in 2003. Two prominent Dalit academicians and poets from P.S. Telugu University, namely Dr.Yendluri Sudhakar and Dr.K. Sanjeeva Rao (Sikhamani) wrote forewords to this book. This is a collection of twenty-nine poems reflecting the Dalit life and written in Telangana dialect. He is in the process of publishing a novel **Sura** with the Dalit theme.

A Call

Dalit! Oh, dalit!
Sounding Dalit, Oh, Blazing Dalit
You read and appreciated our poets'
Heaps of writings without missing a syllable
And you boasted that when our artists
tied anklets and danced, it was a matchless folk dance
And all feet moved in rhythm with it
When they opened their voices in folklore
All voices joined them in a single chorus

Later you ran hither and tither
Till your legs ached
Conducted meetings and shouted
Till you broke your wind pipe
That our intellectuals should change
But when will you realise
that the country owes you
the labour of your body?
When do you get infuriated?
at the grief of your caste?
Which is flowing across the country like a steam?
When will you caste off the mould of caste?
How soon have you forgotten the one
Who tied a cloth round the mouth
removed the upper garment
And wound it round the waist
With a broom hanging down from behind?
Do you need his poisnous food
Why not spit into his bowl
Open your eyes; open up your voice
Sharpen the knife on whetstone
Make a hole to the pot of caste system
Unknot the tangles of caste concept
Shake off the caste pride
Till its last fold is straightened.

(Tr. By. P. Naga Jasmine)

NELAVURI VENKATA RATNAJI (1972 -)

Nelavuri Venkata Ratnaji was born on 10th April 1972 in Dharmavaram of Kovvuru, West Godavari district. He got inspiration from Karamchedu and Chunduru incidents. Initially he read very few Dalit poets like Yendluri Sudhakar, Madduri Nagesh Babu, Pydi Teresh Babu etc., as he doesn't want any Poet's influence on his writing. But he stated that his opinion is wrong and now he is reading almost all Dalit Writings. He has written so far three hundred Poems on Dr. Ambedkar and he intends to write a thousand poems on Ambedkar. He also wrote a few *Haikus* on the theme of Draught. He wishes to write Dalit concepts in Gazals. A long Poem entitled **NO ABCD – Only One Voice**; (March 2005) is a writing against the division of ABCD in Scheduled Castes.

Ascetic Godavari

Oh mother Godavari,
Over brimming with worshippers
Imbued with the overwhelming joy of pushkara festivity.
Oh ever following sacred Godavari!
Just remember one thing,
Some Hindu *Bhajagovindas*
in a frenzy of religious fanaticism
Burnt Godra and took a dip
in your whistling lap
Did not you get the burnt smell
For the doomed Chunduru?
the days of pushkara were over
but the miscreants who escaped law
wore our lives in their chappal
And washed their feet in your holy water
Didn't you shudder?
Tell the no that the ominous uncleanliness
attached to our caste
that touched ihem when they stayed our bodies
Can't be washed off
It seems you are adored as
The feeding Mother (Annapurna) of these areas
Not one or two
When the whole lot of epic poets exalted you,
I felt like laughing when beggars uncountable
Spread their rags in your banks
and beg for alms
Do you think their cries of hunger
Are the mild rumbling of your waves
A gem, a jewel!
The Beauty of coastal line!
Volumes of poetry is written on you

Describing your beauty at dawn and dusk
The eye -feasting sight of rowing boats on you
Impressed by such eulogy
You sauntered by in between the Papihills
But have you ever touched a tillers stomach?
While he is drenched in sweat
The drops titillate these fellows
Dripping from the bodies after a ceremonious dip
In order to enable them offer lumps of food
To the manes (to their dead ancestors).
Our mothers and sisters have become lumps of mud
Whom you never owned
The holiness attached to you
is not yours, it's the voice of our toil
Well, the word 'Voice' reminds me
That you, re equal to Saraswathi
But how can that your rays of Literacy didn't fall on us?
Instead of inscribing your esteemed Sanskrit on our tongues
You scribble ignoble fate on our forehead
Is it because you thought;
Anyway we wouldn't be able to buy your donation studies;
Where have you placed me
on the tuned strings of your harp of learning
It's learnt that you're sanctified and deified
recently when I saw you at Goshpada
You are giving holy dips to devotees
With the saffron flags fluttering all around
when announcements were made for the lost ones
It sounded funny and I felt like laughing
Don't you know that its you
Who have lost the way?
Secularism has floated away
Like a raft on your sacred waters
Oh Sabari, who is doting
in the service of Bhadradri

Haven't you heard about the blood shed at Ayodya?
They say here Nanniah wrote verses
Srinadha poured out Poetry
With fantastic stories upholding your Treatness
Building castles in air
They knit our lives into riddle
Which have no answers
Year after year we take holy dips
Yet our history is streams of blood
Your Pushkaras are nothing new to us.
Crying over the crores of 'lingas' you lost
You content with just Veeresalingam
And keep up your Aryan culture
When the body of Karamchendu was burnt alive
Chunduru heads were beheaded
And faces at Vempadu were charred
Who is left out for us to be content with?
Oh (lord) Pushkara celebrations
Just hand me over those miscreants
Then to the dead heroes of Karamchendu
And the immortals of Chunduru
I'll offer Tarpanam.

1. Pushkara: A festival held once in every 12 years.
2. Pindum/ Lump of food : The oblations that are made to deceased ancestors.
3. Tarpanam: a religious rite; offering of water to mane of the deceased.

(Tr. By. P. Naga Jasmine)

JALLI INDIRA (1972 –)

Jalli Indira was born on 01-08-1972 in the village Chittivanigaruvu of West Godavari district. Her parents are Jalli Venkataramanaiah and Koyye Suseela. She has done her M.A., M.Phil and Ph.D. in the University of Hyderabad. She is writing from her school days. She is interested in dance, literature and painting. There is a flair for painting in her family for three generations. Indira realized that the upper caste dominating society would not allow a Dalit to take up fine arts as a profession and be successful. She read famous writers like Tagore, Gudipati Venkata Chalam, Kodavatiganti Kutumba Rao, and also Russian literature and stories from **The Bible**. She chose Dalit women and the atrocities on them as themes for her research. She completed her M.Phil and the Ph.D thesis is in progress.

Indira observed that Dalit women are looked down upon as characterless due to their dark complexion, hard physical labour and without a *bindi* (an indication of a non-Hindu) etc. In the year 1995, a forward caste boy deceived Sunitha a Dalit girl of the Central University. He promised his love and marriage with her but later deceived her. Sunitha committed suicide as she could not digest this. The students agitated over this issue in the university. Deeply depressed by this incident Indira wrote a poem **Postmortem**. She also wrote an essay entitled **Dalit Feminist Manifesto**. At present Indira is working as an Assistant Professor in the Department of Women's Studies, Sri Padmavati Mahila Viswavidyalayam,Tirupati.

YEDLA PETER PAUL (1972 -)

Yedla Peter Paul was born on 24th December in Narasaraopet of Guntur district. His parents are Sangeetha Rao and Mariamma. He is a Post Graduate and working in the Agricultural department of the State government. He published a collection of poems with the title **Kotha Dari (The New Path)** in 2002. The volume consists of 25 poems and chose Dalit theme for many of these poems. A powerful Dalit poet Madduri Nagesh Babu wrote the foreword to this book. In his foreword Nagesh Babu remarked:

"Perhaps Yedla Peter Paul created a dictionary only for him. With so skillfully he is moulding the pots of poetry, perhaps.

It is pathetic
Could not get the answer

Even after listening to so many lessons.
The feet do not move
To do many adventure trips
Routine ... Routine
While reading such poetry written by Paul, suddenly I thought of Bertolt Brecht.
In the dark times, will there also be singing
Yes, there will be singing
About the dark times.

Expressing the innermost strangle is an agony. If an agony take literary shape there is a choice to disappear it's original shape. In Paul's poetry there is no such situation" (viii).

The poet chooses his own structure, style and treatment for the poems.

DARLA VENKATESWARA RAO (1973 -)

Darla Venkateswara Rao was born on an important date, which is celebrated as the Teachers' day and incidentally he is in the teaching profession. He joined in the Department of Telugu, University of Hyderabad on November 2nd 2004. He was born in Cheyyeru Agraharam of East Godavari district and his parents are Lankayya and Pedanagamma. He did his M.A. M.Phil and Ph.D in Telugu literature from University of Hyderabad in 1997, 1998 and 2003 respectively. At the time of research he received Junior Research Fellowship from UGC, New Delhi by qualifying in the test. He received **Jayanthi Ramayya Pantulu Memorial Prize** and **Veeresalingam Rajalakshmi Memorial Prize** in 1995.

Darla Venkateswara Rao worked as a Part-time News reporter for **Andhra Bhoomi** from 1992-94. As a sub-editor he is involved in the publication of **Sahitimoorthula Prasasthi** published by Dr. S. Sarat Jyothsna Rani in 1997 and **Madiga Chaitanyam**, the first published book of poetry by Madigas in Telugu. Telugu Sahitya Vedika, Vikarabad of Ranga Reddy district published his first collection of poetry under the title **Dalita Tatwikudu** in the year 2004. A poem from this collection is given here.

Dalit Philosopher

When everything seems normal
I can't feel guilty any more
before those who stare at me every time I wear new cloths
Even if they suspect my colour, physique and language
I can't any more lend meaning to "Inferiority"
Like stock themes
the imaginary picturisation of my mother as a servant
and my father as a gardener,
It is better if I treat these picturizations
as mere figments of imagination.
Even if the God himself descends
My first preference is my parents! Now
I am a philosopher of Dalit beauty.
In the struggle for supremacy every time
When language along with ideology loses life
I feel like teaching socio linguistics by making it
a compulsory classical subject
Oh, Great Patriot!
Fearing that my grandsons might
become victims in Freedom Struggle again and again
I am protesting against the mortgaging of the country,
Prepared to sacrifice even my life for the cause.
In your distorted history
I don't hanker for my name and
I won't scramble for pension
I will safeguard my country
even if it means baring my life to batons and bullets
Instead of being listed as a Freedom fighter,
I would be black listed as a terrorist or a criminal!
Your history is all distorted.
In the Anti Arrack Movement of yesterday
which took place right before my eyes,
where is my mother's name?
What is this that

women who don't stir out of their houses to vote
even when their husbands contest, are felicitated
as leaders of the movement?
When so many died in
Kargil's "Operation Vijay"
Why is that the flag of fame
that fluttered for Prof. Padmapani
did not flutter for others?
Brother, all your history is distressing.
"Oh Siva, the culture is
falling to decadence
The universal love
and Valentine's Day is defiling
our orthodox culture.
Stretch out the tongue of Kolkatta Kali,
Take her out on a procession
in the streets of Mumbai,
Lynch people and rape sisters
in Orissa and Gujarat
Mow down people at Charminar crossroads,
No matter what you do
We have to inject anti-virus
In to every vein"
Even though you always hate and harass me
I know only how to love you
At least now, you taste the food
morsels a mother feeds
You dab the milky cheeks of an infant
You go to the shade of a tree on a hot afternoon
You will also know how to love!!
That immortality lies only in loving!!

(Tr. By. Dr. P. Hari Padma Rani)

In his poem **The Collapsing Library** Darla presented a critical and historical conspiracy in the denial of education for Dalits.

The Collapsing Library

How nice it would be if I have had magic or tantra or machine

Then, all the books in the library, fast I would have learnt by heart

The internet like a beautiful Mohini
and the globalization like heaven in the palm
would have been on the other side of Amrutham!

As a baby kicking happy in the mother's warm womb,
As a youth unmelting, stand still for ever,
I feel like staying in the library never leaving.

From a bookrack the Vedas are loudly inviting
the ears that are cleared from lead, to the feast.
Greedily I choose alphabet
if a alphabet is kept on one side.
and food on the other side
Even if the multi folded stomachs of my great grand fathers are stretched
you may find gruel in it, but never a alphabet.
There are danger-signals on the rector scale
There are cracks on the library walls with the vibrations of internet.
At once, I should do something.
Even if I search till another Millennium
I may never find a alphabet again.
My desire to die in the iibrary
and to reborn as a book in it,
perhaps has to die with my birth itself.
(Tr. By. Dr. T. Bharathi)

VEMULA YELLAIAH (1973 -)

Vemula Yellaiah was born in Lingalaganapuram of Warangal. His parents are Butchaiah and Chandramma. He is a Post Graduate in Telugu Literature. He is working as a co-editor to **Mulki**, a Quarterly for minority writing. He is a poet and a novelist. He became popular with the publication of his single novel **Kakka**. This novel is prescribed for students of Post Graduation in Andhra University.

VARRE RANI (1973 – 2001)

Varre Rani was born on 23rd September 1973 in Machilipatnam of Krishna district. Her parents are Venkataramaiah and Sitamma. But she is brought up and educated by Subba Rao and Alivelu Mangatayaru. She is a postgraduate in Sanskrit and she did M.Phil. She taught Sanskrit and Telugu literature in a private college, Vijayawada.

From her childhood she experienced the pangs of loneliness. She observed the society very carefully and sensitively. Her first short poem **Stri (A Woman)** is published in **Andhra Bhoomi** (1996) and received good response from readers. Her other poems are **Vastavamloki (Into the Reality)** and **Jolaali.** She received **Nandini Award** for the poem **Jolaali**. She also wrote short stories. She selected incidents from her experience as plots for her stories. Her poem **Sharpness** is a good example for feminist poetry.

What's it to the village, it will be all right
It's only I
Suppressing hiccups, at a distance
What's it to the landlord, he will be scolding
It's only I in the fields
Becoming tears in the memory of the child in the hut
In my palm that has dug wells and ponds
My tears fall
Instead of water
Instead of tar's smoothness touching my feet
That paved the road
Pierce the thorns of excommunication
Have grown crops
But starvation filled my vessel
instead of rice
I was of use everywhere
But at the temple threshold
I stopped like the slippers
What's it to the country it will be all right on the surface

It's only I who is not part of anything
Wiping tears, at a distance
What is it about development, we have achieved a lot
It's only I
Lying in this corner
Grinding my heart
No use sitting likes this any longer
I will sharpen my sickle! (Tr.By. K.Suneetha Rani)

PACHANURU ANURADHA (1973 -)

Anuradha's forefathers are immigrants in Hyderabad. She is the first child to her parents Durgaiah and Lakshminarasamma. Though she was born and brought up in the state capital she could not get free exposure to education and economic development due to the caste restrictions. She is graduated from Dr. Ambedkar Open University. Her first poem **Aadapilla (A Girl)** is published in **Vanitha** in the year 1995. She is prominently a Dalit feminist writer.

MARY MADIGA (1975 -)

After the establishement of Madiga Dandora Movement, one group in Dalits i.e. Madigas began to suffix the caste identity to their names. In that process Mary also started using her name as Mary Madiga. She was born in the village Raghunandapuram of Nalagonda district. Her parents are Yadagiri and Narasavva. Her family is the first Christian converts in the village. She is a singer. She worked in a voluntary organization called **Young India**. While working in this organization, she wrote a street play in response to the Tsunduru/ Chunduru incident. She has become a woman leader in the Madiga Dandora Movement. She is taking active participation in the Movement along with Krishna Madiga and Kripakara Madiga, the founders of the Dandora Movement. She is elected as a state leader in the first Madiga Women's Meeting held at Yadagirigutta in 1995. She wrote many songs for Madigas and those songs inspired the activists effectively.

VALLABODA NAGAMANI (1975 -)

Nagamani was born in Saheb Nagar of Rangareddy district. Her parents are Jangaiah and Lakshmamma. She did her M.L.I.SC from Osmania University. She is writing since 1995. She is one of the first generation women writers of Telangana writing about the suffering of Madigas. She wrote a limited number of short stories and she got prizes for each one of her story. Her stories are **Manuvugadi Pendli, Aadapilla, Udyogam, Eduruchupu, Aasa** and **Nestam**. She studied Sri Sri's **Mahaprastanam** and Unnava Lakshmi Narayana's **Malapalli.**

MADDELA SWATI MARGARATE (1976 -)

Swati Margarate, a Dalit Christian belongs to Khammam district and her father Dharmaiah worked as MDO and retired as an Accounts officer. Her mother Konakanchi Mary Jnana Bai is retired as Headmistress of a Government school. Swati Margaret says that being a Christian she could not avail the reservation facility and at the same time could not escape the caste discrimination due to her caste. She did her M.A. and M.Phil in the University of Hyderabad. Her doctoral thesis is on **The Presentation of Dalit Women in Telugu Films**. She is writing in free verse from her childhood i.e. from 6th class onwards. Her parents encouraged her in education and creative writing. She is one of the prominent Women Writers that are leading the Dalit Feminism.

** ** ** ** **

It was very difficult to get the biographical details of the following writers either to place them chronologically or to give more details in spite of our sincere efforts. Some of them failed to respond to our repeated requests. It is not fair to leave them out because of their considerable contribution to literature. Hence we placed them here in alphabetical order.

BANNA ILAIAH

Dr. Banna Ilaiah is teaching in the Telugu department of Kakatiya University. His book **Telugu Kavitam – Abhinava Dhrukpadam (Telugu Poetry – The Modern View)** is published in 2001 and it is a research work. His long poem **Nippukanika (Fire-Spark)** is a bilingual long poem translated by K. Damodara Rao, teaching faculty of Kakatiya University, Warangal. The theme of the poem is the suffering of Dalits in the society.

When our lives were shrouded by black clouds
lights sparkled in others' lives
Can you ever look into the depths of life ?
Did you think we were only heaps of bones,
walking zombies ?
Remember the heinous act of chasing corpses,
and killing them again in the open fields?

Whose bed of rights is this soil,
Whose watchdog is this history!

As we were trampled when we were mere buds
you were born and blossomed into flowers.
We were the ones who had no business
with seasons.
We were concerned only with labour
as you ordained.
We were not wanted for anything
except manual work.
When seasons changed, our bodies
duly complied with.

Nature was born of us.
We conquered the forests,
crossed the rivers,
dictated the course of Waters,
and whirled the wind along with us.
Without much ado

you converted our labour
to your advantage: Body is but Panchabhutas
you said, said it repeatedly,
chanted it, and controlled our destiny.
You made an incantation
of our labour. (**Fire-Spark**, 8)

G.R. KURME

G.R.Kurme published a collection of poems **Punadi Rayi (A Foundation Stone)** published in 1994. In his poetry he warned that if the foundation stones were dislocated the entire construction of the society would be destructed. In this collection he presented the life of a Dalit as **Katikapari**, a tax collector in a village and as a person who carries the dead bodies.

Amidst My Own

For me
Living means smearing
all my people like mascara to the eye.
The people that are excommunicated as castes
separated as fields, lands and backyards
Second to none both in profile and profession
that purges their blood with sweat perfume
That drink mixing the water and tears
that loll like black moonlight shadows in the white darkness
Look here! On the screen of my eyeball.
they are passing by now.
If I have to prove that I am alive amidst my own
Isn't it that it must become clear that
My blood drops and my people's sweat drops are of the same blood group!
Aren't my people
That fallen as thunderbolts with my dumb thunder must agree with me.
Aren't they recognized me
When only I became the tongue in their mouth.

Isn't my identification known
When only I lifted my darling dame to their shoulders
And made them carry it.
Aren't my people walked down on me
When only I laid the foundation stone.
Aren't they sensed my responsibilities
When only I bore the tablet. (Tr. By. Dr.Sheela Swarupa Rani)

In another poem titled **I Was Murdered** Kurme very critically analyses traces the well planned exploitation of Dalits.

I was Murdered
When I burnt down the jungle with hey-stack
When the hilly lands were irrigated by erecting bunds against the
Indus River
When huge godowns of the barely-corn were established at
Mohenjodaro
I manifested myself as a son of this soil
When my boat swimmed to the Baharain shore
When I uncovered the parcel of pearls in Mesopotamia
When the world-trade erected me as a sovereign
I wrote my history as the Indus Civilization

When the production flew through my hands
When the copper and the tin became my ribs
When the invasion of the superstition took place on me
I was severely wounded by the blows of the canes of plunder
When Harappa and Hastina were my two feet
When the serpents became the watch-dogs of my infanthood

When encircling the sacrificial fire alone was the oblation

I was murdered in the Indian Ocean*.

(Tr. By K. Purushotham)

*The equivalent of Indian Ocean in Telugu is Hindu Maha Samudram.

The word Hindu is worth noting in the context

(**Kakatiya Journal of English Studies**, Vol 21, 2001)

G. KALYANA RAO

A revolutionary writer, G. Kalyana Rao was born in Aalakurapadu in Prakasam district. His father is a teacher and his mother died when he was still an infant i.e., eleven months old. His grand parents bring him in the early childhood. His grand mother is a storyteller and used to create the stories. Kalyana Rao gives credit to her for his talent as a writer. Perhaps he received the narrative technique from her. He suffered the poison of untouchability during his school days in Munganuru near Kavali. To save his son from this bitter experience, his father took him to Aalakurapadu and admitted him in the school where he is working. He is much influenced by cultural activities in Aalakurapadu. One of his teachers read the Russian novel **The Mother** to the audience in nights. His high-school studies are in Tanbuturu. During that period he took part in plays. He did his Intermediate and degree in Jawahar Bharati College, Kavali. He says that his education in that college is a sweet memory and it is a great inspiration. Every year the students in that college used to enact plays and once Kalyana Rao wrote a play entitled **A Night in Those Days**, there are only three characters in the play. By looking at the title every one looks it as a love theme. As the rehearsals are done very secretly no body could guess the theme of the play. The theme of the play is an incidence during the Telangana

Movement. Like any other youth during those days Kalyana Rao is also influenced by Naxulberry Movement. Under the influence of Srikakulam Movement (Andhra Pradesh) he wrote two plays – **The Early Dawn** and **Let A Hundred Flowers Bloossom. The Early Dawn** has given a hundred shows. Later he became a member in **VIRASAM** (The Revolutionary Writers Association). Though he got selected in APPSC Group-I, due to petty politics he could not get the appointment.

In the year 2005, the Andhra Pradesh State Government headed by Congress Party decided to invite the Maoists for discussions in Hyderabad under the Chairmanship of the Home Ministry of Andhra Pradesh. Kalyana Rao participated in this discussion on behalf of the Maoists.

G. MOHANA RAO

Known with his pen name Spartacus, Mohan Rao became popular with his novel **Khakibatukulu (The Lives of the Police)** written between 1980 and 1983 and published in 1996. Being a Dalit by birth and a Constable by profession it is easy for him to depict the lives of Dalits in the police system. He has to face many problems from his department for writing this novel as it revealed the unbearable realities of the behaviour of non-Dalits towards Dalits. To write about the painful life of the police constable in the novel, he used the ideology of Ambedkar and Karl Marx. The chief character in the novel is Prakasam and he is a police constable during 1940s that is in the British Government. And Spartcus states that he has modeled the chief character, Prakasam on his father. The novelist tried to convince that there is a need for the higher officials to be sympathetic and never to ill-treat Dalits in their profession and the Dalits also should change their life style.

G. SUBBA RAO

Retired as a Sub-postmaster from the Postal

department Subba Rao is now residing in Kothapet of East Godavari district. He is a successful Telugu poet first and a Dalit poet in the second place. He is also a critic of Dalit literature. In the year 2000, Subba Rao brought out a collection of Dalit Poetry with the title **Netturinkaa Errabadutundi**. This book includes forty-one poems. In his preface Subba Rao states that there is no need to discuss whether Dalit writers alone can effectively and powerfully portray the Dalit suffering and feeling than non-Dalits. And at the same time one has to rethink once again, about the non-Dalits writing Dalit literature and participating in Dalit movements. All his poems are collected and brought out as a book in May 2002 with the title **Biyyapu Ginja**. There are forty-one poems in this collection. Some of his poems are published in journals like **Dalit Commando** and **Mool Nivasi Times**.

How long this Candle to be burnt?

The seed that's covered beneath my feet,
Sprout with my sweat, when cared and protected
The fields fill with yield,
You take the yield to your heart
It's my baby too;
Alas, you own the child but didn't even touch the father with hand.
When bring the water from deep below the earth to surface,
You fill your hands with water,
But, you alienate me – Bhagiratha and keep distance.
When the fertile lands were domesticated to give great yields,
You fill your coffers with the booty,
Worship the land that touched your feet,
Earth is my mother too,
You didn't like my presence; what is my sin?
When you had driven us to the outskirts of the village,
We have made "Poleramma" as our goddess,
When you denied entry for us into the temples,

We took up cross as a repentance and built churches for ourselves.
Our ancestors weren't aware, who thought "sinners would die with their sins"
That your sins would become hanging noose for us,
When faced with hunger or dishonour,
Our parents hanged themselves and killed themselves,
We learnt to face and challenge the injustice,
"The wood with fire will burnt the same wood" was our forefather's adage,
One spark is enough to engulf the entire forest.
My grand father and father killed the workers of your neighbouring fields in your water fights;
you groomed your moustache with pride;
Why are you jealous when my son sports a moustache?
Only valiant heroes sport moustache.
When we stitched our skins as footwear and made you wear, you suppressed us beneath your feet
When we wear footwear why do you feel threatened?
When our forefathers laid their lives, you said we have no freedom,
You say the country, which we have protected as soldiers, is not ours,
What's the sacrifice you have made?
What's the treachery we have committed?
I drench my self with sweat every day and get clean,
How can you be cleaner than I am?
I am the one who worship mother earth every day with my labour,
How are you more sacred than me?
What's it that divide us?
Is it your self-esteem, or ego?
People say difficulties are like water pots,
Why there should be misery for some, luxuries for others?
Who's the one that made these false laws?
Who's that "Kapata Mohini" who distributed venom to us and gave elixir to you?

Is it right that to respect few people, so many have to be disrespected?

Who made this treason?

We got hurt when we were plucking the grass for your cattle or ploughing your fields.

Hurts are not new to us.

Feeling hurt is also not new to us.

We wouldn't tolerate if you burn our huts; if you rob our efforts and labour.

I have learnt the strength of valour of brave heart.

Cutting heart into pieces would not be tolerated.

Now,

I don't want to remain as a watchdog to your house.

I don't want to burn as a candle for you.

I want to open my claws like tiger.

I want to burst like dynamite. (Tr. By Ch. Prabhakar)

In the poem **Passover Festival** Subba Rao critically and ironically focuses on deceiving nature in Dalits. He quotes from mythologies how people are self-centred and deceive others for their petty benefits. They are willing to sacrifice the welfare of the group for their individual profit.The poem is given hereunder.

Saying he is our brother-in-law
We take pride in Vasista
who got the statute made
to cut off Sambuka's head that did penance
Kunthi, who borne illegitimate children
and brought the orphan Karna into the world
we worship as Gonthemma.
Pilot, who on behalf of the high priests
got Christ crucified, we leave,
And blame the Judas that kissed the hand
But –
We celebrate pass over with positions
If bribed
countless are the Judas that can handover the saviours!
If threatened a little
all are Peters

Why, only three times?
Before it dawns,
Thirty three times
Deny the one
Who gave them shelter. (Tr.By G. Sheela Swarupa Rani)

GADDAR

Basically a singer with dance steps and specific attire, Gaddar is a popular people's singer. He started identifying himself as a Dalit activist, perhaps after Karamchedu incident. His songs sung between 1997 and 1998 are brought out as a volume in October 1999 with the title **Songs of Gaddar**. There are twenty-one songs in this collection and the popular journalist Potturi Venkateswara Rao and a well-known writer Allam Rajaiah wrote forewords to this anthology. After 1997 he is not very active on the dais as he received bullets in his body and severely hurt and almost experienced death.

GEDDADA NARASIMHA MURTHY

Geddada Narasimha Murthy is the Principal of Sakyamuni Public School, Kotrenikona, East Godavari district and convener of Joshua Sahitya Kala Pitam. He also worked as a Journalist. Narasimha Murthy started his writing career when he was studying IX standard. He did his post graduation in Telugu Literature. He informs that he started writing more actively after reading Dr. Ambedkar's works – **Who are the Sudras?, Value of a Rupee, What Gandhi and Congress Have Done to the Untouchables?** and **The Annihilation of Caste** etc.

Narasimha Murthy is a poet and his poems are published in Telugu News papers and journals. He is also an essayist. In his poem **Democracy** he laments over the common man's suffering even in the democratic form of Government. He starts the poem "After having so many Amendments to the Constitutions/ what is there to be proud of! / The poor man's life is like/ falling into the fire from pan".

KOYI KOTESWARA RAO

Koyi Koteswara Rao a writer from Telangana is working as a lecturer in Government Boys Junior college, Armur, Nizamabad district. In his poem, **Oh! Dalit Warrior** he speaks about the life of Dalits.

After ploughing and planting in the field
Kept the golden crops in heaps.
Alas! The food grain laughed at the wages
Oh! Dalit-warrior! The fountain-life of the earth!
After Knowing the caste and jati of a man
Then alone people talk with him.
Even the dogs roar at the low caste
Oh! Dalit-warrior! The fountain-life of the earth!
A *panchama* is accused as a merit less
The worthless crows cry the same
The uncountable worth in physical labour
Oh! Dalit-warrior! The fountain-life of the earth!
Abused as coolies, their huts destroyed,
Split the hearts saying they are low caste.
In the name of religion, burn a human being
Oh! Dalit-warrior! The fountain-life of the earth!
They worship a cow and call her mother,
They chase him as he is a mala.
In mikes speak loudly about humanity
Oh! Dalit-warrior! The fountain-life of the earth!
You Madiga-fellow! Said the disgusted minister
Bow down with folded hands at election time
Politics is but changing colours
Oh! Dalit-warrior! The fountain-life of the earth!
The conspiracy in asking the thumb
Is so proud while hissing poison
They ask now the death of the colony as *gurudakshina*
Oh! Dalit-warrior! The fountain-life of the earth!
Poured the hot lead in the ears
Tied the spittoon to the mouth
Beaten and chased as per the witness of the palm leaf
Oh! Dalit-warrior! The fountain-life of the earth!
The sun rised in a poor hut

By fighting against the dark night
That created darkness in the lives of poor
Oh! Dalit-warrior! The fountain-life of the earth!
Gurudakshina: Offering or reward to a teacher on completion of a Pupil's Education

(Tr.By T.Bharathi)

M.A.K. BHEEMA RAO

M.A.K. Bheema Rao of Duddivari Agraharam of Amalapuram, East Godavari District is a graduate with the Bachelor of Education. He is the Divisional President of Scheduled Castes Welfare Association and Convener of Konaseema Mala Mahanadu. He is a poet and a playwright. His play **Chaduvuleni Bratuku (A Life without Education)** is telecasted in All India Radio, Visakhapatnam. He regularly participates in Poets' Meet. He is taking active part in Dalit Movements. His poems are published in Poetry Collections, **Dalit Commando** and other magazines. His poem **Untouchable's Valour** is cited here.

When you call me dear brother;
When got my rib bone broken by some body,
My blood vessels were cut and suppressed down below,
My brothers were butchered mercilessly
When the call dear brother itself become a cry in wilderness,
I will revolt and be a Dalit rougue.
When you are engrossed with the sweet talk about your dear sister's childish pranks
And when my sister was raped and honour was crucified to the tamarind tree,
And when tears roll in my moist eyes with her memories,
I will be a revolting Dalit caste rougue.
When the child's love reflect in looks at his mother's breast for milk or love,
When she was paraded 'naked' with dot marks on her breasts as a symbol of your lust,

I will pick up weapons and be a revolting Dalit rougue.
But, brother,
I have no hatred towards you or your caste,
I hate the cunning scoundrels and caste fed fascist fanatics of your caste. (Tr.By.Ch.Prabhakar)

MADDURI VIJAYASREE

Madduri Vijayasree has become popular with her poem **Alisamma**, a bold witness of the atrocities on Dalits in Karamchedu. In this poem she warned the pride dominant-Caste men that if they do not change their attitude, they have to face the cruelty of Dalits. She uses powerful words to show her anger and agony for the exploitation of the dominant castes on Dalits.

Alisama's Curse
For you
It may be surprising
Ridiculous
Irritating
But
I am a new question
I cannot sit in "women's only" seat
though it is empty
Before and after my name
There will not be any respectable address either in calling or in shouting
I am the sorrow that wept rolling in the village
because of victims people's arrogance
I am the one that lighted wicks in the courts of eyes
I am Alisamma
Day before yesterday according to Sri Rama's order
I got my nose and ears severed
Yesterday in Punjab police hands got portrayed as reasonless sorrow
Even today
Between *punnama narakam* and turmeric vermilion*
I become centuries of doubt and crisis

Yes, I am Alisamma speaking
Although it is very painful to you
By your arrogance! By your haughtiness
You beasts
Because of the crime of giving birth to you
Do not make your mothers be abused by people, I say
At least from now on
Take off your tails and fangs
Transform yourselves into human beings, I curse you.

* between male children, who are supposed to rescue from *punnama narakam* the hell after death, and husband, who represents turmeric and vermilion the married woman is entitled to.

(Tr. By K.Suneetha Rani)

NAGAPPAGARI SUNDAR RAJU

Nagappagari Sundar Raju was an active member in Dandora Movement and a powerful poet. While doing his PhD in the University of Hyderabad, he edited a book entitled **Madiga Chaitanyam** published by Madiga Sahitya Vedika – Andhra Pradesh, University of Hyderabad in 1997. There are 25 poems and it is a collection of poems by Madiga poets. Prof. Kolakaluri Enoch, a popular Dalit writer, wrote foreword. The Madiga Sahitya Vedika is believed to be the brainchild of Sundar Raju. In his preface to **Madiga Chaitanyam** he explained the injustice done to Madigas in detail. He is also a short story writer. He died at an early age, while working in S.K. University as a lecturer in Telugu. In the story **Joresavu Katha (The Story of Joresav)**, Sundar Raju Portray the economic reasons for the suicide of Joresav and also tells the inner feelings of untouchable children when that are treated badly by the teachers, fellow students and their parents.

PYDI TERESH BABU

Known as Pydisri, Teresh Babu is one of the important and bold writers among the contemporary Dalit writers. His writing always aims at the emancipation of Dalits. In some of his poems he boldly questioned and warned the non-Dalits for their aggressive behaviour towards Dalits.

Fresh Signature

To construct new mansions without dismantling
This country is not a desert
If asked about my qualifications to rule
I will demonstrate in a picture frame the way I grow crops
If asked how I will revive this corpse
I will show from close quarters how I mend shoes
If asked what material I use to build a new society
I will place the kneaded civilization on my potter's wheel
If asked how I would cure the country's wounds
I will narrate my taking out the thorns
From goats' feet without a pin
If you refuse to step down from the chair
I will illustrate
The process of wood turning into a chair with chisel, adze and saw
As evidence of your sovereignty
If you show your long hair, beard and moustaches
I will take out the knife and whetstone from a barber's pouch
If anyone asks what is my authority on this land
I will awaken millions and millions of sleeping signatures
Buried under layers of soil shouldering this country
To write new sentences without striking out
This country's history is not that pure.

(Tr.By.K.Suneetha Rani,**Indian Literature**, Nov-Dec 2000)

Teresh Babu's short story **The Supplementary Question** published in October 1996 deals with the politico-religious reasons for the division in Scheduled Castes. He accused the political leaders for planning the division among the Dalits that diverted the united fight of Dalits against the dominant castes. Instead of fighting against the dominant castes the two major groups (Mala & Madiga) are fighting with each other. The two groups, who lived harmoniously as brothers so far, now started suspecting one another as enemies. The writer reveals the conspiracy of the dominant castes in the division of Dalits through this brief story. In another story **Savarna Deergha Sandhi**, deals with the theme of intercaste marriage. Sombabu, a dominant caste fellow fell in love with his collegue Syamala, a scheduled caste young woman. As usual when she asks him to marry her after a few months he is upset and begins to think the consequences of their marriage. He discusses the issue with many of his collegues. Syamala demand him to marry her. He is upset with her warning and finally married her. At the conclusion of the story Teresh Babu gives a beautiful twist. When Sombabu asks what would have happened if denied her proposal, she very calmly says "I would have married a man with a strong personality and rejected one, who has no individuality."

In another story entitled **Kondaru Manchi Valla Katha (A Story of Some Good People)**, he projects the life of Yadaiah, a rickshaw driver. He saves money with Subbisetty, a tradesman and when he admits his wife in the hospital, he asked Subbisetty for his money. He refuses to give him on that day because it is Friday. The belief is that money (the Goddess of Lakshmi) should not be given i.e, Lakshmi sent out of the house. Yadaiah requests many people and they refuse to give him on Friday. He goes back to Subbisetty to request him again as his wife's condition is in danger. When Subbisetty refuses again he quarrels and then hit him on his head and he was arrested for one day. Next day Subbisetty comes and withdraws the cash and handover the entire money that Yadaiah saved with him. By the time he reaches the hospital his wife is dead. The writer very ironically states that though the people are good but their beliefs are dangerous and evil as they play with the lives of the poor. Teresh Babu wishes to bring to light how Dalits could not establish their rights.

The Dalits contribute for the national wealth through their hardwork but they never enjoy their rights.

SATISH CHANDER

Satish Chander, the Director of A.P. College of Journalism is a popular writer in Telugu literature in general and later every now and then he is writing on Dalit concepts. So far he published seven volumes of his poetry and some ironical short incidents. They are: **Made in India** in 1992 (an irony), **Panchama Vedam** in 1995, a long poem on Dalit theme, **Iti-hasam** in 1995 (an irony), **Naanna Cycle** in 1996, a collection of poems, **Kanti** in 1999 (Editorials), **Pasupujabilli** in 2002 (poetry) and **Daruvu** in 2002 (an irony).He got popularity with his poem **Panchama Vedam (The Fifth Note)**

The Fifth Note[1]
With hands folded
to my respected teacher
Sir:
You gave me seventeen marks out of a hundred
and failed my hundred-year-life.
You counted on your fingers and taught me
to solve that arithmetic problem, cursing that I will
never get it right even if I die trying.
I understood it only in death.
Whichever way I counted,
I found only four fingers on my hand.
Father didn't have the fifth finger either.
He never made a thumbprint
on my progress report you sent him
with zeros all over.
Mother never fed me finger food
on moonlit nights.
She didn't have a thumb.
Whenever I looked stupid,
you cursed me in that ambrosial tongue[2].
I never developed a taste for ambrosia.

I ate rice.
Tell me,
Who's the fifth caste?
The one that doesn't have the fifth finger?
That's what I learn from my great-grandfather
Ekalavya[3].

2
Forgive me for dying without paying your fee.
What could I give you?
I'd give you my life-breath
if it weren't soiled in my body.
I'd give you my heart
clean and sensitive.
But then, you'd have to die my death.
The best gift is my effigy.
It will protect you from the evil eye
when you eat
a public all-caste meal[4] on Gandhi's birthday.
Ekalavya, too, is an effigy in the *Mahabharata*.

3
Give my greetings to the Pandavas
and Kauravas[5] in the class.
Give my sympathy to Karna[6],
who joined the class with a new
caste certificate.
They're bright kids.
They applauded your verses.
To me they sounded like curses.
To tell the truth
The laws of Manu felt like obscene jokes to me.
Whenever you ran out of words to curse me,
You talked of my mother.
You accepted that I was born of my mother
even in your curses.
We are proud we are our mother's children.
Mother is our goddess.

Kunti
Whom you cast out,
is a goddess in our home.

4
No, it isn't kerosene that burned me,
I burned from pride.
Tell that to the Press.
I couldn't suffer the stink of my own corpse
when it burned.
It was the same odour your living body emitted.
Then I knew the difference between you and me:
caste stinks alive.
My friends say it's no sin to kill you.
But were you ever alive?
When you laughed at me you showed
the teeth in your skull
with no lips around them.
Warrior Ekalavya doesn't kill corpses.

5
One last word.
Give my thanks to the uncles
who attended my funeral.
I heard the town was flooded with their tears.
I was watching their faces.
their makeup washed away,
Their stripes showed.
Their eulogies stank
like mildewed ballot boxes.
But thank them for their help.
They supplied on my ration card
The kerosene to burn me.
I owe them one.
Ekalavya will make up for it.
He'll burn them free of charge,
In the forest.

Notes

1. The fifth in the title plays upon the number five. Brahminic texts call the untouchables Panchamas, the fifth caste. Also the fifth note in Indian music is the most melodious of all. The original title Panchama Vedam includes a pun: the fifth Veda/ the Veda of the fifth caste people.
2. Ambrosial tongue: Sanskrit, the language of Brahminic texts.
3. Ekalavya: A forest tribesman in the *Mahabharata*. He learns archery using the great teacher Drona's icon as his guide and excels Drona's most favourite student Arjuna of the Pandava lineage. Drona comes to know of this and asks Ekalavya's right thumb as teacher's fee, which Ekalavya chops off from his hand and submits. This effectively renders Ekalavya handicapped and Arjuna unrivalled. The poem uses Ekalavya as a symbol of low caste untouchables.
4. Caste-free meal: Public feeding to all castes who sit together to eat, a celebration often held on Gandhi's birthday. Mahatma Gandhi, as is well known, fought for a casteless society and abolition of untouchability.
5. Pandavas and Kauravas: Cousins, protagonists and antagonists respectively of the *Mahabharata* epic.
6. Karna: Illegitimate son of Kunti, the mother of Pandavas. She conceives him before her marriage and abandons him immediately after birth. Found by a low caste charioteer, he is raised as a low caste man, grows up to be a skilful archer and gets recruited to the warrior class by Duryodhana, the Kaurava king who elevates him to kingship.

(Tr. By. Velcheru Narayana Rao,**Indian Literature**, Nov-Dec 2000)

NON-DALIT WRITERS

K.V. NARASIMHAM (1942 -)

Popularly known as KOVENA, formed with the Telugu initials of his name K.V.Narasimham, is a non-Dalit contributing to Dalits through his writings and social activities. He is an ex-Stores Petty officer of the Indian Navy and at present residing in Gudur of Nellore district. His research work **Towards Emancipation** is published in 1987 by Liberation Tigers. In his introduction to this book, Dr. Gurukula Mitra, President of Telugu National Liberation Organisation, Hyderabad remarked:

> This is the era of liberation of nation. Nations are struggling to emancipate themselves from the imperialist stranglehold. Ethnic or socialistic, the struggles are mainly nationalistic in character. The mighty powers are grabbing the weaker nations to subject them to imperialistic exploitation. All the present struggles in Asia, Africa and Latin America are aimed at throwing away these imperialists.

The writer states that the book **Towards Emancipation** is a brief methodical analysis of Politico-socio-economic evolution with an alternative. And this alternative "aims at giving real political power to the oppressed natives who want to better their living conditions" (10). He is working towards the unity of all Bahujans and there by acquire the political power. He also published **The Alternative: Bahujan Revolutionary Strategy** in 2002 and in this he discussed how caste is a lone ugly feature existing in India alone. He also discussed the need for a political party for all the minorities and the oppressed castes. He strongly believes that the practice of Ambedkarism is the only revolutionary ideology in India

G. VIJAYA LAKSHMI (1974 -)

G.Vijaya Lakshmi an important woman writer from Backward Castes, was born on December 3rd, 1974 in Nuziveedu of Krishna district and her parents are Krosuri Dharma Raju and Papa Sugunavathi. She did Post Graduation in Telugu literature and Diploma in Printing. She is working as a proofreader with VGS publishers, Vijayawada. She is a poet and a short story writer. Vijayalakshmi also contributed articles to **Naveena,**

Andhra Bhoomi, Andhra Prabha, Mahila and **Prajasakti**. She is the editor of **Chittaruvu,** a collection of Dalit poetry by 99 poets and 135 poems. She received many Awards for her creative writing. A few among them are **Ranjani Kundurti Award** for her poems **Mamathala Nagisheelu** and **Panjaram lo Pakshulu, Someswara Savithribai Award** for her story **Prema Pushpam, Virangana Savithribai Phule Award** by Bharatiya Dalita Sahitya Akademi for her contribution to Dalit Literature and **Youth Award** by the Collector, Krishna district, on behalf of CMEY, State Government for her contribution to literature.

Vijaya Lakshmi strongly believes that fighting is the right solution for emancipation of woman. She expressed that her experiences are the themes and inspiration for her writing.

BETI SRIRAMULU

Popularly known as B.S. Ramulu, Beti Sriramulu was born in Jagityala of Karimnagar district, to Raju and Lakshmi. He was in Peoples War Group between 1985 and 1990. After coming out of Peoples War Group, in the year 1992 he established an organization for Dalit writers, intellectuals and artists and he is the founder secretary for this organisation. He is a creative writer as well as a social philosopher. His works include poetry, short stories and novels. He also writes essays on Marxism, Ambedkar and Dalitism. He has collected the stories published after 1990 and brought out a collection of short stories entitled **Smruthi** in 1998. B.S. Ramulu is one of the contemporary non-Dalit writers writing a powerful literature with commitment for the emancipation of Dalits. He wrote forewords to many Dalit works and published many Dalit writings on behalf of their organization.

G. LAKSHMI NARASAIAH

G.Lakshmi Narasaiah is a very prominent researcher and a Dalit sympathizer among non-Dalits contributing to Dalit writings. He collected and edited many anthologies.

His anthologies are very helpful to Telugu literature and researchers. When no publisher came forward to publish Dalit writings and when the Telugu literature is not willing to provide any space to Dalit writers, Lakshmi Narasaiah boldly brought out volumes of anthologies in Dalit poetry, short story and a book on Social Philosophy of Dalit poetry. The details of his contribution to Telugu Dalit literature are:

In 1995 along with Tripuraneni Srinivas brought out **Chikkanavuthunna Pata (The Thickening Song)**, a collection of Dalit Poetry with 104 poems from forty six poets. Perhaps this is the first volume to which a number of Dalit poets contributed and one has to remember that the literature published and edited by Lakshmi Narasaiah include not only poets of Scheduled Castes but also Backward Castes and Minorities. **Padunekkina Pata (The Sharpened Song)** in 1996 is a collection of 158 poems from 71 poets and Lakshmi Narasaiah is the chief editor of this volume.

Lakshmi Narasaiah edited Eight Volumes of Dalit stories and he is the sole editor for every volume except volume 1, to which he is the co-editor along with Dr.Rachapalem Chandrasekhar Reddy. Surprisingly these volumes are not published chronologically. For example volume three is published in 1997 where as the fourth volume is published in 1998 and volume number seven is published in 1999 where as volume number six is published in 2000. Each collection of these eight volumes of stories has a specific theme. For example Dalit Stories – 6 deals with the stories related to Personality development and volume number is subtitled as untouchable stories, 1910-1998 and so on.

JULURI GOWRI SANKAR

Juluri Gowri Sankar is yet another promising writer from BC community writing powerful Dalit Literature. In his poem **Paadamudralu** (1993) he narrated the hard physical labour of Dalits and how they are kept at a distance, in the outskirts of the main village. He also warns that one day the Dalits certainly realize the exploitation and revolt against the dominant castes. Gowri Sankar has published a collection of poems by poets from Backward Castes with the title **Ventade Kalaalu**, in 2001. In the preface to this book he remarked that the Scheduled Castes high- jacked the Dalit Poetry as the Backward Castes contributed seventy five percent of Dalit writings so far. He also accused that the Scheduled Caste writers instead of opposing the caste-society are working towards the establishment of the caste system. All the prominent Backward Caste writers contributed to this volume.

K. LAKSHMI NARYANA

Dr.K. Lakshmi Narayana also brought out two volumes of Dalit Poetry. The first volume of Dalit Poetry consists of seventy poems from Dalit Bahujans and in the Second Volume there are Eighty-Seven Poems. B.S.Ramulu wrote the foreword to the second volume and Katti Padma Rao to the first volume and in this volume the poems are selected from Sri Krishnadevaraya's **Mala Dasari** and included many predecessors and contemporary writers. The second volume began with Palkuriki Somana's **Surasani Katha (Story of Surasani)** and recorded the contemporary poets.

OTHER DALIT WORKS

In 1992 a few students of the University of Hyderabad established a literary Organisation namely **Vispotana.** Under this organisation **Dalita Manifesto**, a collection of poetry is brought out on 14th April 1995. In the introduction to this anthology the definition of Dalit poetry is discussed. The poems written after 1980s to 1995 are included in this collection. There are 51 poems and these poems are mainly written with Dalit concept by Scheduled Castes, Backward Castes as well as non-Dalits. As **Vispotana** is the eruption from the death of Sunitha (a student of Central University, and she is already referred earlier in this book), G. Kalyana Rao in the **Dalit Manifesto** presented a poem about her even before the foreword. In his foreword Kalyana Rao confesses:

> Truly, I am a prohibited human being in every sense. I am Karamchedu. I am Indravelli. I have revolution and Untouchability, both in my life. A completely prohibited man I am. I am writing the foreword to my life. That is why the foreword to **Dalit Manifesto** reminds me of so much. The past and the present both together as tears and blood; in every corner of life there are insults, exploitation and oppression of the crores of Untouchables in order and a dark conspiracy.

Sunki Reddy Narayana Reddy of Nallagonda edited **Bahuvachanam: Dalit Bahujana Poetry** in 1996. There are 54 poems by Dalit Bahujans (Scheduled Castes, Backward Castes and Minorities) in this collection. This is dedicated to Nagna Muni and Siva Sagar. G. Lakshmi Narasaiah in his foreword to this anthology referred Nietzsche to justify the need for understanding life from various angles. He quoted: "There is no single category in terms of which everything is ultimately to be explained. Perhaps, reality is pluralistic". He also wished that **Dalit Manifesto** would remain as a milestone in the history of modern Telugu Literature. The foreword as well as the preface is very important to understand the ideology of Bahujans.

The Gosangi Publications published an anthology of Dalit Bahujan poems in February 1998. There are thirty-three poems in this volume and it is dedicated to **Sunkam Achhalu** (1923 – 1983) a Member of Parliament in 1952. Except a brief dedication there is neither a preface nor a foreword that give some information about the book or the publisher. There is no specific editor too.

OTHER DALIT POEMS

The following are the writers whose poems in translation or in original we could get from some magazines. It was not possible to contact them as the addresses or phone numbers were not published in those journals/magazines.

Arundhatis

Dunna Yadagiri
Translation: P. N. Jasmine

The face tattooed all over
The teeth turned black with snuff powder
Hay like hair for want of grooming
The unkempt nauseous body
with not even ash as it
Clad in blanket like coarse
sarees of sober colours
Hand-cuff like anklets
thick cheap glass bangles upto elbows
The stalk of neem leaf for a nose ring
A strip of straw for ear studs
Taught to walk with a hunch
We've made our beautiful mothers unsightly
To save them from your lustful eyes
When your lured looks fall on our women folk
Like those of a bull on a cow-herd
We made our women chew tobacco
so that atleast you'll be repulsed by its smell.
Have you noticed what flags does the time bear now
The time which so far had wrapped our mothers
in the dirty rags of wretched lives?
When your heart quake
at the sound of *Dandora* beats
atleast now you can identify
who the blazing Arundhatis are!

Dandora: A movement started by Madiga (one of the Scheduled Castes) for a specific division among Scheduled Castes.

The Background Mourning

Gunturu Yesupadam
Translation – G. Sheela Swarupa Rani

Some body has left the shackles in the darkness under my eye
If the eye lids are lifted, there are sounds of palm leaves,
None to be seen anywhere.
Some old woman's choked voice
from some graveyard or sleeping volcano
Some one, unknown haunting me and mocking at me;
Filling my pen with their tears
Paying my letters as rent
no one is visible, yet
they crawl along my back bone.
If eyes are closed burst out in the dreams
if eyes are opened
Stab like arrows of questions in the heart
They say my life is theirs
waiting to overcome me
No one is visible...
Yes –
The termites eaten nether reminders in the annals of history
the thrown away *vistharas* at the outskirts of the sacred land
My people that are being crushed under the polyster feet of formless giant
to no one they are visible.
They spill over from the dripping blood
Come out roaring from the letter's womb.
Appearing like questions
They pass by lighting my eyes.

Visthara: a leaf plate

The Bloomed Dalitam

Kalluri Ananda Rao
Translation: P.Naga Jasmine

Do not make men deities

the touch of the hands
the flowed wine in cana's wedding are no more.
No matter how many mountains
do you turn into churning sticks
The holy cows [Kamadhenus] that fulfill your desires
The holy trees [Kalpa vrukshalu] that yield you limitless treasure
won't come out of the sea
No Alladin's lamp can create
castles on the sand hillocks any more
Don't treat men as cattle
The gorgeous colours of the caste system are fading
And since the proud feelings of caste supremacy
are no longer of any value
They are receding to a corner*
If you look around intently
you can hear the Ox that so far
quietly went round the grinding stone blindfolded, bellowing
You can see the oxen that ploughed the land
with a muzzle round their snout's
jerking their horns
You may wonder why mention all these now
Just now our inner eyes have started
looking through our bodies
The folk lore that we have sung so far
are burning us from within rousing self esteem
When we were labelled 'The people of unmentionable caste'
we thought may be it was true
Later when called a sudra, a cursed one,
a chandala, an out caste, the fifth one,
The least of marking, the loathsome one,
a pariah, an ablative, a filthy one, an abominable one
We thought we were gods with
a thousand and one names
While living as cobblers, farm labourers,
scavengers, weavers, bonded labourers

the guards of graveyards, coolies,
rickshawallas, beggers and theives
We thought we were the Narayanas
Who took multiple incarnations
We thought our hands are an emblem of dignity of labour
Our feet are the strengthy feet of Vamana
that can till the very mountains
But infact
The living waters of our labour and vitality
Dried up in the exploiting mouths of 'Agastyas'
The Vamana feet having turned limp
were listlessly dodging towards the graveyards
But now
Being revitalised, affirming second to none
We let our inner vision look through our bodies
We gather the sparkles of fire and pour down
Our folk songs turn into songs of self esteem
Lo, heed and mind
We know to skin off
We know to strike off
We know to carry the body to the graveyard
and to lead the soul to liberation as well
Yes, we are
Tanners
Cobblers,
Labourers
Watchmen at graveyards.

Prisoner's song

Krupa
Translation: M. Revathi

Untouchability flowing into night
locks me up
Myself turn into a tool
break these narrow mines
Amidst the crowd I bury the loneliness with vengeance

I pass on in open place, after yawning, into the darkness
Again beasts are getting another prison ready
Oil lamps in the huts
Trembled the shadows
Birds sing in the early hours
I sing loudly

The redemption and *Bhupalam**.

Bhupalam: One of the ragas in classical music used to wake people from sleep.

Dalit Manifesto

Salandra
Translation: K. purushotham

You've said that
I should not enter the temple of your god
O.K., whatever it is
it's nice I became an atheist
You've said that
I should not be educated.
If I read, you have ordered to
cut my tongue off
If I hear, you have ordered to
pour hot lead into my ears.
O.K., whatever it is
it's nice that I have known
what a stupid you are
how broad-hearted you are.
You have asked me to
take care just the rites of the burial of the dead.
O.K., whatever it is
it's nice that I have known
how to bury your lives as well.
You have asked
my wife, my better-half
to live just by selling her body
O.K., what ever it is

it's nice that by distancing
myself from the cultured bastards
I found an opportunity
to meet the people of my class.
You have asked me to
live forever outside the village,
O.K., whatever it is
it's nice that
I am in the forest*
While one has called me an untouchable
another fellow termed me a harijan
one more bastard
calls me a vile person
I am habituated to it.
What if I am called by whatever name:
When I become a drop of tear
blossomed in the eye of a comrade
When I imagine the goals of the martyrs in my wounds
Yes,
what if whoever calls me by whatever name?

* Forest is associated with the leftist armed struggles.

(taken from **Kakatiya Journal of English Studies,** Vol 21, 2001)

Dalit Song

Suryavamsi

Translation: K. Purushotham

Oh clouds, do not leave, rain here too
Our streets too are a part of this country
Do not let anyone cover a shroud on the memories of the past
Having got up now and then, they are frightening us
In our own country, we are victimised by your colonial invasion
We remained refugees, and you the citizens
We too have asked for entry into the hearts of the temple but

Not only to the gods, to the human beings too distant we became
Rented houses also have rejected us
Choultries too have honoured us by throwing out
Let the tap-water flow onto the drainage
It would be an offence if we collect it in our hands
When spat upon one cheek, we showed another cheek
But, we show cyclone in the silence blasted now!
(taken from **Kakatiya Journal of English Studies**, Vol 21, 2001)

Works Cited

Ambedkar, B.R.. "Annihilation of Caste", **Dr.B.R. Ambedkar Writings and Speeches Vol 1**. Govt. of Maharastra: Education Department, 1989.

Bhimanna. Boyi **Gudeselu Kalipothunnai (The huts are Burning)** Lalitha Press, Khairatabad, Hyderabad 1973)

————**-Paleru**. Hyderabad: Padmavati Printers, 1988.

Ilaiah Banna,. **Fire-Spark (Bi-lingual long poem)**. Bapatla: Sree Lakshmi Press. 1998

Jadhav, R.G "Some reflections on Dalit Literature". N.M.Aston Ed. **Dalit Literature and African-American Literature**. New Delhi: Prestige, 2001.

6
Conclusion

Prior to Independence movement there were only few references about Dalits in various texts and during the Independence struggle some writers like Kusuma Dharmanna, Gurram Joshua, Boyi Bheemanna wrote protest literature. Dalit literature produced after 1980s is revolutionary and militant in its presentation. The literature aims at Brahmanism and its injustice towards Dalits. The protest against the hegemony of dominant castes, anger, self-respect, in search of roots, social exploitation etc., are the predominant themes in Dalit Literature. Certainly all the writers of this category are much influenced by Ambedkarism. Ambedkar perhaps, is a well-known Dalit to realise and voiced against Hindu Dharma Sastras very systematically. In his book on *Annihilation of Caste*, he aptly said, "the Indian society was formed with an ascending scale of reverence and descending scale of contempt" (p. 47). It is quite ironical to note that though the lower castes are the basis for every manual work, unfortunately they are looked down. Dalits now realised their importance in the society and they want to assert their right place in the society.

The Dalit literature has become a powerful protest literature after the brutal incidents of Karamchedu, Tsunduru Chunduru and Neerukonda. The establishment of Dalit Mahasabha gave a strong support to the so far voiceless Dalits by propagating and publishing the atrocities on Dalits at national and international level.

There is no doubt that the Dalit Mahasabha of Andhra Pradesh is influenced by Dalit Panthers of Maharastra and guided by Ambedkar's ideology.

During 1980s when Dalit Mahasabha is established the word Dalit is used for all those who are oppressed and suppressed in the society. Hence the Scheduled Castes, Scheduled Tribes, Backward Castes, Minorities and Women came under the umbrella of Dalits. But later, perhaps from the second half of the 1990s onwards the activists and writers restricted the usage of the word Dalit only to untouchable castes. Hence the phrase – Dalit Bahujan is coined to refer the Scheduled Castes, Scheduled Tribes, Backward Castes and Minorities. Scheduled Castes and Other Backward Castes and Minorities agree upon this phrase. The argument for this division of Dalit and Bahujans is that the Scheduled Castes alone suffer untouchability - the most cruel, inhuman social evil in the human world. Hence the Scheduled Castes cannot be treated on par with the Backward Castes and Minorities who are touchables. Moreover these touchables do not like to be grouped with untouchables for fear that they will loose their status and respect. Hence there is a clear-cut division between Dalits and Bahujans.

The next important point to be noted here is that in the year 2000 the Scheduled Castes were divided into four groups— A, B, C and D by the state government under the Chief Ministership of Nara Chandra Babu Naidu. After this the Dalits are broadly divided into two groups the **Dandora** and the **Mala Mahanadu**, in favour of the division and against the division respectively. Subsequently under the banner of Dandora, Madigas started writing the history of Madigas, and how they are backward under the non-division and how Malas dominated and enjoyed the fruits of reservations. A strong bitter enemity began between **Dandora** and **Mala Mahanadu**. Even the writers are divided and started writing in favour of their groups. The **Mala Mahanadu** challenged this act of division by the state government in the Supreme Court and won the case. Now the Dandora Movement is pressurising the political parties to make a law and support the division of the Scheduled Castes. The agitation is still active.

The strong united Andhra Pradesh Dalit Movement that fought against the dominant castes in Karamchedu and Tsunduru/ Chunduru later divided into two groups. The **Madiga Reservation Porata Samithi** (MRPS) also known as **Madiga Dandora** was established on 7th of July 1994 in Edumudi Village of Prakasam district. The main demand of MRPS is the categorization of Scheduled Castes of Andhra Pradesh in to four groups – A, B, C and D. They demanded that the reservations have to be given proportionately. Manda Krishna Madiga is the founder president of MRPS. The accusation of **MRPS** is that within the Scheduled Castes there exists a social hierarchy and Mala and Adi Andhra castes alone reaped more benefits of reservation in education and employment. Responding to the demand of MRPS, the then government of Andhra Pradesh appointed a commission. Justice Rama Chandra Raju, a retired Judge is appointed as the one man commission. With in a span of two months Justice Ramachandra Raju submitted his report to the state Government. The criticism against this Commission was that the Commission did not consult even the National Commission of SC/ ST. On the basis of this report the Government of Andhra Pradesh divided the Scheduled Castes in to A, B, C& D groups in the Month of June 1997. The 15% reservation of SCs was distributed in the ratio of 1: 7 : 6 : 1 on the basis of population.

There are 59 Scheduled Caste groups in Andhra Pradesh. Among these 59 castes a large number of people belong to three castes and they are Madiga, Mala and Adi-Andhra. The percentages of there castes are Madiga 45.8%, Mala 37.9% and Adi-Andhra 6.8%. The remaining 56 castes constitute 9.5% ; hence the details of these castes are not known.

(Source: ***Encyclopedia of Dalits in India****, ed. Mamta Rajawat Vol:4, P:206, Anmol Publications: New Delhi, 2004.)*

One has to understand the reservation policy in the Constitution before discussing the division within the Scheduled Castes. Initially the reservations are provided for the Scheduled Castes and Scheduled Tribes with certain financial limitation for ten years as per article 335 of the Indian Constitution. After that the reservations are still continued through constitutional amendments in the years 1959, 1970, 1980, 1990 and 2000. The reservation facility to the Scheduled Castes and Scheduled Tribes is extended in their promotions in the employment as per the 77th Amendment. The Constitution has provided 15 per cent reservation to Scheduled Castes in the nation. The **Madiga Reservation Porata Samithi** (MRPS) states that a specific caste i.e. Malas alone are enjoying the reservations in Andhra Pradesh. Hence severe injustice is done to Madigas and its sub-castes. Based on this argument the Telugu Desam Government under the leadership of Nara Chandra Babu Naidu categorized the existing 59 castes listed under the Scheduled Castes into A B C and D in the year 2000.Against this division of Scheduled Castes the Malas under the banner **Mala Mahanadu** filed a case in the Supreme Court. On the 6th November 2004 the Supreme Court of India declared the divisions invalid and suspended the State Government's order.

A five-Judge bench of the supreme court in E.V. Chinnaiah Vs state of Andhra Pradesh held the act 20 of 2000 as unconstitutional.

The Supreme Court said two points .

1. Apportionment of the reservations made to SCs or STs to subgroups within cannot be done by the state legislatures. Only parliament has the competence to do so.
2. But even Parliament does not have the competence to do so since the Constitutional has intended that the SCs and STs are an indivisible, homogeneous entity

Article 341 says: 1. The president may with respect to any State or Union Territory, and where it is a State, in consultation with the governor thereof, by public notification, specify the castes races, or tribes, or parts of or groups within castes, races or tribes which shall for the purpose of this Constitution be deemed to be Scheduled Castes in relation to that State or Union Territory, as the case may be. (2). Parliament may by law include or exclude from, the list of Scheduled Castes specified in a notification issued under clause (1) any caste, race or tribe or part of or group within any caste, race or tribe, but save as aforesaid a notification issued under the said clause shall not be varied by any subsequent notification.

Nagam Kumaraswamy a Research Scholar in Osmania University has brought five points in connection with the A B C D division of Scheduled Castes in Andhra Pradesh in his article published in **Vaartha,** a Telugu Daily News Paper on 27th January 2006. His contention is: (1) The Madigas accused that the Malas are enjoying the reservation facility more than any other group in the Scheduled Castes for the last fifty years. Now they are placed before Madigas in the order of the division. If the accusation is true why are they not placed in the last position in the order of priority? This clearly shows that it is a mere political trick. (2) When all the 59 castes do not spread in the three regions i.e. Rayalaseema, Andhra and Telangana, in that case, Is the categorization scientific? (3) This problem does not pertain to Andhra Pradesh alone: It is a nation-wide problem. So, has the intellectuals sought out a reasonable solution to satisfy all the sub castes of Scheduled Castes in India? (4) Is it that Malas and Madigas of Andhra Pradesh alone are Scheduled Castes? If not, should there be another movement for social justice for the other sub-castes of the Sheduled Castes in India? How long it will be? (5) There are non-Dalit intellectuals who declared that they are fighting for the liberation of Dalits against the oppression and attacks by the upper caste in the entire nation. What type of solution have they found out for this nation-wide problem?

Kumaraswamy expresses that if possible there should be an ordinance that extends social justice to all the categories in Scheduled Castes. He also suggests some changes in the categorization of Scheduled Castes in Andhra Pradesh. He says that in the present categorization Mala and its sub-castes have to be placed under D instead of C. In Telangana Relli and Adi Andhra (A&D) castes do not exist. Hence in that region the 15% of reservations should be equally distributed between Mala and Madiga castes. In the other places the distribution should be on equal basis where all the four categories exist.

G.R.Kurme, the founder member of the **Dalit Writers, Artists and Intellectuals' United Front** put forward some issues related to the categorsation of Scheduled Castes. He stated that the then Andhra Pradesh government took a wrong decision in the categorization without consulting the National SC and ST Commission appointed as per the Article 338 of the Indian Constitution. The Commission is given an extensive power to safe guard the Scheduled Castes and Scheduled Tribes. The constitution declared that neither the central government no the state government has a right to take decision to process the Scheduled Castes and Scheduled Tribes as per clause (9) of article 338. Hence with out consulting the National Commission for SCs and STs even the Constitutional Amendment is also not possible.

It is difficult to apply this categorization to the entire nation. There is a vast difference in the socio-economic status of Malas and Madigas of Andhra Pradesh and Chamars and non-Chamars in the North India. If Malas are developed in Andhra Pradesh the Chamars are developed in the north and they are even dominating over the non-Chamars.

Kurme further argues that as per the article 341 of the constitution, the Parliament alone has the power to take a decision for the welfare and development of Scheduled Castes or to add new sub castes or to delete any sub-caste from the list of Scheduled Castes. If it is done that will be applicable to the entire nation but not to some castes alone. He further emphasizes that according to the Constitution it is not a right decision to give a special reservation policy for Madigas of Andhra Pradesh alone.

The Usha Mehra Commission appointed by the Central government visited different places in the State and met Dalit activists and Social /Dalit organizations in the month of July 2007 to study the issue of the categorization of Scheduled Castes. The leaders of **Mala Mahanadu** and **Dandora** met the committee and presented their arguments. The result is awaited

It is not a right understanding that the creation of Dalit literature is slowly reduced. Dalit literature which started as a powerful protest literature is now expanding its boundaries in various angles for the over all development of Dalits in the society. Though in the beginning there was confusion in the usage of the word Dalit, now there is a clear understanding in the usage of Dalit and Bahujan. These broad categories are trying to fight unitedly. This unification and understanding is clearly visible among Dalit Bahujan writers.

Annexure – I

Government of Andhra Pradesh – Social Welfare (H) Department.

Memo. No. 24282/H1/95-1 Dated: 20-12-1995

Sub:- Social Welfare Department – Not to use the term 'Harijan' and use 'Scheduled Caste' instead – Instructions issued – Reg. Ref : -

1. Ministry of Welfare O. M. No. 12025/14/90 SCD (RL Cell) dated 16-8-1990.
2. Govt. Memo. No. 24090/H1/90-1 S. W (H1) Department, dt. 25-10- 1990.
3. Statement of Hon'ble Chief Minister made on the floor of Assembly on 19-12-1995.

* * *

1. Government have decided that under no circumstances, the word 'Harijan' should be used in any official matters, dealing, certificates etc., or in any manner whatsoever by any department in Government or by any official. Instead, the word 'Scheduled Caste' should invariably be used.
2. All the departments are hereby requested to take necessary action for removal of the 'Harijan' wherever existing the text books, official documents, Government offices, on the school/Institution buildings, application forms etc and instead the word 'Scheduled caste' be used.
3. Government view that any violation of these instructions would be dealt with severely. All the Heads of the Departments, District Collectors are requested to communicate the decision of the

Government in this regard to all the subordinate offices for strict implementation.

S. Ray,
Principal Secretary to Government.

Annexure – II

The Bhopal Declaration

Adopted unanimously by The Bhopal Conference, 'Charting a New Course for Dalits for the 21st Century', held at Bhopal, Madhya Pradesh, India, 12-13 January, 2002

We intellectuals and activists assembled at the Bhopal Conference, 12-13 January, 2002, to deliberate the issues concerning the welfare of and justice to the 250 million are:

Declaring our belief in Babasaheb Dr B. R. Ambedkar's ideal of Social Democracy and his prophecy that, "A democratic form of Government presupposes a democratic form of society. The formal framework of democracy is of no social democracy",

Endorsing the ideals of civil society enshrined in the Constitution of India, particularly its Preamble that declares the Indian State's commitment to Justice, Liberty, Equality and Fraternity,

Recognising that the principles established by the Universal Declaration of Human Rights and various other charters of the United Nations which our nation has acceded to also emphasise the same principles,

Recognising also the tribals' legitimate and historical rights over forest and forest-produce,

Acknowledging the role of tribal communities, particularly tribal women, to the protection and conservation of the country's rich biodiversity and natural resources as well as its culture and civilization

Acknowledging also the need to ensure that SCs and STs are given due representation in all bodies of decision making,

Recalling the struggles that Babasaheb had waged for the emancipation of his people and the historic rights he had won for them,

Mindful of the fact that even after 54 years of Independence, the Dalit community is denied of its basic human rights and is also at the receiving end of the most brutal and oppressive forms of discrimination and exclusion,

Reaffirming that concerted action by society as a whole – especially coordination among the political leadership, officials and grassroots activists – is necessary for the overall development of the most oppressed of India,

Bearing in mind the responsibility to take forward our struggle at this critical juncture in spite of the fact that most political formations are reluctant to pursue any policy favourable to the Dalits,

Recognising that the social consensus over the Dalit cause – reluctantly agreed upon at the time of Independence – has by and large broken down,

Convinced that informed and democratic discourse at all levels is essential to re-negotiate a new consensus over redeeming the pledges of the founding fathers of the Republic to do justice to Dalits,

Convinced also that the national psyche and public discourse in the country accepts uncritically the rigid hierarchy and discrimination caused by caste and thereby denies that caste is a major source of prejudice and brutal violence,

Emphasising that Babasaheb's stress on struggle through democratic and constitutional means is relevant today,

Regretting that the post-Ambedkar Dalit intelligentsia has failed both in carrying forward his emancipatory movement as well as making a dent in the country's intellectual life,

Recognizing the need for Dalits to make common cause with other liberation and human rights movements in and outside the country,

Conscious of the hurdles that caste-Hindu society – and its tentacles in government, media, voluntary sector, etc., – are likely to hurl at any serious movement that challenges the entrenched system of discrimination and exclusion,

Noting that women – especially Dalit women – represent the most oppressed sections of our society, and that they face multiple forms of discrimination, including caste-based, religious and patriarchal ideology and practices,

Welcoming the winds of change the world over that are conductive to Inclusion, Equal Opportunity, Diversity, Democratisation and Civil Society, and against discrimination, stereotype, stigma, exclusion and caste society,

Hoping that this country will no longer remain an exception to the global norm of Progress, Equality, Justice, Peace and Social harmony, and

We hereby Solemnly proclaim that while we rededicate ourselves to work in unison to achieve the basic rights of Dalits, we are convinced that unless the following issues are resolved, no amount of activism on our part and pro-active measures from the State can liberate the community from the scourges of untouchability and exploitation.

We therefore demand ...

21 – Point Action Agenda for the 21st Century

1. Ensure that each Dalit family will own enough cultivable land for socio-economic well-being. The government should pursue all possible measures, including the distribution of surplus land, government revenue lands and temple lands within a specific timeframe. If the need be, the government should purchase cultivable land and distribute it among Dalits.

2. Enact legislation and enforce it stringently to enable Dalits to have an equitable share in the appropriation and use of rural and urban common property resources. The law must be amended to ensure that lengthy litigation with the ulterior motive of denying Dalits legal redressal is not resorted to.
3. Enact legislation and enforce the right of Dalit agricultural labourers to living wages, to gender parity in wages, to job security, to better working conditions and welfare measures, and ensure punitive measures against offenders.
4. Appoint Statutory Committees at the national and state level to identify within a specified time-frame all the Depressed Calss lands occupied by non-Dalits, to assess the quantum of compensation to be paid by non-Dalits for their illegal utilization of lands, to identify the original owners and their nearest kith and kin for resorting these lands back to them, to expedite legal proceedings in courts specially appointed for this purpose against the illegal occupants and to ensure punitive measures against them.
5. Ensure the restoration of alienated lands to tribals, restore their rights over forest and forest-produce, provide them with compensation and rehabilitation measures, extend resources and capacity building measures for the gainful utilization of their lands and forests and make those Dalits displaced due to construction of dams/ developmental projects shareholders of such enterprises.
6. Democratise the capital so as to ensure a proportionate share for SCs and STs. Make budgetary allocation for SCS and STs to enable them to enter the market economy with adequate investment resources, and develop their capacities and skills for such market enterprises.
7. Enforce with stringent measures the Bonded Labour System (Abolition) Act, 1976, and abolish forthwith child labour to ensure freedom with dignity for all

Dalits, and accordingly make suitable amendments in the appropriate legislations.

8. Amend Article 21 of the Constitution of India: Fundamental Rights so as to include the following rights for all citizens, but with special emphasis for SCs and STs, and on the basis of two criteria, namely low economic income and without religious discrimination: the rights to a standard of living adequate for the health and well-being of women and men equally, including food, safe drinking water, clothing, housing, public health and medical care, social security and social services; the right to living wage and the right to own five acres of cultivable land or to gainful employment.
9. Implement compulsory, free and high quality education for all Dalits immediately, make allocation of the funds proportionate to the number and level of the illiterates, ensure compensation to those families which forfeit their income from child labour, increase the number and amount of scholarships, and provide better infrastructural facilities in SC and ST schools and offer market-oriented vocational and technical education.
10. Make the reservation quota applicable in all public and private educational institutions from primary to technical and professional institutions from primary to technical and professional levels. Every SC/ST child with low income base must be given quality free education at the State's expense. And every English medium school must implement Diversity in Admissions.
11. Recognise SC and ST women as a distinct category among women, and accordingly make segregated data on Dalit womenavailable in census reports, action taken reports and progress reports, evolve national and state level perspective plans for mainstreaming SC and ST women in developmental programmes, market enterprises, financial allocation, reservation facilities in education, employment and health facilities, and

mandate the National and State Commissions for SC and ST for Women to study and report specifically the status of SC and ST women in their annual reports.

12. Implement effectively in letter and spirit the SC and ST (Prevention of Atrocities) Act, 1989, and Rules 1995, especially with regard to atrocities against Dalit women, and accordingly prosecute dominant caste leaders and their minions who stoke the fire of caste clashes and police officials acting in connivance with them. In cases of atrocities against SCs/STs, a system of collective punishment has to be evolved as oppressors enjoy community support and protection and escape the law.
13. Ensure diversity or due representation of SCs/STs in all public institutions of India, whether universities or academic or autonomous or registered bodies. Those institutions which do not abide by the principle of Affirmative Action must lose recognition and state funding. All private industry/ corporate houses must accept and implement Diversity in workforce immediately.
14. Ensure that in all state and national budgets allocations are made as per the proportion of SC and ST population and penal action taken against unutilisation or diversion of funds meant for these sections.
15. Every government and private organisation must implement Supplier Diversity from socially disadvantaged businesses and Dealership Diversity in all goods and services.
16. The State must assume sole responsibility in protecting the SCs and STs. The State must identify those atrocity prone areas and deploy forces. In addition, provide arms licences to the SCs and STs as stipulated in the Atrocities Act for self-defence purposes, make the setting up of Dalit self-defence groups from village onwards mandatory, and specially train Dalit women to handle weapons in self-defence against the perpetrators of crimes and atrocities.

17. Eliminate the humiliating practice of manual scavenging on an urgent footing through effective rehabilitation, alternative and sustainable employment measures and developmental programmes, and prosecute violators of the Employment of Manual Scavengers and Construction of Dry Latrines (Prohibition) Act, 1993, especially the gross violators, Railways Defence and Urban Local bodies.
18. Make it statutory for Parliament and State Assemblies to debate on the annual Reports of the National and State level Commissions for SC/ST and Safai Karamcharis within the following year, and ensure that these annual reports and the action-taken reports of the government are made public.
19. Make reservation mandatory in the private and corporate sector in the same proportion as in the public sector and government institutions and develop the capacities and skills of Dalits to help them cope up with the demands of these different sectors.
20. Implement a policy of reservation to SCs and STs at all levels of the Judiciary and Defence Forces. And make transparent appointment processes in Judiciary by doing away with the nomination system.
21. Bring out a Truth Paper in two years on the status of reservation during the past 25 years and place it before the Parliament and State Assemblies for debate, and on a war footing fill immediately all the backlog posts meant for Dalits and that, too, only with Dalit candidates.

India Together
January 2002

Annexure– III

Vancouver Declaration: International Dalit Conference, 2003

Adopted Unanimously by the International Dalit Conference, Vancouver, BC, Canada, May 16-18, 2003

WE, THE DALITS, from all over the globe having assembled at the International Dalit Conference, to deliberate the issues concerning the 250 million Dalits (Scheduled Castes and Scheduled Tribes) of India and their future in the 21st century,

INSPIRED by that great thinker and philosopher of the oppressed, Babasaheb Ambedkar,

REDEDICATE ourselves to his mission to bring about a democratic and peaceful transformation of India whereby all its citizens, irrespective of their gender, caste, creed, language and region, will enjoy the fruits of equality and justice,

WHEREAS the world has entered the third millennium and is progressing towards accomplishing the goals of Liberty, Equality and Fraternity, and whereas India has failed to eradicate untouchability and caste-and descent-based discrimination and is yet to achieve basic fundamental human rights,

CALL UPON the Dalits of the world to unite in their activism in the true spirit of interfaith and multiculturalism, and resolve to work tirelessly for the upliftment of the community,

AFFIRM that every human being has the inherent right to life and dignity and that Black is beautiful and Dalit is Dignified,

MINDFUL of the fact that the Dalits and Tribals

accounting for a fourth of India's one billion population, continue to be the victims of manifold discriminations and violence,

MINDFUL also that women belonging to these sections are the victims of gender-caste discrimination,

SINCERELY BELIEVE that the caste problem is not the problem of Dalits alone but also of the entire nation and without the Annihilation of Caste and the elimination of other primordial identities, India will not be able to realise its full socio-economic potential and claim its rightful place among the community of nations,

UPHOLD our unwavering belief in the Indian Constitution as well as the unity and integrity of India,

TAKE cognisance of the universal ideals enshrined in several international and national covenants and treaties – from the Universal Declaration of the Human Rights to the Bhopal Declaration – and

ENDORSE wholeheartedly the Bhopal Declaration in letter and spirit,

AFFIRM our mission to support the struggles of oppressed people worldwide and muster all possible support from anywhere for the advancement of the Dalit cause,

RESOLVE to propagate knowledge of Babasaheb as a philosopher of emancipation to all the oppressed anywhere in the world, and to fulfil the pledge,

RESOLVE also to build our own educational, cultural and other institutions for the advancement of the community, we

REDEDICATE ourselves to institutionalise the process started in the conference through constant coordination and by setting up a formal institutional structure for better networking among the Resident and Non-Resident Indian Dalit community as well as to make use of international institutions and processes to sensitise the world about the plight of the Dalits and Tribals in India,

WE therefore Demand,

1. The rightful and proportionate share of Dalits and Tribals in India's national institutions, wealth and capital must be recognised. Economic exclusion hitherto practised in the name of caste must be done away with. The community should have equitable access to means of production and economic empowerment.
2. Since no development is possible without gender justice, women of these groups must be given priority in all developmental activities. They must have formal, legally sanctioned rights on par with men.
3. Private Corporations and Multinational Corporations operating in India must recognise and accept their social responsibilities.
4. The United Nations and its affiliates, and non-governmental agencies concerned with human rights, social and economic development, must recognise that the Dalits are a special group and create separate Dalit divisions managed by the Dalits themselves. Their programmes and projects should have special Dalit components as well as special focus in their reports.
5. Dalit Studies must be included in Indian and international educational and research institutions, especially in North America and Europe, and universities should recognise the need to admit Dalit students on priority.
6. The World Bank and other International Financial Institutions should attach conditional special component clauses and must ensure the rightful share of the Dalits in the funds they lend to India for socio-economic and sustainable development.
7. The international governmental and non-governmental development aid agencies should focus on Dalit development and empowerment with initiatives to be inbuilt in their system and adopted in the funding programmes.
8. Sustained efforts must be made at the United Nations to expedite the process of formally equating caste-

based discrimination with racial discrimination.

9. Untouchability is practised in many countries such as Bangladesh, Nepal, Pakistan and Sri Lanka. No effort must be spared to address the problem by the world community.
10. Reorganise the National and State Commissions for SCs and STs as the SC and ST Vigilance Commissions and the decisions of these Commissions should be binding.
11. All laws, rules and regulations meant for protecting the rights of the Dalits must be included in the Ninth Schedule of the Constitution of India, to prevent unjust and lengthy litigation processes, which always go against the community.

Annexure – IV

Addresses of some of the writers and activists

Banna Ilaiah,
Professor & Head,
Dept of Telugu,
Kakatiya University,
Vidyaranya Puri,
Warangal-506009

Bhupati Narayana Murthy,
Maliki Puram,
East Godavari (dt) – 533253

Bhutam Mutyalu (Teacher),
H.No. 8-98,
Near Electricity Sub Station,
Nampally (Village & Mandal),
Nallagonda (Dt) - 508373

Bojja Tharakam,
Plot No.1, Bal Reddy Nagar,
Toli Chowk, Hyderabad-500008.
Ph.(R) – 040-23562525

Boya Jangaiah,
5-9-214, Manyamcheluka,
Nalgonda-508001.
Ph. 0868- 232515

Challapalli Swarupa Rani,
P.S. Telugu University,
513101

Chilukuri Devaputra,
28-4-678
Government Quarters, B1
Anantapur.

D.M Leela Kumari,
H.No. 4-16-551,
Mahati Sadhan,
18/3 Arundal Pet,
Guntur-522002

Darla Venkateswara Rao,
Lecturer Dept. of Telugu,
Central University,
Gachibowli,
Hyderabad-500046,
Ph.08416-253933.

Dunna Yadagiri,
H.No.2-1-83,
Jama Masjid,
Nallagonda-508001

G. Syamala,
2-2-18/49, D.D. Colony,
Bag Amberpet,
Hyderabad – 13,
Ph: 040-27423168

G.Subba Rao,
16-106/9,
Opp. To Girls High School,
Near Old state bank Colony,
Kotha Peta-533223,
East Godavari (Dt)

Gaddar,
Venkatapuram (Post),
Cantonment Area,
Secundrabad.
Ph. 040-27797629

Gaddhada Narasimha Murthy,
MA Telugu,
Nadava Palli (Village & post),
Kotrani kona Mandal-533212

Guda Anjaiah,
H.No.1-9-19/152,
Ram Nagar,
Opp. To Karthik Appartment,
Hyderabad-500048,
Cell.92462709, Ph.040-27620869

Hemalatha Lavanam,
Nasthik Kendram,
Benz Circle,
Vijayawada-8

J.Gowtham,
Editor,
Mahajana Monthly
H. No. 1-9-69
Street No: 18, Ramnagar,
Hyderabad – 500048
Ph. (O) 9949265939.

K. Sanjeeva Rao (Sikhamani),
Associate Professor,
Centre for Comparative Studies,
Telugu University,
Public Gardens,
Nampalli, Hyderabad -500004

K.G. Satyamurthy,
Q.No. 421-C, Sector 8,
UKKU Nagar,
Visakhapatnam-530032.
Ph. 0891-2510672

Kalekuri Prasad,
12-11/108/C,
Padmanabha Nagar,
Mehidipatnam,
Hyderabad.

Katti Padma Rao,
Lumbini Vanam,
Ponnuru – 522124,
Guntur (Dt),
Ph: 08643-244659

Katti Swarna Kumari,
Lumbini Vanam,
Ambedkar Nagar,
Ponnuru-522124

Koyi Koteswara Rao,
Telugu Lecturer,
Govt. Boys Junioa college,
Armur, Nijamabad (Dt).
Ph.08463-225666

M.A.K Bheema Rao,
Dudduvari Agraharam,
Amalapuram-533201.
Ph(R) 235693,
Cell:9440123093

Madduri Vijasyasree,
C/o Madduri Nagesh Babu,
H. No. 13-2-73,
VenkatReddy Colony,
NersaRao Pet,
Guntur (Dt) – 522601.

Masterji,
Flat No. 256, South End Park,
L.B Nagar,
Hyderabad-500001

Moka Rathna Raju,
11-6-8,
Rockdale Layout,
Maharanipet,
Vizag – 530002.

Nathala Pratap Kumar,
Teacher & Poet,
Ambedkar Sahitya Akademi,
Tanuku,
West Godavari (Dt) – 534211

Nelavuri Venkata
Rathnaji(Venkoji), Writer,
Chagallu (Village & post),
West Godavari-534342.

P.Ram Babu,
Raja gruha,
Official Colony,
Ramachandra Puram,
East Godavari –533255

Peidi Teresh Babu,
Flat No.303, H.No.1-1-128,
Pattabhi Residency,
Ashok Nagar, Street No.9,
Hyderabad -500020

Potla Hemalatha,
Plot No.1 Leo Tower
Appartments,
Near KORA Residential,
Tilak Road, Rajahmundry

Sarella Venkata Rathnam
(SAVERA),
Dalita Chaitanya Vedika,
Vankata Krishna Puram
Colony,
Amalapuram-533201,
East Godhavari(Dt)

Satish Chandar,
A.P College of Jounalisam,
Adjacent to Oxford Grammar
School, 3-6-712/2/3, Street
No-11,
Hymayat Nagar,
Hyderabad-29

Surepalli Manohar,
184, Pylon,
Nagarjunasagar-508203

Swarana Latha Devi,
Dept.of Telugu,
T.J.P.S College,
Guntur, Ph.2351602, 2231942

Talluri Laban Babu,
Kusumanjali Publications,
3-6-348 Jana Priya Colony,
Bahadurguda,
L.B. Nagar,
Hyderabad – 500074

Therasa Devadanam,
Rami Reddy Thota,
Kotta Peta, Guntur

Vemula Yellaiah,
FCI.BSC Godown,
Gollagudem,
Nalgonda-508001

Yedla Peterpal,
Venkat Reddy Nagar,
NarsaRao Peta,
Ph.No.08647-231865
Cell.9849317112

Yendluri Sudhakar,
Associate Professor,
Telugu University,
Bommuru,
Rajahmundry – 533124

Bibliography

Primary Sources

Anjaiah, Guda. *Uuru Manadira*. Hyderabad: Hema Sahiti Publications. 1999.

Bhemanna, Boyi. *Gudeselu Kalipothunnai* (*The Huts are Burning*) Hyderabad: Lalitha Press. 1973.

———. *Paleru*. Hyderabad: Padmavati Printers, 1988.

———. *Panchama Swaram*. Hyderabad: Bhimanna Sahithi Nidhi, 2000.

———. *Paramatma : The Super Soul*. Hyderabad: Bhimanna Sahithi Nidhi, 2002.

———. *Sankharavam*. Hyderabad: Bhimanna Sahithi Nidhi, 2001.

Devadanam, Teresa. *Asprusyulu Avaru? Thappevaridi?* (np) 1982.

———. *Arundathi Vani- Antaranithanam Nirmulana*. (np), 1985.

Devaputra, Chilukuri. *Panchamam*. USA: First ATA Telugu Conference & Youth Convention American Telugu Association, 1998.

Ilaiah, Banna. *Fire-Spark*. Warangal: Bodhi Publlications, 1998.

Jangaiah, Boya. *Uppu Neeru*. Hyderabad: Boja Publications, 2002.

———. *Boja Kavithalu*. Nalgonda: Boja Publications, 2001.

Joshuva, Gurram. *Christhu Charitra*. Madras: Diocesan, 1963.

———. *Gabbilam*. Vijayawada: Insaan Printers, 1987.

———. *Kotha Lokam*. Vijayawada: Joshuva Foundation,1996.

———. *Munthajamahalu*. Vijayawada: Insaan Printers, 1993.

———. *Naa Katha*. Vijayawada: Joshuva Foundation,1996.

Kalyana Rao G. *Antarani Vasantam*. Vijayawada: Viplava Rachayatula Sangham, 2004.

KOVENA. *Pratamnayam*. Nellore: Vijaya Graphics, 2002.

———. *Towards Emancipation*. Madras: Liberation Tigers, 1987.

Laban Babu, Talluri. *Madiga Vari Charitra*: *The Chamârs of AP* Hyderabad: Kusumanjali Publications, 2001.

Narasaiah, Lakshmi G. & Srinivas, Tripuraneni Ed. *Chikkanavuthunna Paṭa*: *Dalita Kavitvam*, Vijayawada: Dalita Sana Publications, 1995.

———. *Padunekkina Pata*: *Dalita Kavitvam*, Vijayawada: Dalita Sana Publications, 1996.

———. *Dalita Kathalu-3*: *Asprusya Kathalu* Anantapur: Rama Publications, 1997.

———. *Dalita Kathalu-4*: *Ardhika, Rajakeeya Kathalu*. Anantapur: Rama Publications, 1999.

———. *Dalita Kathalu-6*: *VyakthitvaVikasa Kathalu* (*1910-2000*). Anantapur: Rama Publications, 2000.

———. *Dalita Kathalu-7*: *Hakkula Sadhana Kathalu*. Anantapur: Rama Publications, 2000.

Manohar, Surepalli. *Nallagonda Naayamma*... Telangana: Telangana Rachayitala Vedika, 2002.

Muthyalu, Bhutham. *Dugili*: *Dalita Kavitvam*. Nalgonda: Gumpu Sahiti Samstha, 2003.

Narayanamurthy, Bhupati. *Brahmana Bhavajalam Pi Kshatriyula Tirugubatu*.Nidamarru: Lokayuta Printers, 1993.

———. *Dalita Vimukti*. Malikipuram: Telugu Praja Samithi Publications, 1993.

———. *Dalitula Pai Damana Kanda*. Malikipuram: Telugu Praja Samithi Publications, 1993.

———. *Dalitula Asalu Jathi Nagulu*. Malikipuram: Telugu Praja Samithi Publications. 1993.

————. *B.C. Mandal Commission Nivedika*. Malikipuram: Telugu Praja Samithi Publications, 2004.

Nagesh Babu, Madduri. *Meerevutlu*. Narasaraopet: Sreeza Publications, 1998.

————. *Naraloka Prardhana*. Guntur: Bhasyam Publishers. 2002.

————. *Racha Banda* Ponnuru: Lokayata Publications. 1996.

Peter Pal, Yedla. *Kotha Dari* (*The New Path*). Hyderabad: Anupama Printers, 2002

Padma Rao, Katti. *Kulam Pratyamnaya Samskruti* Ponnuru: Lokayatha Publications, 1997.

————. *Nalla Kaluva*. Ponnuru: Lokayatha Publications, 1996.

————. *Pithruswamya Vyavasthalo Stri*. Ponnuru: Lokayatha Publications, 1998.

————. *Ambedkar-Budhudu*. Ponnuru : Lokayatha Publications, 2002.

————. *Mulla Kireetam*. Ponnuru : Lokayatha Publications, 2002.

————. *Neelikeka*. Ponnuru: Lokayatha Publications, 1998.

Pratap Kumar, Nethala. *Palakamki*. Tanuku: Sahiti Publishers, 2003.

Ramachandra, Darla.. *Kirrucheppulu*. Jagitiyal: Vishala Sahitya Akademi, 2002.

Ratnaji, Nelavuri. *Oke Gonthu*. Rajahmundry: Sudha Offset Printers, 2005.

Rathna Raju, Moka. *Neevu – Nee Sthanam*. (np), 1988.

————. *Gunde Kolimi*. (np), 2002.

————. *Poddu Podupu*. Amalapuram: R.K. Printers,1994.

Sambuka. *Poyedemilenoollam* Vijayawada: Dalita Vimochana Samiti, 1992.

————. *Charitralo Kristhavam*. Vijayawada: Mythri Book House, 2004.

Satish Chandar. *Daruvu* Hyderabad: Smiles & Smiles Media Pvt. Ltd, 2002.

SAVERA. *Dalita Chaithanya Lahari.*,Amalapuram:Dalita Chaitanya Vedika, 2004

————————. *Dalita Jathula Dharma Yuddham.*, Amalapuram:Dalita Chaitanya Vedika,1991.

————————. *SAVERA Padya Manjari*. Amalapuram: Dalita Sahitya Vedika, 2003.

Sikhamani. *Kirrucheppula Basha*. Hyderabad: Milinda Publications, 2000.

Sivasagar. *Sivasagar kavitvam*. Hyderabad : Bahujan Book Syndicate, 2004.

————————. *Ambedkar Suryudu*. Hyderabad: Dr. Ambedkar People's Educational Trust, 2004

Subba Rao, G. *Biyyapu Ginja*. Kakinada: Visalandra Publishing House, 2002.

Sudhakar, Yendluri. *Nalla Draksha Pandiri*. Secundrabad: Sri Sri Printers, 2002.

————————. *Vargikharanam*. Rajahmundri: Manasa-Manogna Publications, 2000

Swarooparani, Challapalli. *Mankena Puvvu*. (np), 2005

Tharakam, Bojja. *Na Lage Godavari*. Hyderabad: Janapada Vignana Kendram, 2000

————————. *Bregil Prajala Bhuporatam*. Hyd: Sakhi Human Rights Watch, 2000.

Omprakash.Valmiki, *Joothan: A Dalit's Life* Kolkata: Mandira Sen for SAMYA, 2003

Venkateswara Rao, Darla.. *Dalita Tatvikudu*. Vikarabad:Telugu Sahitya Vedika, 2004.

Secondary Sources

Ahir, D.C. *Dr. Ambedkar on Christianity in India*. New Delhi: Blumoon Books, 1995.

Ambedkar, B.R. "Annihilation of Caste", *Dr. B.R. Ambedkar Writings and Speeches Vol 1*. Govt. of Maharashtra: Education Department, 1989.

Ambedkar, B.R. *The Rise and fall of the Hindu Woman*. New Delhi: Blumoon Books, 1999.

Ambedkar, B.R. *Castes in India: Their Mechanism, Genesis and Development*. New Delhi: Dalit book Trust, 2003.

Ambrose, S.J, Hanumantha Rao, V., Sankaran, S.R., Sachidananda, Thorath, Sukhadev. (Eds). *Samskarana Vuubhilo Munigipothunna Dalita Sakshemam*, 2001.

Anand, Dinesh.S. *Origin of Scriptures*. New Delhi: Blumoon Books, 2000.

Anthoniraj, Thumma. *Breaking Barriers*. Delhi: ISPCK, 2000.

————. *Voices of the Victims*. Delhi: ISPCK, 1999.

Asmitha. *Neelimeghalu*. Hyderabad: Vipula Computer services, 2003.

Aston N.M. Ed. *Dalit Literature and African-American Literature*. New Delhi: Prestige, 2001.

Balasubramanyam, G. *Telugu Sahityamlo Dalitula Samasyalu*. Chittoor: Srinivasa Publications, 2000

Basham. A. L. *A Cultural History of India*. New Delhi: Oxford University Press, 2003

Bathula, B.R. *Bharata Rathna, Baba Saheb Dr. B.R. Ambedkar*. Hyderabad: Sowjanya Publications, 1990.

Berwa, Lakshmi N. *Asian Dalit Solidarity*. Delhi: ISPCK, 2000.

Brown, William . *Telugu- English Dictionary*. New Delhi, Madras: Asian Educational Services, 2001.

C.V. *Dalita Udyama Vythalikudu Kusuma Dharmanna Kaveendrudu*. Vijayawada: Jayanthi Publications, 2000

Chandrasekhar Reddy, Rachapalem. *Adhunikandhra Kavithvam: Udhyamalu – Sandharbhalu*. Hyderabad: Annupama Printers, 2002.

Clarke, Sathianathan. *Dalits and Christiyanity*. New Delhi: Oxford University Press, 1999.

Deliege, Robert. *The Untouchables of India*. New York : Berg Publishers,1999

Deshpande, G.P. (Ed). *Selected Writings of Joti Rao Phule*. New Delhi: Left Word Books, 2002.

Dumont, Louis. *Homo Hierarchicus: The Caste System and its Implications*. New Delhi: Oxford University Press, 1988.

Gopal, Ram and Gadkar Ravindra Devendra Singh, Ed. *Restoration of Human Rights and Dignity to Dalits*. Delhi: MANAK Publications, 2004.

Gopi, D. *Gudesa Yeosebu: Dalita Kathalu*. Vijayawada: Dalit Women Literary Parishat, 1996.

Gosangi. *Mogi: Dalita Bahujana Kavitvam*. Nalgonda: Neelisahithi, 1998.

Gupta, Dipankar. *Interrogating Caste*. New Delhi: Penguin Books, 2000.

Hanlen, Rosalind.O. *Jyothi Rao Phule*. Hyderabad: Hyderabad Book Trust, 1993.

Hemalatha, Lavanam. *Jashuva Kalam Cheppina Katha*. Vijayawada: Nasthik Kendram, 1998.

Hooks Bell. *AIN'T I A WOMAN: Black Women and Feminism*. London: Pluto Press, 1981.

Hughes, Marnie and Warrington. *Fifty Great Thinkers History*. Chennai: Routledge, 2004.

Human Rights Watch(ed). *Broken People*. Bangalore: Books for Change, 1999.

Ilaiah, Banna. *Telugu Kavitha- Abinava Drukpadam*. Warangal: NaaNee publications, 2001

Ilaiah, Kanch. *Buffalo Nationalism*. Kolkata: Samya, 2004

————. *God as political Philosopher*. Calcutta: Samya, 2001.

————. *Why I Am Not A Hindu* Calcutta: Samya,2003

Jaiswal, Suvira. *Caste*. New Delhi: Manohar Publishers, 1998.

Jha,Vivekananda."Stages in the History of Untouchables". *Indian Historical Review*,Vol.2,pp.14-31.

Jhunjhunwala, Bharat. *Varna Vyavastha: Governance through Caste System*. New Delhi: Rawat Publications, 1999.

Keer, Dhananjay. *Dr. Ambedkar Life and Mission*. Mumbai: Popular Prakashan Pvt.Ltd. 2003.

Kesavakumar, Sathyanarayana. K. (eds). *Dalita Manifesto: Kavita Sankalam* Hyderabad: Vispotana Publications, 1995.

Kothari, Rajani. Ed. *Caste in Indian Politics*. Hyderabad: Orient Longman, 2001

Narasaiah, G Lakshmi. *The Essence of Dalit Poetry*. Hyderabad: Dalit Sana Publications, 1999.

Narayana, K Lakshmi. *Dalita Kavitvam-1*. Anantapur: Rama Publications, 2000.

———————. *Dalita Kavitvam-2*. Anantapur: Rama Publications, 2002.

Lal, A.K. Dalit in Action. *New Delhi: Concept Publishing Company. 1997.*

Leelakumari, B.M. *His Thoughts*. Guntur: Dalit Women Literary Parishat, 1993.

Macdonell, Arthur Anthony and Arthur Berriedall Keith. *Vedic Index of Names and Subjects*, Vol. 1, London, 1912.

Madhava Rao. K. *Joshua's Gabbilam (Bat)*. Hyderabad: Joshua Foundation, 1998.

Majumdar, D.N. *Races and cultures of India*. 4th ed., Bombay, 1961.

Mallayya, Kaluva. *Kaluva Mallayya Navalalu*. Karimnagar: Telugu Vachanam Publications, 2001.

Masthan Rao, Devarapalli. *Dalita Dasabdham*. Ponnuru: Srujana Printers, 1997.

Mohanty, Manoranjan. *Class, Caste and Gender*. New Delhi:Sage Publications, 2004.

Moon, Vasant. *Growing up Untouchable in India: A Dalit Autobiography*. New Delhi: Vistaar Publilcations, 2001.

Mowli, V. Chandra. *B.R. Ambedkar – Man and His Vision*. New Delhi: Sterling Publishers Pvt. Ltd. 1990.

Omvedt, Gail. *Dalits and the Democratic Revolution*. New Delhi: Sage Publications, 1994.

———. *Ambedkar towards an Enlightened India* New Delhi:Penguin, 2004.

Ortiz, Bobbye S. and Gupta, Tilak D. *History as it Happened*. Kharagpur: Cornerstone Publications,1998.

Perez, Rosa Maria. *Kings and Untouchables*. New Delhi: Chronicle Books. 2004.

Prasad, Kalekuri. *Dalita Udyamam- Dalita Sahityyodhyamam*. Hyderabad: Sakshi, Human Rights Watch, 1999.

Prashad, Vijay. *Untouchable Freedom*. New Delhi: Oxford University Press, 2000.

Price, John. "A History of the Outcaste: Untouchability in Japan". Ed.s.George De Vos and Hiroshi Wagatsuma, Japan's Invisible Race:Caste in Culture and Personality.University of California Press,1972.

Quigley, Declan. *The Interpretation of Caste*. New Delhi: Oxford University Press, 1999.

Rajshekar, V. T. *Christians & Dalit Liberation* Bangalore: Dalit Sahitya Akademi, 2000.

Raju ,Maddela. *Mastarji Dalita Geethalu*. Hyd: Padmasri Graphics, 1998.

Ramachandraia, I. *Ambedkar Bodhanalu*. Andhra Pradesh: Ambedkar Dharma Poraata Samithi, 2002.

Rambabu, P. *Aadi Bharatiyulu*. Ramachandrapuram: Chandra Graphics, (nd)

————. *Chandala*. Ramachandrapuram: Chandra Graphics, 2005

Ramulu, B.S. *Bahujana Tathvam*, Hyderabad: Visala Sahitya Academy, 2004.

————. *Visala Sahiti Samagika Chaitanya Patalu*. Hyderabad: Visala Sahitya Academy, 2004

Reade, Winwood *The Outcast*. New Delhi: Rupa & Co, 2003.

Robb, Peter. Ed. *Dalit Movements and the Meanings of Labour in India*. New Delhi: Oxford University Press, 1993.

Sakshi, Team Ed.*Dalit Human Rights Monitor 2000-2003, Andhra Pradesh*, Sakshi Publications, 2003.

Samel, Swapna. *Dalit Movement in South India(1857-1950)*.New Delhi:Serials Publications, 2004.

Samsan, Pilli. *Dalita Sahitya Charitra*. Guntur: Union Printers, 2000.

Sankruthyan, Rahul. *Olga Nunchi Gangaku*. Hyderabad: Visalandra Publishing House, 2002.

Sangeetha Rao, R. *Ambedkar and Marx*. New Delhi: Blumoon Books, 1996.

Shah, Ghanshyam,ed. *Caste and Democratic Politics in India*. Delhi: Permanent Black, 2002.

Sharma. H.D *B.R. Ambedkar: A Crusader for Equality*. New Delhi: Rupa & Co., 2002.

Sharma, R.S. *Sudra Varna m Yela Puttindhi*. Hyderabad: Hyderabad Book Trust, 1992.

Sikhamani ed. *Maddela Santhayya Kavitvam: O.C. Kreesthu*. Hyderabad: Maddela Santhayya Memorial Trust, 2002.

————. *Santhayya Kosam*. Hyderabad: Maddela Santhayya Memorial Trust, 2003.

Singh, Yogendra. *Social Stratification and Change in India*. New Delhi: Manohar Publishers, 1997.

Srinivas, M.N . *Caste – Its Twentieth Century Avatar*. New Delhi: Penguin Books, 1996.

Subba Rao G. ed. *Nethurimka Yerrabadutundi*. Samarlakota: Ramsha-Sireesha Publications, 2000.

Sudhakar, Kakani , Subba Rao, Kuurapati. Eds. *Sambhuka Sakam*. Vijayawada: Mythri Publications, 2005

Sudhakar, Yendluri. *Ambedkar Alochana Vidhanam*. Secundrabad: Ambedkar Publications Society,2000.

Suryanarayana, V. *The President Speaks*. New Delhi: Blumoon Books, 2000.

Syamala, Gogu. *Nalla Poddu*. Hyderabad: Hyderabad Book Trust, 2003.

Tharakam, Bojja. *Brazil Prajala Bhuporatam*. Hyderabad: Sakshi Human Rights Watch, 2000.

Videhi, Dr. Alladi. *Andhrula Sangheeka Ardika Charitra*. Hyderabad: Neelkamal Publications Pvt. Ltd, 2003

Venkata Subbaiah, Vallampati. *The Contemporary Literature of Rayalaseema: A Socio-cultural Analysis*, Anantapur, 2006.

Vijaya Bharathi, B *Baba Saheb Ambedkar* Hyderabad: Navya Printers, 1999.

Zelliot, Eleanor. *From Untouchable to Dalit*. New Delhi: Manohar Publishers, 1996.

———. *Dr.Babasaheb Ambedkar and The Untouchable Movement, New Delhi: Blue Moon 2004.*

Journals

Palanati, S.R. *Bahujana Keratalu*. Ongole August 15, 2004.

Rajasekhar, V.T. ed. *Dalit Voice*. Bangalore Vol. 23 No. 2 January 16- 31, 2004.

Shiva Prakash, H.S. ed. *Indian Literature – Sahitya Akademi*, Nov-Dec, Vol. XLIII No. 4, July-Aug. 1999.

————. *Indian Literature – Sahitya Akademi* Nov-Dec, Vol. XLIV No. 6, 2000.

Srinivas, V. ed. *Kakatiya Journal of English Studies*. Vol. 21, 2001.

————. *Kakatiya Journal of English Studies*. Vol. 23, 2003.

Sudharsan,Y. ed. *Dalita Sankharavam*. Madanapalli Vol. 7, June– July2004.

—————. *Dalita Sankharavam*. Madanapalli. Vol. 8, August 2004.

——————. *Dalita Sankharavam*. Madanapalli. Vol. 10, Nov-Dec 2004.

——————. *Dalita Sankharavam*. Madanapalli. Vol. 11, April 2005.

Index

N